Institutional Change and Globalization

John L. Campbell

PRINCETON UNIVERSITY PRESS

PRINCETON AND OXFORD

LIBRARY OF CONGRESS CATALOGING-IN-PUBLICATION DATA

Campbell, John L., 1952–
Institutional change and globalization / John L. Campbell.
p. cm.
Includes bibliographical references and index.
ISBN 0-691-08920-5 (cloth : alk. paper)—
ISBN 0-691-08921-3 (pbk. : alk. paper)
1. Social institutions. 2. Organizational change.
3. Globalization. 4. Economics—Sociological aspects. I. Title.
HM826.C36 2004
302.3′5—dc22   2004042851

British Library Cataloging-in-Publication Data is available

This book has been composed in Sabon

Printed on acid-free paper. ∞

pup.princeton.edu

Printed in the United States of America

1 3 5 7 9 10 8 6 4 2

To Kathy

———————————————

CONTENTS

FIGURES

TABLES

PREFACE

THIS BOOK IS about some of the most important problems confronting social scientists who study institutions and institutional change. It is also about globalization, particularly the frequent claim that globalization is transforming national political and economic institutions as never before. In both respects, this book is a direct extension of *The Rise of Neoliberalism and Institutional Analysis* (Princeton University Press, 2001), a project that I organized with my colleague Ove K. Pedersen, in which we and a small group of adventurous scholars tried to see how well different institutionalist paradigms could account for the emergence of neoliberal changes around the world during the late twentieth century. It was during the completion of that project that I began fully to appreciate the common problems that confronted all the main types of institutional analysis, or neoinstitutionalism, as it is called frequently today.

I also realized that I had been struggling with these problems for many years in other research projects, particularly those in which I had tried to explain institutional change in the political economies of the United States and postcommunist Europe. To this degree, the book also has roots that extend back to a variety of earlier papers, lectures, and seminars that I delivered at various universities, but particularly at the Center for Public Organization and Management in Denmark, where I was twice a visiting scholar, thanks to grants from the Danish Social Science Research Council, and also at the Institute for Political Science at the University of Copenhagen, where I am an Adjunct Professor. I am indebted to all of these organizations for their financial and intellectual support. More immediate financial support for the completion of this book was provided by Dartmouth College in the form of a Senior Faculty Grant for which I am also very grateful.

As this book makes clear, there are several traditions of institutional analysis: rational choice, historical, and organizational institutionalism. As a graduate student, I was trained in the paradigm of historical institutionalism just as it was coming into vogue during the late 1970s and early 1980s. Later, I came to appreciate the contributions of other institutionalist paradigms, even if I did not embrace all aspects of them. So this book is also based on the belief that institutionalists, including myself, can learn much by paying attention to each other's work, even though it might fall outside their own paradigm. In particular, I think institutionalists of all paradigmatic stripes share common problems that need to be resolved to improve the enterprise of institutional analysis in general. Not all institutionalists embrace such an eclectic position—especially those who believe that pushing one paradigm to the limit against the arguments of others is the best way to advance social science. I certainly respect this view. But I think that this is what institutionalists have been doing for a long time and that now it is time to begin searching for common ground and possibilities for cross-fertilization. One way to begin doing this is to acknowledge our common problems and try to fix them. I hope this book helps in that regard.

As for the ideas presented in this book, I am indebted to several people for comments, suggestions, questions, and discussions over the years. They include Denise Anthony, Mark Blyth, Paul DiMaggio, Frank Dobbin, Francesco Duina, Peter Evans, Eva Fodor, Bob Forster, Marshall Ganz, Peter Hall, Doug Hechathorn, Peter Kjaer, Joel Levine, Eleanor Lewis, Michael Macy, Uli Mayer, Victor Nee, Klaus Nielsen, Hans Peter Olsen, Charles Perrow, Dietrich Rueschemeyer, Vivien Schmidt, Adam Sheingate, Jim Shoch, Bradd Shore, Andrew Schrank, Mike Smith, Yasemin Soysal, Sven Steinmo, Richard Swedberg, Ivan Szelenyi, Charles Tilly, Andy Van de Ven, and the students who took my graduate seminars on institutional analysis. In a few extraordinarily generous cases colleagues read early drafts of the entire manuscript and offered wise criticism and advice. For this I would like to thank Michael Allen, John A. Hall, Edgar Kiser, Ove Pedersen, W. Richard Scott, Marc Schneiberg, and two reviewers for Princeton University Press, Elisabeth Clemens and Neil Fligstein. In particular, I have had many fruitful discussions and much correspondence with Mike and Ove over the years that helped me work out the ideas in this book and bring them into focus. Ian Malcolm, my editor at Princeton University Press, provided much encouragement and support throughout the course of this project. So did my editor at Akademisk Forlag A/S, Carsten Wulff, who showed great patience as I prepared the manuscript for Danish translation. Leon Lindberg first introduced me to institutional analysis when I was in graduate school, a gift for which I will always remain grateful. Finally, in addition to offering methodological advice at a critical moment, Kathy Sherrieb, my wife, supported me in more ways than I can count while I worked on this project, as she always has. This book is dedicated to her with much love and affection.

John L. Campbell
Lyme, New Hampshire

Institutional Change and Globalization

Chapter 1

PROBLEMS OF INSTITUTIONAL ANALYSIS

INSTITUTIONS ARE the foundation of social life. They consist of formal and informal rules, monitoring and enforcement mechanisms, and systems of meaning that define the context within which individuals, corporations, labor unions, nation-states, and other organizations operate and interact with each other. Institutions are settlements born from struggle and bargaining. They reflect the resources and power of those who made them and, in turn, affect the distribution of resources and power in society. Once created, institutions are powerful external forces that help determine how people make sense of their world and act in it. They channel and regulate conflict and thus ensure stability in society.

Without stable institutions, life becomes chaotic and arduous, as people learned, for example, following the demise of the communist regimes in Eastern Europe after 1989. The sudden weakening of old political constitutions, property rights, law enforcement, and other institutions generated tremendous confusion as these countries began to move toward capitalism and democracy. National politics were inundated suddenly with dozens of political parties and interest groups vying for power in unstable coalitions. Economies were besieged with all sorts of mafia, scam artists, and other shady characters that made commerce unpredictable and sometimes dangerous. Even a simple thing like taking a train from one city to another was suddenly fraught with possible attacks by bandits and uncertainty about schedules. As a result, building new political and economic institutions was one of the most urgent tasks for the postcommunist countries (Elster et al. 1998). This should not be surprising. After all, Max Weber, Karl Marx, Emile Durkheim, Karl Polanyi, and many other scholars have shown that capitalism itself is impossible without a solid institutional base.[1] This is one reason why institutional analysis has become such an important perspective in the social sciences in North America and Europe.

As this example suggests, institutions change. Sometimes they change radically. Sometimes they evolve more incrementally. Sometimes they are quite stable. This book is about institutional change, how to recognize

---

[1] For instance, see Weber ([1927] 1995), Marx ([1887] 1973, chap. 28), Durkheim (1933, chap. 7), and Polanyi (1944).

different types of institutional change when we see them, and how better to understand some of the forces that make institutional change happen or not. As we shall see, scholars from various intellectual and social science backgrounds share common conceptual, theoretical, and methodological problems when it comes to these issues. Indeed, institutional analysis has been criticized repeatedly for having an inadequate understanding of institutional change (e.g., Lieberman 2002; Scott 2001, 181; Thelen and Steinmo 1992, 15). Among other things, we sometimes have trouble recognizing institutional change for what it is, mistaking evolutionary developments for more revolutionary shifts and failing to appreciate fully how much continuity there often is during episodes of institutional change, even across big events like those that occurred in postcommunist Europe after 1989. As such, this book is intended to confront and help rectify some of the most important analytic problems facing institutional analysis today. In doing so, it also offers a new theory of institutional change that combines insights from several versions of institutional analysis.

This book also confronts, however, a more concrete problem: the phenomenon of globalization. Much has been written about globalization and much of this writing suggests that the forces of globalization have triggered what amounts to a revolutionary change in national political and economic institutions.[2] Some scholars intimate that this threatens the utility of institutional analysis for understanding today's world. I disagree. Much of this literature has overestimated the extent of institutional change associated with globalization. Why? Because much of it either has failed to take institutional analysis into account, or has failed to elaborate institutional analysis along the lines suggested in this book.

Broadly speaking, then, this book does two things. First, it identifies serious problems that are central to institutional analysis and offers some conceptual, methodological, and theoretical tools for solving them—tools that help improve the analytic power of institutional analysis, especially for understanding change. Second, to demonstrate the utility of these tools, it applies them to the phenomenon of globalization to show how they can help us improve our understanding—and reduce our misunderstanding—of how phenomena like this produce institutional change, or not, in the world around us.

But what do I mean by institutional analysis? Today there are three major versions of institutional analysis: *rational choice, organizational,*

---

[2] The literature on globalization is vast. However, for a sampling of work that suggests that globalization has unleashed forces for revolutionary institutional change in the world, see Giddens (2000), Guéhenno (1995), McKenzie and Lee (1991), Ohmae (1990, 1995), and Sassen (1996).

and *historical institutionalism*.[3] To be precise, these are often referred to as new forms of institutional analysis, or neoinstitutionalism, because each one descends from an old version of institutional analysis. Each one also cuts across sociology, political science, and economics. Their utility is evident from the extraordinarily wide range of things that they have been used to explain: the development of art museums and other cultural organizations, the rise of modern corporations, the organization of labor unions, the adoption of affirmative action policies, the diffusion of business management models, the progression of forms of corporate governance, the rise of health care systems, the creation of markets, the transformation of property rights, the growth of economies and nation-states, the making of economic, fiscal, social, technology, and other public policies, the growth of social movements, the ability of groups to preserve natural resources, the variation that occurs in national economic performance and national responses to economic crisis, the operation of national and international security regimes, the diffusion of citizenship rights, the dissemination of world culture, the effects of globalization, and much more.[4]

Despite the important insights of the three new institutionalist paradigms, there has been much bickering among their supporters as to which is the best approach and what each one's strengths and weaknesses are (e.g., DiMaggio and Powell 1991; Kiser and Hechter 1991; Thelen and Steinmo 1992). Indeed, some of us even disagree about what institutions are in the first place. For instance, some rational choice institutionalists define institutions as a strategic equilibrium. By strategic equilibrium they

---

[3] Several excellent collections are available that illustrate each paradigm. For rational choice institutionalism, see, for example, Brinton and Nee (1998) and Knight and Sened (1998a). For organizational institutionalism, see Powell and DiMaggio (1991). For historical institutionalism, see Steinmo et al. (1992). The collection by Campbell and Pedersen (2001c) presents examples from all three paradigms.

[4] For examples of institutionalist accounts of cultural organizations, see DiMaggio (1991); for modern corporations, see Fligstein (1990) and Williamson (1985); for labor unions, see Hattam (1993) and Orren (1991); for affirmative action, see Dobbin et al. (1993) and Edelman (1990); for business management models, see Guillén (1994a); for corporate governance, see Campbell et al. (1991); for health care systems, see Scott et al. (2000); for markets, see Fligstein (1996) and Fligstein and Mara-Drita (1996); for property rights, see Barzel (1989); for economies and nation-states, see North (1990) and Skowronek (1982); for economic policy, see Hall (1986); for fiscal policy, see Levi (1988); for social policy, see Skocpol (1992); for technology policy, see Campbell (1988) and Ziegler (1997); for social movements, see Keck and Sikkink (1998), Kitschelt (1986), and Tarrow (1996); for the preservation of natural resources, see Ostrom (1990); for national economic performance and crisis response, see Gourevitch (1986) and Katzenstein (1978); for national and international security regimes, see Katzenstein (1996b); for citizenship rights, see Soysal (1994); for world culture, see Boli and Thomas (1999a); for globalization, see Wade (1996) and Keohane and Milner (1996).

mean a situation where no persons would unilaterally choose to alter their current behavior given the available alternatives and given their expectations about how others might respond if they began to behave differently (Bates et al. 1998, 8–10; Calvert 1998, 57–60). Other rational choice institutionalists view institutions as sets of formal and informal rules and the monitoring and sanctioning mechanisms that cause actors to comply with these rules (North 1990, 3). Similarly, historical institutionalists take institutions to be the formal and informal rules and procedures that structure conduct (Thelen and Steinmo 1992, 2). Finally, although organizational institutionalists recognize that institutions include formal rules, many of them see institutions as informal, common, and taken-for-granted cultural frameworks, scripts, and cognitive schema (Jepperson 1991).[5]

Regardless of these and other disagreements, beginning in the late 1990s scholars began calling for a *second movement* in institutional analysis, that is, a more constructive dialogue that explores the ways in which these paradigms might complement and connect to each other (e.g., Campbell and Pedersen 2001b; Hall and Taylor 1996; Immergut 1998; Peters 1999, 149–51; Suchman 1997; Thelen 1999). The hope was that such a conversation might lead to a reconciliation and perhaps a new and more unified approach for studying institutions.

The premise of this book is that an important part of a second movement in institutional analysis involves recognizing that these three paradigms share a common set of problems that need to be resolved. By recognizing these problems, institutionalists should see that they have much more in common and at stake together than they thought previously. Moreover, for reasons discussed later, unless these problems are resolved, institutional analysis is not likely to advance much beyond its current stage of development. At least three important analytic problems require attention: the problems of change, mechanisms, and ideas. Globalization constitutes a fourth problem, but of a much different order.[6] This book

---

[5] All of these definitions are at odds with the more popular understanding of institutions, which tends to equate institutions with well-established organizations, as in the phrase, "Lou's Restaurant is a local institution." From an institutionalist's point of view, Lou's is really an organization, a group of people that produces goods or services. It exists within a set of institutions that make up its surrounding environment, such as the rules established and enforced by government regarding the restaurant's health, accounting, labor, and other practices as well as the taken-for-granted local customs regarding the appropriate way to treat customers, employees, and suppliers. For further discussion of the distinction between organizations and institutions, see Perrow (1986, 167–77, 2002, chap. 1) and Jepperson (1991).

[6] These four problems do not constitute all of the important problems confronting institutional analysis. But I focus on these because they cut clearly across all three institutionalist paradigms. Furthermore, they are the ones that have challenged me the most in my own work. I suspect that this is true for other researchers too.

examines each one of these problems and suggests how we might begin to rectify them. To my knowledge, although many scholars have compared the strengths and weaknesses of one institutionalist paradigm to another, virtually no one has examined in detail the common problems that all three paradigms share. Nor have they tried to offer solutions for them. Let me elaborate briefly on each of these problems and how the book is organized around them.

First, institutionalists debate about the best way to describe institutional *change*. For instance, some of us argue that it tends to follow an evolutionary pattern characterized by the gradual accumulation of small, incremental changes over long periods of time. Others say that it conforms more to patterns of either punctuated equilibrium or punctuated evolution. These patterns are more revolutionary than evolutionary in the sense that they are characterized initially by prolonged periods of either equilibrium and stability or evolution that are interrupted suddenly by a crisis that throws things into turmoil until a radically new set of institutional arrangements is established, which then remain in equilibrium or evolve slowly for another long period of time (Blyth 2002, chap. 1; Hay 2001; Krasner 1984). No matter what our position is on the issue, we often fail to explain adequately how to distinguish among these and other patterns of change. That is, we fail to specify one of the most important dependent variables with which institutionalists are concerned. As a result, it becomes difficult to establish the degree to which a given episode of change is actually evolutionary, revolutionary, or something else. This has been true even with respect to some of the most important institutional changes in the twentieth century. For instance, there has been much debate about the degree to which institutional change in postcommunist Eastern Europe during the 1990s constituted a sharp, revolutionary break with the communist era, or something more evolutionary that still bore a strong resemblance to past institutions (e.g., Campbell and Pedersen 1996; Crawford and Lijphart 1995; Hanley et al. 2002; Stark 1996). Chapter 2 explores what institutionalists mean by institutional change and how we might better recognize different patterns of change when they occur. Resolution of this problem is critical if we want to adjudicate among competing claims about the nature of institutional change in specific empirical cases, including globalization, and, in turn, if we want to test theories that seek to account for different patterns of change.

Second, institutionalists rely on causal concepts but often without clearly specifying the underlying *mechanisms* or processes by which change occurs. As a result, these concepts resemble mysterious black boxes whose contents need to be unpacked and examined. Unless we do this, vague concepts end up carrying much of the argument when, in fact, mechanisms should be doing the work. This is an important problem in the social sciences in general (Hedström and Swedberg 1998a; McCloskey 1985) and especially for institutionalists insofar as critics charge that the neglect of mechanisms undermines the empirical and theoretical credibility of institutionalists' arguments (Hirsch and Lounsbury 1997; Hirsch 1997; Knight 2001). It also undermines the credibility of arguments about globalization. Chapter 3 discusses how we might think more clearly about the mechanisms underlying some of the most important causal concepts that institutionalists use. In particular, it focuses on the concepts of path dependence and diffusion. It also addresses, albeit in less detail, other concepts, such as how institutions enable, empower, constitute, and constrain action. Resolution of this problem is critical if we want to develop tighter and more convincing causal arguments about institutional change.

Third, many institutionalists have taken a cultural turn recognizing recently that *ideas*, broadly construed, as well as self-interests drive change (Campbell 2002). Whether norms, intellectual paradigms, policy frames, world views, and other types of ideas affect institutional change are issues that have spawned new research agendas and much debate among institutionalists working in comparative politics, international relations, political economy, and political, economic, and organizational sociology.[7] Many of us, however, have been hobbled in these efforts because our work on ideas suffers from conceptual and methodological problems (Blyth 1997; Finnemore 1996; Yee 1996). Notably, what we mean by ideas and what the mechanisms are by which ideas affect behavior are often confusing. And it is not always clear in the first place what the difference is between ideas and interests. Chapter 4 clarifies how we might better think about all this, particularly how we might better study the effects that ideas have on political, economic, organizational, and other types of behavior. Insofar as this chapter discusses the ideational mechanisms associated with institutional change, it also addresses some of the issues raised in chapter 3. Resolution of this problem is critical if we want to determine how ideas—such as norms, paradigms, and frames—as well as self-interests affect institutional change, and the degree to which they do this.

By grappling with the problems of change, mechanisms, and ideas, this volume offers conceptual, theoretical, and methodological insights that can help institutionalists better understand important social phenomena in the world around us. To demonstrate this, I apply these insights in chapter 5 to an analysis of *globalization*. Why pick globalization rather than some other empirical phenomenon? Many institutionalists have ar-

---

[7] For example, on comparative politics, see Berman (1998); on international relations, see Katzenstein (1996b); on political economy, see Blyth (2002), Goldstein and Keohane (1993a), and McNamara (1998); on political, economic, and organizational sociology, see Campbell (1998), Dobbin (1994), and Fligstein (1990).

gued that differences in national institutions are an important cause of variation across countries in political and economic performance. Globalization is a fourth problem for institutional analysis insofar as some people now claim that the forces of globalization, notably increased international capital mobility and trade, are leveling these institutional differences across countries. As a result, they intimate that much institutional analysis is becoming irrelevant for understanding societies during the late twentieth and early twenty-first centuries (e.g., Giddens 2000; Guéhenno 1995).[8] If we accept this argument, then our desire to improve institutional analysis will likely diminish and scholars will turn to alternative analytic approaches. Utilizing the lessons from chapters 2, 3, and 4, chapter 5 shows that claims about the leveling effects of globalization are mistaken and that institutional analysis can help us understand why this is so. Resolution of this problem through the application of the analytic tools developed earlier in the book is critical if we want to demonstrate that institutional analysis is still relevant for understanding how societies are changing during the globalization era.

Two clarifications are necessary about the problem of globalization. First, this problem is of a fundamentally different order than the other three. The problems of change, mechanisms, and ideas are *internal* to the logic, conceptual apparatus, and causal arguments of institutional analysis. The problem of globalization is *external* to these arguments in the sense that a change in the empirical reality of the world, that is, increased capital mobility and trade, appears to some observers to pose a threat to the relevance of institutional analysis per se for understanding societies nowadays. Second, although the analysis of globalization in chapter 5 develops insights and arguments specific to the debates about globalization, its primary purpose is to illustrate how the concepts, methods, and arguments of previous chapters can be used fruitfully in doing empirical research on important real-world problems. It is not intended to be a full-blown or exhaustive critique of the globalization thesis.

While chapter 5 demonstrates the utility of my arguments for empirical research, chapter 6 weaves them together into a theory of institutional change that integrates insights from all three institutionalist paradigms

---

[8] This is especially a problem for rational choice and historical institutionalists who work in the comparative politics and comparative political economy traditions. It is also crucial for organizational institutionalists who focus on national institutional differences as key explanatory variables (e.g., Dobbin 1994; Soysal 1994). But it is less a problem for those organizational institutionalists, such as John Meyer and his colleagues (e.g., Thomas et al. 1987), who maintain that the increasing integration of the world polity is leading to the global diffusion among nation-states of a common set of institutional practices. For them, globalization is a problem insofar as it does *not* result in greater institutional homogeneity across countries.

thereby advancing the second movement—that advocating a sustained three-way dialogue—in institutional analysis. In brief, this theory suggests how institutional change is a process of *constrained innovation*. By this I mean, on the one hand, that institutions tend to constrain the range of options from which actors are likely to choose as they engage in institutional innovation. But, on the other hand, institutions also provide principles, practices, and opportunities that actors use creatively as they innovate within these constraints. I present this theory as a series of analytic propositions about the antecedents that initially trigger episodes of institutional change and the complex processes by which it unfolds. This is a deliberate attempt to advance the second movement in institutional analysis. Based on these propositions, I also offer some suggestions about how institutionalists can fruitfully orient their work in the future.

Although the problems of change, mechanisms, ideas, and globalization are the central focus of this book, it will become evident that each one involves a variety of secondary problems that also occasionally require attention. Briefly, the problem of change requires that we think about the appropriate time frames we use in analysis and the important institutional dimensions we choose to track over time. The problem of mechanisms requires that we confront the relationship between social structure and agency and that we acknowledge the relative advantages and disadvantages associated with different levels of analysis in our research. The problem of ideas requires that we consider carefully how we should define ideas, identify the actors who use them, specify the causal mechanisms that involve them, and develop the appropriate methodologies for studying their impacts. The problem of globalization requires that we consider all of these things carefully in studying how international economic pressures may affect national political and economic institutions. The secondary problems underlying the four primary problems around which this book is organized will not all receive equal treatment. This is not because one is necessarily any more or less important than another, but because I deal with them on an ad hoc basis and only insofar as is necessary to address the four primary problems with which the book is concerned.

In sum, this book makes six important contributions. It focuses attention on some of the most pressing theoretical and methodological *problems* that threaten to block the further development of institutional analysis. It suggests *solutions* for how these problems might be resolved. It demonstrates the utility of these solutions for better understanding how institutional change happens by applying them to the phenomenon of *globalization*. It offers a *theory* of institutional change. And in doing so it contributes to the *second movement* in institutional analysis by raising common issues and questions about which proponents of the three institutionalist paradigms need to think carefully in order to advance their collective enterprise. To illustrate my arguments, I give throughout the book a variety of empirical examples of policy-making and institution building in the United States, Europe, and Asia. Many of these examples are historical or cross-national and are drawn from comparative politics and political economy, economic and political sociology, organizational sociology, and, to a lesser extent, international relations. As a result, this book also offers a *guide* for students and scholars interested in some of the most exciting debates and empirical work being done today in institutional analysis.

THE RISE OF INSTITUTIONAL ANALYSIS AND ITS PROBLEMS

How extensive are the problems that I have identified in the new institutional analysis? This will become clear in subsequent chapters. But to begin to answer this question it is helpful to understand how each paradigm developed and what it stands for intellectually. Institutional analysis has deep roots in sociology, political science, and economics. My intent here is not to review this history in great detail or to develop an exhaustive comparison of all the important similarities and differences among these paradigms. This has been done at length elsewhere.[9] Nor do I intend to elaborate the complexities of each problem here. That will be done systematically in later chapters. Instead, my purpose in the remainder of this chapter is to provide a brief thumbnail sketch of each paradigm and its origins. Because much has been written about the differences among paradigms, I discuss them only briefly.[10] Instead, my primary goal is to show that all three paradigms tend to focus on similar patterns of institutional change, rely on similar causal concepts, and recognize the need for a better understanding of how ideas—such as norms, values, and cognitive structures—as opposed to self-interests affect behavior in general and institutional change in particular. Insofar as all three paradigms share common ground in this regard it should not be surprising that they also share common problems. Because, as noted above, the problem of globalization is of a fundamentally different order than the problems of change, mechanisms, and ideas, I will not discuss it in my review of the three paradigms.

[9] Several comprehensive discussions of the intellectual history of institutional analysis are available. Most attend closely to comparing and contrasting the old and new versions of institutional analysis within a particular paradigm. For rational choice institutionalism, see Nee (1998) and Rutherford (1994); for organizational institutionalism, see DiMaggio and Powell (1991), March and Olsen (1989, chap. 1), and Stinchcombe (1997); for historical institutionalism, see Skocpol (1985) and Thelen and Steinmo (1992).

[10] For detailed discussions of the differences among the three institutionalist paradigms, see Campbell (1997), Campbell and Pedersen (2001a), Hall and Taylor (1996), Peters (1999), and Scott (2001).

The discussion is summarized in table 1.1, which represents each paradigm as an ideal type. Keep in mind, however, that each paradigm consists of a vast literature. Although I will generalize about each one, there are always exceptions to these generalizations and considerable variation within each paradigm.[11] Occasionally, there are also scholars whose work cuts across paradigms (e.g., Campbell 1998; Clemens 1997; Keck and Sikkink 1998). Hence, although sufficient for present purposes, the following discussion is intended to reveal only some of the broad contours of each paradigm. And again, it tends to emphasize similarities rather than differences among paradigms.

Rational Choice Institutionalism

In economics, institutional analysis emerged during the late nineteenth and early twentieth centuries. It was based on the insights particularly of Max Weber, but also Karl Marx and other nineteenth-century scholars. Among the most influential institutional economists were John R. Commons, Thorstein Veblen, and Wesley C. Mitchell, all of whom shared a devotion to empirically based research, an interest in the changing nature of economic institutions, habits, and norms, and a belief in the ability of informed concerted action to improve human welfare (Hodgson 1994, 58–60). Indeed, several institutionalists in the United States, notably Commons, played important roles in the New Deal during the 1930s—a time during which institution building was high on the national political agenda because it was viewed as a way to extricate the United States from the clutches of the Great Depression.

This old version of institutional analysis was juxtaposed to neoclassical economics, which stressed the need for simple theoretical models that abstracted from reality through the use of formal deductive analysis and mathematics. In contrast, the old institutionalists eschewed the elegance, rigor, and parsimony of formal deductive modeling for thick description, historical analysis, and inductive reasoning that, in their view, more accurately captured the true nature of fundamental historical processes. The old institutionalists were also less inclined than the neoclassicists to make simplifying assumptions about human rationality. Neoclassicists argued that it was reasonable to assume, at least for purposes of formal mathematical modeling, that people were motivated by self-interest and operated according to a cost-benefit rationality. Institutionalists argued that

---

[11] For discussion of variations and debates *within* these paradigms, see Knight (1998) and Hechter and Kanazawa (1997) on rational choice institutionalism; Schneiberg and Clemens (forthcoming) on organizational institutionalism; and Peters (1999, chap. 4), Hall and Taylor (1996, 1998), and Hay and Wincott (1998) on historical institutionalism.

TABLE 1.1.
Similarities and Differences in the New Rational Choice, Organizational,
and Historical Institutionalism

	Rational Choice Institutionalism	Organizational Institutionalism	Historical Institutionalism
Similarities			
Favored Patterns of Change	Punctuated equilibrium, evolution	Punctuated equilibrium, evolution, punctuated evolution	Punctuated equilibrium, evolution, punctuated evolution
Favored Causal Concepts	Path dependence: Based on feedback, increasing returns, and choice within institutional constraints	Path dependence: Based on constraining and constitutive aspects of institutions	Path dependence: Based on feedback, learning, and choice within institutional constraints
	Diffusion: Based on information contagion, feedback, and imitation	Diffusion: Based on mimetic, normative, and coercive processes	Diffusion: Based on learning and coercive processes
Role of Ideas	Increasing: Cognitive structures, beliefs, and norms constrain actors (and make institutions inefficient).	Substantial: Taken-for-granted cognitive and normative structures constrain (and enable) actors.	Increasing: Policy paradigms and principled beliefs constrain actors.
Differences			
Theoretical Roots	Neoclassical economics	Phenomenology, ethnomethodology, and cognitive psychology	Marxist and Weberian political economy
Definition of Institution	Formal and informal rules and compliance procedures; strategic equilibrium	Formal rules and taken-for-granted cultural frameworks, cognitive schema, and routinized processes of reproduction	Formal and informal rules and procedures
Level of Analysis	Micro-analytic exchanges	Organizational fields and populations	Macro-analytic national political economies
Theory of Action	Logic of instrumentality	Logic of appropriateness	Logics of instrumentality and appropriateness
Theory of Constraint	Action is constrained by rules, such as property rights and constitutions, and bounded rationality.	Action is constrained by cultural frames, schema, and routines.	Action is constrained by rules and procedures, cognitive paradigms, and principled beliefs.

human motivation and rationality was more complex, that people operated sometimes according to altruistic principles, and that the language
people thought in affected how they perceived themselves and, thus, their
interests. Finally, the old institutionalists insisted that one cannot understand the economy by focusing just on individual market actors. Instead,
they argued for a more holistic account that also paid attention to the
roles played in the economy by corporations, labor unions, trade associations, banks, and other organizations as well as the unequal distribution
of wealth, power, and information among them (Yonay 1998).

The professional competition between institutional and neoclassical
economics grew particularly intense during the period between the two
world wars. After the Second World War, the intellectual sway of institutional economics declined. By the late 1950s it had become marginalized
and neoclassical economics had become dominant in North America and
Europe in part due to the rising popularity of econometrics and mathematical modeling (Yonay 1998).

However, a new brand of institutional analysis, the so-called new institutionalism in economics, emerged beginning in the 1970s in reaction to
persistent problems for which neoclassical economics seemed to have either little interest or few solutions. In particular, Oliver Williamson (1975,
1985), Douglass North (1981, 1990), and others recognized that competitive markets did not always produce the most efficient economic behavior.
They argued that under certain conditions, such as small numbers bargaining or limited information about suppliers and customers, markets
were in fact typically inefficient insofar as monitoring and enforcing transactions could be done at lower cost through different institutions like
corporate hierarchies or long-term subcontracts. By institutions they
meant systems of formal and informal rules and compliance procedures
(e.g., North 1990, 3; Rutherford 1994, 182). Hence, whereas the neoclassicists had pushed institutions aside and argued that unfettered markets
were generally the most efficient arena for economic activity, the new
institutionalists disagreed and wanted to bring the analysis of institutions
back into economics.

The new institutional economics also held that although transactions
could be organized through a variety of institutions, no institution was
necessarily going to be optimally efficient. Why? First, because political
elites are self-interested and want to maximize tax revenues and other
benefits of office, they frequently create property rights and other institutions that constrain the behavior of market actors in ways that undermine
long-term economic growth. For instance, North (1981, 185), who won
the Nobel Prize in economics for his work, argued that the domination
of politics in Western countries by pluralist interest groups, which
emerged from the struggle among workers, farmers, and businesses, gen-

erated a system of property rights that favored income and wealth redistribution at the expense of economic efficiency. Second, for a couple of reasons, once institutions are established they evolve slowly in a path-dependent manner. On the one hand, institutions are expensive to create and change. On the other hand, once established, institutions tend to generate positive feedback and support from constituents as well as institutional elites who derive increasing financial returns and other benefits from them. Hence, influential people are often reluctant to modify institutions in fundamental ways—even if institutions are discovered to be inefficient relative to the possible alternatives. Instead, people tend to make only marginal adjustments to their institutions that result in path-dependent change.

The causal concept of path dependence suggests that once people are on a particular institutional path they tend to stick to it rather than jump to another one. Thus, evolutionary change becomes the norm (Arthur 1994; North 1990). According to North (1990, 90), even when major disruptions occur to the institutional status quo, such as a severe price shock or political crisis of the sort that are central to punctuated equilibrium models, the changes that result are often less discontinuous and more evolutionary than they appear on the surface as a result of path-dependent effects. Of course, this is not to say that the new institutionalists reject completely the possibility of truly revolutionary change that constitutes a sharp break from the past. Williamson (1985), for instance, suggested that a sudden increase in transaction costs will be followed by a rapid shift from markets to vertically integrated firms as the principle means of governing economic exchange. And even North (1998, 19) accepted that on at least some occasions abrupt changes may occur that resemble the punctuated equilibrium model, mentioned earlier.

It is important to note that scholars in this tradition occasionally discuss another causal concept that is closely related to path dependence. That is the concept of diffusion (e.g., Coleman et al. 1966). For instance, Brian Arthur (1994, chap. 5) explained that under some circumstances the diffusion of an economic practice through a market may be driven by "information contagion," that is, informal word-of-mouth information sharing about what the best practice is. He argued that buyers who seek such information tend to learn about practices that previous buyers have already adopted and with which they are already familiar. Hence, buyers are likely to learn more about a frequently used practice than one with few previous users. In this way, certain practices are more likely to diffuse through the market than others as a result of an information feedback process that is much like those that are associated with path-dependent change. However, researchers who are influenced by the tradition of the new institutional economics and who are sympathetic to diffusion arguments point out that little attention is paid in this literature to whether the practice in question is transformed in the process of diffusing from one context to another and, if so, how this happens (Kiser and Abel 2002). As we shall see, this is also a problem in other versions of institutional analysis.

The new institutional analysis in economics did not constitute a complete rejection of the neoclassical tradition. In particular, North, Williamson, and their followers embraced methodological individualism—the idea that micro-level individual actions give rise to institutions. They also accepted in modified form the neoclassical assumption that individual action is motivated by an instrumental rationality, that is, a decision-making logic based on an interest in maximizing benefits relative to costs. The modification was that rational decision making was limited by the availability of relevant information and the cognitive ability of actors to process it (Langlois 1986; Rutherford 1994, chap. 3). Institutions, they argued, are built to advance actors' self-interests. By self-interests they meant an actor's concern with improving his or her well-being (Coleman 1990, 28–29; Scharpf 1997, 40).[12] Once institutions are built, actors continue to pursue their interests as best they can within the constraints imposed on them by these institutions. In contrast to the old institutionalism, the new institutionalism was more abstract, formal, individualist, and oriented toward rational choice and economizing models (Rutherford 1994, 4). As a result, this view represented a rational choice approach to the study of economic institutions.

In sociology and political science the development of rational choice institutionalism was heavily influenced by these ideas. In sociology it was also a reaction against the legacy of Emile Durkheim (1933, 1938) and the structural functionalists, notably Talcott Parsons (1951), who argued that social structure and institutions generate individual action, not the other way around. Rational choice institutionalists in sociology rejected this view in favor of methodological individualism (Coleman 1990; Hechter 1987; Nee 1998). So did their counterparts in political science. Furthermore, in political science, rational choice institutionalists reacted against an earlier institutionalist tradition of the late nineteenth and early twentieth centuries, illustrated, for instance, by Woodrow Wilson's scholarly work. Like the old institutionalists in economics, the old institutionalists in political science were intent on describing in rich detail and understanding the development of formal institutions like constitutions, cabinets, and parliaments in non-abstract and often atheoretical terms.

---

[12] This is a controversial point. Some rational choice scholars argue that interests need not be hedonistic. An actor's preferred course of action may be intended to improve the well-being of others rather than herself (Elster 1989, 23–24).

They did so with a strong normative emphasis that was often rooted in moral philosophy, and their work paid little attention to the development of testable propositions (Peters 1999, chaps. 1, 3; Scott 2001, 6–8). Given its reaction against the older views, it is not surprising that much rational choice institutionalism in political science, and to a lesser extent in sociology, is now characterized by formalized and abstract game-theoretic modeling (e.g., Calvert 1998).

Rational choice institutionalists in sociology and political science also paid much attention to how individuals build and modify institutions to achieve their interests (e.g., Kiser and Kane 2001; Knight 1992, 1998). Some accepted that patterns of punctuated equilibrium occur occasionally and cause fairly revolutionary and abrupt institutional changes (Moe 1987; Shepsle 1986). However, many others maintained that path-dependent evolutionary change is the norm (e.g., Ingram and Clay 2000, 527). For example, in a discussion reminiscent of North's objections to punctuated equilibrium models, political scientist William Riker (1998, 121) argued that even brand new and apparently revolutionary institutions are not created de novo, but contain vestiges from the past. Riker showed that the U.S. Constitution evolved from the Articles of Confederation, the national government of the Continental Congress, the thirteen state governments, and British colonial administration. But regardless of whether they focus on evolutionary or revolutionary change, rational choice institutionalists find that both norms and more formal institutions emerge and are enforced as a result of self-interested behavior (e.g., Brinton and Nee 1998, part I; North 1981, chap. 5; Ostrom 1990, chap. 6).

Perhaps the most important contribution that sociologists and political scientists have made to the rational choice paradigm is to develop the so-called choice-within-constraints approach—a view that takes seriously that institutions, including informal norms as well as formal rules and regulations, limit the range of choices individuals are likely to make as they pursue their interests (Alt and Shepsle 1990a; Nee 1998; Scharpf 1997). For example, Margaret Levi (1988) argued that political rulers are predatory insofar as they are interested in maximizing the revenues they collect from citizens. Their ability to maximize revenues is constrained, however, by the type of political institutions within which they operate. During the Middle Ages, English monarchs eventually had to negotiate with parliament over tax policy. This lent tax policy a degree of credibility and legitimacy that was absent in absolutist states, such as France, and so English rulers were able to tax more effectively than the French. Variation in institutional constraints made the difference.

It is worth mentioning briefly that rational choice theorists who are especially interested in game theory do not always follow the choice-within-constraints approach. Instead of viewing institutions as rules that constrain behavior, they argue, as noted earlier, that institutions are strategic equilibria—situations where no one sees an advantage in changing his or her behavior. As game theory has become increasingly popular among political scientists, even those who initially adopted the choice-within-constraints approach, such as Margaret Levi, have shifted toward this new definition of institutions (e.g., Bates et al. 1998, 8–10).

Finally, there has been much talk among rational choice institutionalists about the need to better incorporate an analysis of "ideas" into their work (e.g., Garrett and Weingast 1993; Goldstein and Keohane 1993b). Many have acknowledged that cognitive structures, belief systems, and other sorts of ideas influence how actors perceive their interests and options in the first place, including which institutions they might prefer to build and sustain under different circumstances. Notably, the concept of bounded rationality, which rational choice theorists invoke frequently, often alludes to these sorts of cognitive constraints. Bounded rationality refers to the limited capacities of actors to collect and process important information and use it to make well-informed decisions (Jones 1999). Yet, according to some rational choice institutionalists, although interest in the issue of cognition is increasing, their colleagues have failed to incorporate adequately an analysis of these sorts of ideas into their work (Knight and North 1997).[13]

In sum, although there are several varieties of rational choice institutionalism in the social sciences (e.g., Alt and Shepsle 1990b; Knight and Sened 1998b), they all tend to share basic features that relate to the problems in institutional analysis raised earlier. First, many rational choice institutionalists examine how institutional change typically follows an incremental and evolutionary pattern rather than a punctuated equilibrium pattern. Others attend to more dramatic and abrupt changes. In either case, however, little attention has been paid to how we can tell whether change is evolutionary or not. Indeed, a recent review of the literature on rational choice institutionalism makes no mention of this issue (Ingram and Clay 2000). Second, rational choice institutionalists believe that change tends to be evolutionary because it occurs through the path-dependent mechanisms of feedback, increasing returns, and choice within constraints (Knight 1992, chap. 4; North 1998). Some also extend the discussion of path-dependence to the process of diffusion. Nevertheless, reflecting on the state of the art, North (1998, 21) complained that rational choice institutionalists "simply are ignorant" about the mechanisms involved in path-dependent institutional change. As noted earlier, the same seems to be true for diffu-

---

[13] North (2001) has gone so far as to argue that, with the exception of some branches of psychology, all of the social sciences have neglected the importance of cognitive process and that we need to develop a "cognitive social science" to correct this deficiency.

sion insofar as they neglect how institutional practices may be transformed as they are adopted into local contexts. Third, according to North, a better understanding of these mechanisms requires rational choice institutionalists to pay much closer attention to the normative and cognitive processes by which actors perceive the range of choices available to them. In other words, they need to take ideas as well as self-interest much more seriously than they have to date. In particular, although some rational choice institutionalists have recognized increasingly that cognitive structures, belief systems, and the like constrain change, most theorists, in North's view, have paid rather limited attention to how ideas like these come into play and understand very little about how they operate (North 1990, 42–44; Knight and North 1997).

Organizational Institutionalism

One way organizational institutionalism differs from rational choice institutionalism is in its much greater emphasis on normative and cognitive ideas. Organizational institutionalism's roots stretch back to Weber, Durkheim, and several mid-twentieth-century organization theorists (DiMaggio and Powell 1991; Perrow 1986, chap. 5; Scott 2001, chaps. 1, 2). Prominent among them was Philip Selznick (1949), whose classic study of the Tennessee Valley Authority (TVA) is frequently identified as a cornerstone of the old institutionalism in organizational analysis. In constructing a detailed case study of the development of the TVA, Selznick argued that organizations are not always rational. That is, they do not always act independently in the interest of accomplishing their official goals. Instead, organizations often change in response to the pressures and values imposed on them by powerful constituents in their environment. As organizations are infused with these values, their real objectives diverge from their officially mandated goals and they come to serve the values and interests of these constituents. In turn, as organizations become more important for actors in their environment who depend on them, they become institutionalized along with the values they embody.

According to Selznick, the TVA was established ostensibly to facilitate regional development through democratic planning. However, he showed that to maintain control, consent, and ultimately its authority, the organization coopted local citizens and included representatives of powerful agricultural interests among its leadership. As a result, contrary to the organization's initial charge, its programs ended up serving more affluent and powerful agricultural constituents at the expense of its official and more populist goals. Following Selznick, a number of early organizational institutionalists documented that organizations respond to environmental pressures by altering their initial goals in order to survive (e.g., Zald and Denton 1963).

What is important here is that much of the old institutional analysis in organization studies maintained that norms and values were an important part of institutional life. Organizations responded to the norms and values in their environment in ways that resulted in behavior that did not fit traditional theories of organizational decision making, which rested on rationalist and utilitarian assumptions. These were the same assumptions that underpinned neoclassical economics and the new institutionalism in economics (March 1996, 281–83). Thus, according to organizational institutionalists, organizations sought to act appropriately vis-à-vis their cultural environments rather than instrumentally vis-à-vis their official goals.[14]

The difference between a logic of appropriateness and a logic of instrumentality is central to new versions of organizational institutionalism (March and Olsen 1989, chap. 2). Building on the idea that organizations act in response to the norms and values in their environment, John Meyer and Brian Rowan (1977, 340) argued that

> organizations are driven to incorporate the practices and procedures defined by prevailing rationalized concepts of organizational work and institutionalized in society. Organizations that do so increase their legitimacy and their survival prospects, independent of the immediate efficacy of the acquired practices and procedures.

In other words, organizations adopt whatever practices they believe their institutional environment deems appropriate or legitimate regardless of whether these practices increase organizational efficiency or otherwise reduce costs relative to benefits, as rational choice institutionalists contend.

Meyer and other new organizational institutionalists have generated a vast number of empirical studies arguing the basic point that the behavior and formal structure of business firms, schools, nation-states, and other organizations are defined by their institutional environments and that these organizations seek legitimacy from their environments to ensure their survival (e.g., Boli and Thomas 1999a; Scott and Meyer 1994; Thomas et al. 1987). In contrast to the old institutionalists like Selznick,

---

[14] The distinction between logics of instrumentality and appropriateness was eventually accepted by some rational choice institutionalists who argued that once actors determine the range of appropriate choices before them, they then proceed to pick one on instrumental grounds (Ostrom 1991). In contrast to this sequencing argument, other rational choice institutionalists have suggested that both logics may operate simultaneously in institution-building episodes. Jon Elster (1998b), for example, claimed that state delegates to the U.S. constitutional convention in Philadelphia were motivated sometimes by a concern for treating states fairly and sometimes by a concern for advancing their state's interests.

who focused on individual organizations, the new institutionalists shift their attention to entire fields or populations of organizations within an institutional environment. For them, institutions include informal and common cultural frameworks, symbolism, and taken-for-granted cognitive schema as well as formal rule systems. Importantly, institutions also contain routines and processes that sustain these frameworks, symbols, schema, and rules and, therefore, reproduce themselves over time (Jepperson 1991, 145). Moreover, because organizations of a common type, such as art museums or business firms, share a common institutional environment, they all tend to adopt similar structures and practices over time. Hence, fields or populations of organizations gradually become isomorphic or homogenous. This is not because they all instrumentally seek the most efficient way of operating or try to maximize benefits relative to costs, as rational choice institutionalists would expect, but because they seek to conform to the culturally appropriate scripts, schema, and organizational models in their environment. For instance, organizational institutionalists have argued that the field of state governments in the United States adopted very similar enabling legislation for the establishment of health maintenance organizations because they perceived that it was the legitimate thing to do within their political environment (Strang and Bradburn 2001).

The distinction between normative and cognitive factors is important for organizational institutionalists. Whereas much of the old organizational institutionalism emphasized that actors respond to the normative and value-laden pressures in their environments, and do so deliberately and self-consciously, new versions of organizational institutionalism additionally stressed cognition and how actors' perceptions of what is an appropriate practice depend on the taken-for-granted scripts, schema, habits, and routines that they possess and through which they interpret the world (Scott 2001, chap. 2). Indeed, actors may not have a clear sense of what their self-interests or goals are at all, particularly during periods of great uncertainty and information scarcity, and so they may act in unreflective ways according to these taken-for-granted cognitive structures. Hence, institutionalized scripts and routines are said not only to constrain action but also to enable or constitute it by providing actors with models to guide their behavior (Clemens and Cook 1999). In this regard, the new organizational institutionalism also differs sharply from much rational choice institutionalism and draws heavily from phenomenology, ethnomethodology, and cognitive psychology (DiMaggio and Powell 1991; DiMaggio 1997).[15]

---

[15] A European variation on this theme is represented by the discourse analytic tradition of institutional analysis, which emphasizes how systems of symbolic meaning codified in

Reliance on normative and cognitive factors has not been without its problems. For example, despite its importance within this paradigm, some organizational institutionalists have admitted that the distinction between normative and cognitive ideas is often blurred; that it is not clear when norms become so taken for granted that they become part of a cognitive structure (Clemens and Cook, 1999, 445–46). Critics, such as Paul Hirsch (1997), have also suggested that the mechanisms by which normative and cognitive structures affect behavior are often poorly specified.[16] In any case, insofar as taken-for-granted institutions are said to constrain behavior, on the one hand, and to enable or constitute it, on the other, in ways that lead to the unreflective reproduction of behavior over time with only minor variations, some organizational institutionalists have embraced the idea that institutional change generally occurs in path-dependent evolutionary ways (Powell 1991, 189–94).

Another branch of organizational theory, although one not always associated with institutionalism, also argues that institutional change tends to follow an evolutionary pattern. Population ecologists maintain that principles and practices become institutionalized as they diffuse through populations of organizations and thus become taken for granted cognitively as the legitimate mode of operation (e.g., Carroll and Hannan 1989). Adopting concepts from evolutionary biology, the population ecology view holds that diffusion is driven largely by competitive selection. Organizations adopting the principles and practices that best fit their environmental niche will be the ones most likely to survive. Although most organizational institutionalists distance themselves from this approach, ecologists argue that the two views are compatible once we realize that populations of organizations may evolve as they seek to adopt principles and practices that confer legitimacy on them as social actors (Hannan and Freeman 1989, 34–35). The problem, they admit, is that while they know a good deal about selection processes, they know much less about the processes that lead to the creation of new organizational principles and practices in the first place (Hannan and Freeman 1989, 20–21). In other words, this approach neglects an analysis of creative innovation, entrepreneurial activity, and agency. The same criticism has been leveled against organizational institutionalists who talk about how cognitive schema and other institutions constrain change in path-dependent ways (Hirsch 1997).

---

language influence how actors observe, interpret, reason, and act (e.g., Campbell and Pedersen 2001a, 8–14). Discourse analysis has a particularly strong affinity with organizational institutionalism insofar as both are concerned with how actors behave in institutionally appropriate ways and how taken-for-granted linguistic patterns, intellectual paradigms, or other kinds of ideas shape how actors understand the world (e.g., Pedersen 1991).

[16] Hirsch's criticism is among the most extended and fully developed, and is targeted specifically at W. Richard Scott's representation of the paradigm as presented in the first edition of his book, *Institutions and Organizations*.

However, organizational institutionalists are less sanguine about evolutionary change than many rational choice institutionalists. To be sure, many argue that evolutionary change is the norm and that even apparently revolutionary institutional changes may, upon closer inspection, stem from the gradual accretion of many incremental path-dependent adjustments (e.g., Van de Ven and Garud 1993)—an argument very much like Riker's rational choice analysis of the U.S. Constitution. But others argue that when change occurs, it is more likely to follow a punctuated equilibrium or punctuated evolution pattern. That is, change is episodic and marked by a brief period of crisis or critical intervention followed by a longer period of stability or path-dependent evolutionary change (Powell 1991, 197).

For example, Neil Fligstein (1990) showed that the development of corporate America followed a pattern of punctuated equilibrium. Periodic bouts of market and price instability, severe competition, and overproduction triggered a series of crises for U.S. corporations throughout the late nineteenth and twentieth centuries. In response to each crisis, corporate managers shifted from one conception of corporate control to another. For Fligstein (10), conceptions of control were "totalizing worldviews" through which managers interpret their situations. Direct control of markets through holding companies and horizontal mergers gave way in the early 1900s to a manufacturing conception of control that was based on vertical integration and price leading. This was replaced by a sales and marketing approach during the 1930s that emphasized product diversification. Then, during the 1960s, a financial conception of control emerged that privileged conglomerate mergers. In each case, a crisis upset the institutional equilibrium and precipitated a search for a new corporate order that, once institutionalized, ushered in a new period of institutional equilibrium.

Regardless of whether they subscribe to an evolutionary, punctuated equilibrium, or other view of change, the new organizational institutionalists generally agree that fields of organizations adopt common institutionalized practices as a result of three essential processes by which practices diffuse through the field. First are mimetic processes in which organizations facing uncertainty lack a clear idea of what they should do and so copy the practices of other, apparently successful, organizations in their field. Second are normative processes in which organizational leaders have been professionalized to share similar views on what constitutes appropriate organizational practice. Third are coercive processes in which organizations adapt to pressure from other organizations around them to conform to institutionalized standards (DiMaggio and Powell 1983; Mizruchi and Fein 1999). Diffusion is the operative concept here. So, for example, Pamela Tolbert and Lynne Zucker (1983) argued that civil service reform began to diffuse during the late nineteenth century across municipal governments in the United States because it was seen as a way to reduce political conflict and improve government operations. However, as the reform model was adopted by an initial set of governments, it became institutionalized. Later, when other governments adopted it, they did so more to obtain social legitimacy and because they simply took for granted that it was the appropriate way to organize their operations. As noted earlier, the problem with the diffusion approach, according to critics, is that it appears to be a mindless and excessively mechanical transfer of principles and practices from one organization to another. In other words, the underlying mechanisms of transfer are underspecified, and again there is little room for an account of actors and agency (Hirsch 1997; Rao et al. 2003).[17]

Organizational institutionalism was developed and elaborated primarily by sociologists. To be sure, a few economists have relied in part on notions of culturally specific, taken-for-granted routines, practices, and norms to explain variation in economic structure and performance across organizations and countries and over time (e.g., Best 1990; Hodgson 1988, chap. 5; Lazonick 1991; Nelson and Winter 1982; Whitley and Kristensen 1997). However, outside of sociology it is probably in the area of international relations that this approach has been most influential (e.g., Finnemore 1996; Katzenstein 1996b). For instance, Alexander Wendt (1992; see also Jepperson et al. 1996) argued, in contrast to more rational-choice or realist views, that states interact with one another through their representatives and through these interactions they develop a set of intersubjective understandings about themselves and each other. That is, they develop identities and worldviews at the cognitive level through which they define situations, their interests, and subsequent courses of action. According to Wendt, through this identity formation process states decide whether to pursue self-help security strategies, such as defending themselves without assistance from other states, or more cooperative strategies, like NATO, in which they work with other states for mutual defense. Furthermore, work in international relations has suggested that international norms also influence state security strategies and other decisions, such as whether states should procure and deploy nuclear or chemical weapons systems (e.g., Eyre and Suchman 1996; Price and Tannenwald 1996).

---

[17] There are, however, some recent exceptions (e.g., Greenwood and Hinings 1993, 1996); Hironaka and Schofer 2002). For instance, Hironaka and Schofer argued that national state bureaucrats and decision-makers enjoy considerable latitude—depending on their resources, state capacities, and values—in implementing policy models that diffuse to them from the international environment, and claimed that implementation is often a politically contested process.

To review, first, while some organizational institutionalists accept that institutional change follows a punctuated equilibrium or perhaps punctuated evolutionary pattern, others argue that institutional change often tends to be evolutionary. Second, both path dependence and diffusion are important concepts that organizational institutionalists use to account for change. Proponents of both concepts have been criticized generally, however, for overemphasizing the importance of institutional structure, failing to demonstrate the mechanisms by which these structures affect actors, and, therefore, neglecting that actors and agency are important ingredients in episodes of institutional change (Finnemore 1996, 339; Di-Maggio and Powell 1991; Hirsch 1997; Hirsch and Lounsbury 1997; Stinchcombe 1997). Third, the new organizational institutionalists emphasize the importance of cognitive schema and normative principles as determinants of behavior and change. In contrast to rational choice institutionalists, they often put much more emphasis on ideas like these than they put on self-interest as motivational forces. Still, as we have seen, this has not been without its problems—notably, a failure to differentiate clearly between normative and cognitive ideas.

Historical Institutionalism

Historical institutionalism is derived from classical political economy, particularly the historical materialism of Marx and the comparative institutional history of Weber. It has been developed primarily by political scientists who have studied how political and economic decision making is affected by the institutional arrangement of states, including the organization of government agencies, parliaments, constitutions, and electoral rules; by the institutional arrangement of economies, including the organization of labor unions and business associations; and by the institutional connections between states and economies, including economic policy, business regulations, and property rights (e.g., Katzenstein 1978). In this view, institutions are sets of formal and informal rules and procedures, such as those codified in the law or deployed by bureaucratic organizations like states and business firms (Thelen and Steinmo 1992, 2).

Much historical institutionalism has been developed in a macro-level comparative context. For example, many scholars have shown how variation in national political institutions affected the level and progressivity of tax codes across countries (Steinmo 1993), the development of welfare states (Weir and Skocpol 1985; Skocpol 1992), differences in national health care systems (Immergut 1992), and the responses of different governments to international economic crises (Gourevitch 1986). Of course, some researchers have made important insights by focusing on a single state, such as Stephen Skowronek's (1982) analysis of the development of the U.S. civil service, regulatory, and military institutions during the early twentieth century, and how these developments affected the capacity of the federal government to pursue its goals. In all of these instances, and in contrast to organizational institutionalism, historical institutionalists have focused more on broader societal and state structures than on organizations per se. The important point in much of this work is not that institutions directly determine outcomes like these but, more modestly, that institutions constrain them. In a classic statement of the position, Kathleen Thelen and Sven Steinmo (1992, 3) declared that, "what is implicit but crucial in this and most other conceptions of historical institutionalism is that institutions constrain and refract politics but they are never the sole 'cause' of outcomes." This view resembles the choice-within-constraints approach of rational choice institutionalism, discussed earlier.

Historical institutionalism differs from the old institutionalism in political science of the late nineteenth and early twentieth century. As noted earlier, the old institutionalists were concerned primarily with the formal aspects of government, especially the law, how government worked, which institutions worked best, and how government might be improved. Notably, Woodrow Wilson, one of the earliest presidents of the American Political Science Association, wrote several essays about what the U.S. government could learn from European governments that might improve democracy and governmental performance. Given its normative concerns, the old institutionalists were often engaged in progressive and good government movements. Most of their work was very descriptive and lacked much theoretical development or hypothesis testing (Peters 1999, 3–11). In contrast, the recent historical institutionalists are less concerned with these normative issues. They are more interested in studying the informal as well as the formal aspects of government, analyzing the determinants of policy and its outcomes, particularly in historical and comparative perspectives, and developing and testing theories of political institutional development and policy performance. For instance, historical institutionalists have been engaged in heated theoretical debates about the origins of welfare states (e.g., Skocpol 1992; Weir et al. 1988).

However, historical institutionalism emerged mainly in reaction to several streams of thought that had become ensconced in political science and political sociology after the Second World War. First, it took exception with the behavioralism of the 1950s and 1960s, which explained politics in terms of the behaviors of political leaders, interest groups, social classes, or other actors without considering the institutional context within which they operated and how it might affect the interests and behaviors of these actors (Skocpol 1985). Second, it was an effort to move away from functionalist, Marxist, and other forms of grand theorizing that did not adequately explain cross-national variation in how interest groups and social classes were organized and why a particular group or class might demand different policies in different places and at different times (Thelen and Steinmo 1992). Third, it was a reaction against rational choice theory. Historical institutionalists were concerned that material self-interest was not the only motivation for action and that what needed to be explained was not just how institutions shaped actors' strategies, but also how it shaped their preferences and goals in the first place (Thelen and Steinmo 1992). Fourth, much of the ground-breaking work in this paradigm was done in an effort to understand why some advanced capitalist countries were more likely to suffer stagflation than others after the collapse of the Bretton Woods agreement and the oil embargos of the 1970s. Building on earlier work in comparative political economy (e.g., Shonfield 1965), many scholars argued that differences in economic policy and national economic performance during the late 1970s and 1980s depended on whether liberal, statist, or corporatist institutions were in place (e.g., Gourevitch 1986; Katzenstein 1978; Lindberg and Maier 1985). Finally, and more recently, historical institutionalists emphasized the importance of understanding institutional change as well as stability, and thus sought to improve their own work by theorizing how institutions developed in the first place (Thelen and Steinmo 1992).

Central to this perspective is the notion that the institutions that guide decision making reflect historical experience (Hall 1986; March and Olsen 1989, chap. 2). In other words, once institutions have been established through complex struggles and bargaining among organized groups, they have a continuing effect on subsequent decision-making and institution-building episodes. For example, Ira Katznelson (1985) argued that the early provision of voting rights for white men in the United States and a decentralized federalist system of government established by the Constitution mitigated the formation of working-class consciousness and, therefore, a national working-class political party. Workers could obtain social services and other benefits through community-based political machines that traded patronage for votes and that typically organized workers along racial and ethnic rather than class lines. Coupled with the fact that workers did not have to organize politically to obtain the vote, there was little interest for organizing a national labor party. In contrast, the British working class had to struggle for the vote and had to cope with a more centralized national government to obtain government services and protections. As a result, British workers formed a national labor party. Consequently, the presence or absence of a labor party had profound long-term effects on national policy-making in both countries.

As this example suggests, historical institutionalists embrace the idea that policy-making and institutional change tend to be path-dependent processes. This is because institutions constrain the choices available to decision makers; because decision makers incrementally adjust their policies and institutions in response to feedback they receive from their constituents; and because decision makers learn gradually which policies and institutions best suit their purposes (Heclo 1974; Pierson 2000a, 2000b). Insofar as historical institutionalists have emphasized the importance of policy learning, particularly as policy models travel from one country to another, occasionally with a coercive push from powerful states, some of them have recently begun to discuss policy diffusion (e.g., Djelic 1998; Duina 1999). Especially notable here is Peter Hall's (1989a) volume on the diffusion of Keynesianism across the advanced capitalist democracies. In this regard historical institutionalists have begun to develop similarities with a sizeable literature on cross-national policy transfer (e.g., Dolowitz and Marsh 1996).

However, historical institutionalists have also been very interested in abrupt and revolutionary shifts in policy and institutions that represent sharp breaks from the past. (Indeed, Theda Skocpol [1979], one of the major proponents of this paradigm, began her career with an important comparative study of social revolutions.) Historical institutionalists frequently describe patterns of stability and change as punctuated equilibrium (e.g., Baumgartner and Jones 1993; Hall 1993; Krasner 1984). According to some critics, this has created problems for them insofar as their explanations of rapid, revolutionary change do not square well with an analytic framework that talks much about path-dependence. Put in slightly different terms, if institutions are so important in constraining policy-making outcomes at one moment, how can they suddenly become so unimportant at another (Peters 1999, 65; Thelen 1999)? For this and other reasons, some historical institutionalists have complained that the concept of path dependence is often used rather loosely without a clear specification of the mechanisms involved (Pierson and Skocpol 2000; Pierson 2000b; Thelen 2000a).

Recognizing the importance of path dependence, some historical institutionalists have followed Douglass North in maintaining that what may appear initially as a sudden episode of policy-making or institutional punctuated equilibrium and dissonance often turns out to be one of much more evolutionary change. Certainly an interest in the evolutionary pattern of change is consistent with a long-standing tradition in political science that policy-making and institutional change are best conceptualized as being incremental in nature (e.g., Lindblom 1959; Witte 1985). Notably, Paul Pierson (1994) argued that what appeared initially to many scholars as an abrupt and radical overhaul of U.S. welfare policy in the early 1980s turned out later to be considerably less dramatic and more evolutionary. Still other scholars have argued that there is some truth to both views and that the best way to describe institutional change is as a pattern of punctuated evolution (Hay 2001).

Researchers working in the historical institutionalist tradition have long accepted that self-interest motivates behavior and institutional change. Increasingly, however, they have also emphasized that ideas and principled beliefs, such as convictions about what constitutes good public policy and good government, also influence decision making (e.g., Derthick and Quirk 1985). In this regard, they are clearly related to organizational institutionalists in recognizing that a logic of appropriateness may be just as important as a logic of instrumentality (Hall 1993; March and Olsen 1989, chap. 2). In a few cases they have made efforts to deploy an analysis of ideas to help account for those moments when institutional equilibrium is punctuated by a crisis and eventually gives way to fundamental policy and institutional change. Mark Blyth (2002), for instance, showed how struggles over foundational economic theories during moments of economic crisis resulted in intellectual paradigm shifts among academic and political elites that contributed to the overhaul of economic policy during the late twentieth century in the United States and Sweden. Following Peter Hall (1993), Blyth argued that cognitive paradigms constrain the choices available to actors until they no longer provide answers to the problems these actors face. Then a search is launched for a new paradigm that, when found, ushers in a new set of policies and institutions (see also Hay 2001). In other words, although the instrumental pursuit of interests guides reform, so does the sensitivity of decision makers to what they believe are the appropriate blueprints for reform.

To summarize, first, historical institutionalists debate whether institutions vacillate in patterns of evolution and incrementalism, punctuated equilibrium, or punctuated evolution. Yet, as the next chapter shows, it is not always clear for them how we should determine how much change has occurred in a given historical episode or which pattern best characterizes it. Second, although historical institutionalists embrace the notion of path-dependent change, they also recognize that much work remains to be done to specify better the mechanisms involved. As we shall see in chapter 3, the mechanisms underlying diffusion also require attention. Third, historical institutionalists can be located somewhere between rational choice and organizational institutionalists in the sense that they seek to offer a more balanced treatment in their work of the interplay between ideas and a logic of appropriateness, on the one hand, and interests and a logic of instrumentality, on the other hand (e.g., Goldstein and Keohane 1993a). Still, as critics have charged (e.g., Blyth 1997; Yee 1996) and as chapter 4 shows, they often run into difficulty conceptualizing and studying how ideas affect decision making and institutional change.

Conclusion and a Look Ahead

Overall, it is clear that within each of the three institutionalist paradigms scholars tend to debate whether evolutionary, punctuated equilibrium, or other patterns of institutional change are the most prevalent. To my knowledge they have not established clear guidelines for how this debate should be reconciled. They also tend to adopt similar causal concepts, notably path dependence and diffusion, to explain institutional change but have been criticized for poorly specifying the underlying mechanisms involved. Finally, in varying degrees, they have all acknowledged that ideas other than that of self-interest need to be included in accounts of decision making and institutional change, although concerns exist as to how this ought to be done. In other words, the problems of change, mechanisms, and ideas are shared by all three paradigms. Once these problems are reconciled, we will see that institutional analysis can be used to shed new light on the nature of change associated with important empirical phenomena like globalization.

Let me preview more specifically the arguments that lie ahead. In chapter 2, I explain that to determine more accurately how much change occurs in any given case and whether it is more evolutionary or revolutionary, we need to specify carefully the important dimensions along which we seek to observe change, establish the time frame during which we conduct our observations, and then see how many dimensions change during that period of time. In chapter 3, I argue that to understand better how institutional change occurs in path-dependent ways and through diffusion, we need to recognize that it rarely starts from scratch. Typically, institutional change involves the recombination of old institutional elements and sometimes the introduction of new ones as well. I refer to these processes as bricolage and translation, respectively. In chapter 4, I identify four different types of ideas that affect institutional change. I also discuss the actors that create, transform, and mobilize them, and some of the mechanisms through which each type of idea exerts its effects.

In chapter 5, I pull all of these arguments together and demonstrate their utility for understanding important empirical phenomena, in this case globalization. I show that if we identify important institutional dimensions associated with globalization and track them over an appropriate period of time, we find substantially less institutional change at the level of national political economies than much of the globalization literature suggests. Furthermore, the change we see is much more evolutionary than revolutionary. This is because national institutions affect how decision makers respond to the pressures for change that are often said to be associated with globalization. Hence, change has been much less pronounced than many people have assumed because it has happened in ways that are heavily path-dependent; it has happened in ways that involve much translation and bricolage; and it has happened in ways that illustrate how ideas as well as formal institutions facilitate and, more importantly in this case, constrain change. Finally, in chapter 6, I present a theory of institutional change based on arguments developed in the previous chapters. It explains how institutional entrepreneurs and others innovate in response to the problems they confront; how they define and frame these problems as well as possible institutional solutions; how this creative process is constrained by the social, organizational, and institutional contexts within which it occurs; and how all of this affects the probabilities that an episode of institutional change will be relatively more evolutionary or revolutionary.

Throughout this book I draw material from different institutionalist paradigms and synthesize it in various ways to make my arguments. This sort of synthetic move is necessary if we agree that it is time for a second movement in institutional analysis where we begin to think seriously about building bridges among these paradigms.

That said, my aim is *not* to offer some sort of all-encompassing Grand Synthesis where everything in the three institutionalist paradigms is combined into a new theory that completely dissolves the distinctions among paradigms and results in a fully unified view that all institutionalists will accept. Why? There are some real differences among proponents of the three different paradigms. For instance, some institutionalists have fundamental disagreements over the micro-foundations of social action. Some rational choice institutionalists assume that people are motivated strictly by individual, material self-interest and that institution building results from the pursuit of these interests (Ingram and Clay 2000, 529). In contrast, many organizational institutionalists assume that people are motivated by collective identities and cultural frames and that these drive institution building in ways that do not fit neatly with explanations based simply on the pursuit of rational self-interest (Fligstein 2001b, 106). In some cases, these differences may be so extreme as to be irreconcilable (e.g., Hay and Wincott 1998).

The same may be true for disagreements *within* paradigms. Some positions are more extreme and hard-core than others and, therefore, less susceptible to synthesis. For instance, some rational choice institutionalists make the very strong assumption, often as an admitted convenience for building mathematical models and abstract game theories, that actors behave in a fully rational manner and are in fact able to maximize benefits relative to costs. Others make the weaker, yet more realistic, assumption that actors behave only in an intendedly rational manner. In other words, actors try to behave as rationally as possible given the fact that they make decisions under conditions of bounded rationality due to cognitive and other limitations on their ability to calculate costs and benefits accurately (e.g., Williamson 1985, 44–47). The latter is more compatible with historical and organizational institutionalists who are interested in how cognitive schema, norms, and the like affect institutional change. And, of course, there are other differences that may affect the possibilities for synthesis. Some rational choice institutionalists are more interested than others in how history shapes behavior in path-dependent ways; some are more interested in getting their hands dirty with data than in simply engaging in abstract theorizing; and, as noted earlier, some define institutions as rules that constrain action whereas others insist that institutions are strategic equilibria.

My point is simply that some things may be more amenable to synthesis than others. As a result, writing this sort of a book is much like institutional change itself. It involves a process of bricolage. That is, it involves selecting various ideas from different places and combining them in ways that yield something new. Of course, this is not an unbiased process. I draw more heavily from historical and organizational institutionalism, the traditions that I have studied the longest, than I do from rational choice institutionalism. And within the rational choice tradition I tend to find the work of institutionalists like North and others who follow in his footsteps to be more useful than the work of the more abstract game theorists. This is because the former have more realistic assumptions about the micro-foundations of human behavior, are more sensitive to the path-dependent nature of institutional change, take norms and cognitive structures more seriously, have a greater affinity to empirical research rather than to abstract theory construction, and define institutions as rules rather than strategic equilibrium. As a result, the former have more in common with historical and organizational institutionalism in the first place and, therefore, offer more immediate synthetic possibilities. Other people might have a different selection bias and, as a result, might come up with different synthetic insights. I encourage them to do so. But this does not negate my basic argument that all three institutionalist paradigms share common problems and that an important step toward resolving them involves synthesizing portions of each.

Chapter 2

THE PROBLEM OF CHANGE

WHAT IS INSTITUTIONAL CHANGE? How do we know it when we see it? What does it look like when it occurs? Is it evolutionary or revolutionary? These questions lie at the heart of much institutional analysis. Because institutionalists are concerned with developing theories that identify the causes of institutional change, answering these questions is tantamount to specifying the critical *dependent variable* for much of our work. As discussed in chapter 1, institutionalists have described and tried to account for different patterns of institutional change, such as evolution and punctuated equilibrium. And several preeminent institutionalists have spent considerable time trying to map changes in the institutional arrangements of politics, economics, health care, culture, and other areas of concern to social scientists.[1] Institutionalists have offered surprisingly little discussion and guidance, however, about how we ought to determine empirically which pattern of change has occurred.

Why is distinguishing among different patterns of change important? First, being careful empirically to distinguish patterns of change when we see them will help us avoid mistaking revolutionary for evolutionary change, and vice versa—a problem that plagues, for example, much of the literature on globalization, as we shall see in chapter 5. Second, institutionalists have become interested recently in deducing hypotheses and theories that try to specify the conditions under which different patterns of change are likely to occur, including specifically patterns of evolution and punctuated equilibrium (Greenwood and Hinings 1996). However, if we want to test these theories, then it is incumbent on us to explain how we know different patterns of change when we encounter them. Third, failure to identify correctly which pattern of change we are observing can lead to much confusion not only in what we are trying to explain, but how we try to explain it. For instance, if we take a more inductive approach to theory construction and think that we are witnessing an episode of punctuated equilibrium and revolutionary change, then our theoretical explanation of what caused it may be much different than if we think we are witnessing a period of evolutionary and incremental change. Assuming

---

[1] For example, on institutional change in politics, see Skocpol (1992) and Skowronek (1982); in economics, see North (1981); in health care, see Scott et al. (2000); in culture, see DiMaggio (1986).

that change follows a punctuated equilibrium pattern might compel us to search for major events and disruptive processes that trigger change. Assuming that change follows an evolutionary pattern might compel us to search for minor events and path-dependent processes.

This chapter is about how to detect different patterns of institutional change when they occur—that is, how to specify one of most important dependent variables with which institutionalists are concerned. Thus, the chapter focuses on some of the chief methodological problems confronting institutionalists today. Subsequent chapters will deal with issues of causality and explaining how institutional change happens. In this chapter, I argue that describing patterns of institutional change is by no means straightforward. It requires more thoughtful consideration than it has received in the past. Indeed, serious conceptual and methodological issues are involved for research in determining which patterns occur. Unless these are resolved, it will remain difficult to determine whether specific episodes of institutional change are evolutionary, revolutionary, or something else, and our work will suffer as a result.

I begin by reviewing the basic patterns of institutional change with which institutionalists have been most concerned. One is continuous (evolutionary) and two are discontinuous (punctuated equilibrium, punctuated evolution). Continuous patterns of change are those that characterize change as a smooth and gradual process whereas those that are discontinuous paint a much different picture consisting of sharp shifts from one institutional arrangement to another (Meyer et al. 1990). Of course, there are other patterns of change, such as cyclical, accelerating, spiraling, and random patterns of change (Sztompka 1993, chap. 1). Most institutionalists, however, have not articulated theories of these sorts of change, and so I do not address them here. Second, I argue that to determine which of these patterns best characterizes institutional change in empirical cases, we must, on the one hand, clarify what we mean by an institution, that is, specify the critical *dimensions* of the institution in question that may be subject to change. On the other hand, we must define the appropriate *time frame* over which change in these dimensions may have occurred. Hence, institutional change and stability are defined in terms of how much variation occurs, or not, in these dimensions over a given period of time. More specifically, revolutionary change or punctuated equilibrium consists of simultaneous change across most, if not all, dimensions of an institution over a given period of time; evolutionary change consists of change in only a few of these dimensions over a given period of time; and stability consists of the absence of change in most, if not all, of these dimensions. While institutionalists have paid at least some attention to the issue of differentiating among dimensions, we have virtually ignored the issue of time frames. Third, I show that carefully specifying important dimensions and appropriate time frames can yield important theoretical insights into the nature of institutional change regardless of whether researchers rely on qualitative, quantitative, or a mixture of techniques.

Scholars have made strong claims about which pattern of institutional change tends to occur most frequently. For instance, several have argued that evolution is the norm and that even apparently revolutionary periods during which change seems to be radical and abrupt often turn out to be quite evolutionary upon further inspection (North 1998, 19–20, 1990, 90; Riker 1998). These sorts of claims cannot be substantiated without dealing with the methodological issues raised in this chapter. However, my intent is not to provide hard and fast *rules* for specifying dimensions and time frames in every case. I am not sure that is possible. Instead, the discussion that follows simply raises issues and offers *guidelines* that, if taken seriously, can improve how we think about and make choices about the dimensions and time frames we use in our work. Our understanding of patterns of institutional change will improve accordingly and we will be less likely to mistake one pattern for another.

PATTERNS OF INSTITUTIONAL CHANGE

Several basic patterns of institutional change exist.[2] Among the most frequently discussed by institutionalists is the incremental or *evolutionary* pattern. This entails continuous change that proceeds in small, incremental steps along a single path in a certain direction (North 1998; Sztompka 1993, 13–14). Change is evolutionary in the sense that today's institutional arrangements differ from but still closely resemble yesterday's because they have inherited many of their predecessors' characteristics (e.g., Nelson and Winter 1982). For years, it has been argued that institutions are sticky and prone to inertia and, as a result, change quite gradually (e.g., Braybrooke and Lindblom 1963; Lindblom 1959). According to this view, decision makers often suffer from insufficient information about the problems at hand, poor methods for evaluating policy effectiveness, and other difficulties—conditions that rational choice and organizational institutionalists regard as problems of bounded rationality (e.g., Jones 1999; March and Simon 1958, 137–170). Consequently, decision makers are generally reluctant to make sweeping policy decisions that would dramatically transform institutions. Instead, they make decisions that lead only to marginal changes from the institutional status quo. These changes

---

[2] By patterns of change, I am simply referring to a description of how the configuration of an institution changes over time, not the causal processes that precipitate such change. For an effort to do both simultaneously, see Van de Ven and Poole (1995).

accumulate gradually over time resulting in an evolutionary process of institutional change. Thus, for example, despite occasional calls by decision makers for sweeping tax reforms in the United States, we tend to get much more modest changes that often amount to little more than a fine-tuning of already existing tax law (Witte 1985).

Some scholars recognize, nonetheless, that relatively rapid and profound institutional change does occur sometimes (e.g., Astley 1985; Baumgartner and Jones 1993; Campbell and Lindberg 1991; Tushman and Anderson 1986). They often describe this discontinuous pattern of change as *punctuated equilibrium*.[3] For instance, several researchers have argued that a Fordist model of industrial production—a set of institutions based on the principles of mass production, large vertically integrated firms, and centralized union contracts—was institutionalized during the first half of the twentieth century in the advanced capitalist countries and remained in place for decades. It was not until the mid-1970s that rapid changes in technologies, energy prices, and market demand sparked a dramatic shift toward post-Fordist institutions based on the principles of decentralized corporate structures, flexible inter-firm networks, and an attack on conventional union contracts (Lash and Urry 1987; Piore and Sabel 1984). In this case, the mid-1970s marked a turning point between two fundamentally different institutional eras of capitalism.

A few scholars have suggested recently that the periods of equilibrium occurring between punctuations are better characterized as evolutionary rather than static. Hence, they favor a *punctuated evolution* pattern that considers the possibility that there may be two types of change, each driven by different dynamics (e.g., Kaufman 1998). The evolutionary periods are characterized by social learning during which self-reflexive actors gradually adjust their institutions in ways that are constrained by already-given institutional practices, rules, routines, and cognitive schema. These periods are punctuated occasionally by crises that involve open struggles over the very core of the institutional status quo and that eventually result in truly fundamental institutional transformations (e.g., March and Olsen 1989, 170–171). For instance, during the early 1970s the onset of stagflation in Britain caused the Labor Party to experiment with a new economic model, monetarism, although the party continued to stick largely to its long-standing Keynesian principles. In this sense, taken-for-granted assumptions about the appropriate approach to macroeconomic policy began to evolve slowly in a neoliberal direction as a result of trial-and-error learning but was constrained all the while by a well-

---

[3] The concept of punctuated equilibrium has roots to debates in biology about the nature of evolutionary change. See, for instance, Eldredge and Gould (1972), Gould and Eldredge (1977), Gould (1982, 1989), and Eldredge (1989).

institutionalized Keynesian framework. Assumptions about the appropriate macroeconomic model began to weaken, but only at the margins. As stagflation worsened, however, a crisis mentality set in and swept Margaret Thatcher's Conservative Party into power in 1979. The new government broke dramatically with Keynesianism to pursue a full neoliberal agenda, including monetarism, sharp cuts in taxes and social spending, balanced budgets, economic deregulation, and the privatization of state services—a fundamentally different set of institutionalized assumptions and priorities than those that characterized the previous Labor government period (Hay 2001).

Adjudicating among these patterns of institutional change might appear to be simple. That is, in a given empirical case, such as the shift from Keynesianism to neoliberalism, or from Fordism to post-Fordism, simply see how dramatic or abrupt a change has been. Unfortunately, this is not as easy as it might seem. It requires that we determine whether there have been critical turning points that differentiate among relatively stable time periods—a task that requires us to identify historically specific patterns among variables (Abbott 1997, 1992, 1988; Isaac 1997). In turn, this demands that we carefully specify the important dimensions of the institution in question and how they must change in order for evolutionary or punctuated patterns of change to occur. It also means that we need to pay close attention to the time frame over which we track change in these dimensions.

The problem is that how this should be done is not always evident. For example, researchers who focus on only a few dimensions of an institution, or who track these dimensions over relatively brief periods of time, may detect radical institutional shifts. Others with a more multidimensional and temporally longer approach may not. Hence, observers of the Reagan administration's welfare reforms concluded from changes in budget allocations during the first few years of the 1980s that a new and fundamentally more austere set of welfare institutions had begun to develop. However, those who adopted a more multidimensional view that examined budget allocations as well as structural changes in welfare programs and did so across the entire decade disagreed, believing that much more evolutionary change had happened (Pierson 1994, 13–17). As this example shows, how we specify institutional dimensions and time frames can be very important. But how should we go about doing this?

SPECIFYING INSTITUTIONAL DIMENSIONS

We often take for granted that we know what institutions are, but there is debate about how we should characterize them. For instance, W. Richard Scott (2001, chap. 3), an organizational institutionalist, contends that institutions are comprised of three basic dimensions or pillars. The regulative pillar consists of legal, constitutional, and other rules that constrain and regularize behavior. The normative pillar involves principles that prescribe the goals of behavior and the appropriate ways to pursue them. The cultural-cognitive pillar entails the culturally shaped, taken-for-granted assumptions about reality and the frames through which it is perceived, understood, and given meaning. Other organizational institutionalists differentiate among material, symbolic, instrumental, and normative logics of institutions (Friedland and Alford 1991). Douglass North (1990, 45), a rational choice institutionalist, describes institutions as embodying formal rules and procedures as well as informal codes of conduct (see also Moe 1987; Ostrom 1990, chap. 6). Even formal property rights, the regulative institution with which North is often most concerned, consists of a bundle of dimensions that can be conceptually disaggregated into rights of ownership, usage, and appropriation (Barzel 1989; Campbell 1993b). Historical institutionalists, such as Karen Orren and Stephen Skowronek (1994), recognize that institutions consist of various formal and informal dimensions characterized by conflicting institutional logics. Thus, although institutionalists may quibble over what the basic dimensions of an institution are, it should be clear that institutions are multidimensional. As such, if we want to determine how much institutional change has occurred and what pattern it has followed, it is imperative that we carefully specify all the important institutional dimensions and then see how much each one changes.

This is also true for rational choice game theorists even though they have a much different definition of institutions than other institutionalists. While most institutionalists define institutions as sets of formal or informal rules, broadly construed, that constrain behavior, I noted briefly in chapter 1 that some game theorists define institutions as situations of mutually beneficial strategic equilibria where no one sees an advantage in changing their behavior given the likely costs and benefits of doing so. Specifying institutional dimensions is just as important for them insofar as an institution involves several dimensions of behavior around which strategic equilibria are negotiated.

To digress briefly, I will refer frequently to Scott's typology throughout this book because it is often cited and used by researchers, and because it encompasses phenomena of concern to a wide variety of institutionalists. This should not be surprising insofar as he derived it in part from a comprehensive review of the different institutionalist paradigms. As just noted, however, there are a variety of schemes available for distinguishing among institutional dimensions. In the remainder of this chapter, I provide several examples from empirical research to illustrate my arguments. Unfortunately, because different researchers distinguish among institutional dimensions in different ways, readers may find the number of schemes for making these distinctions somewhat maddening to follow. This is a reflection of the diversity of schemes used in the literature and, therefore, unavoidable. Nevertheless, what is important to remember is not the different schemes themselves, but the fact that differentiating among dimensions—regardless of how that is done—is the necessary metric for determining methodologically which patterns of change are operating in empirical cases.

Specifying institutional dimensions is an exercise that involves several considerations. First is the analyst's *theoretical perspective*. Following Scott, for example, if we are concerned with the cultural-cognitive pillar of corporate institutions, then steps need to be taken to track them empirically, as Neil Fligstein (1990) did when he investigated the intellectual backgrounds of U.S. corporate managers from the late nineteenth through the twentieth centuries to determine how their cognitive conceptions of corporate control, that is, their taken-for-granted views on how to run a successful corporation, were changing. Mauro Guillén (1994a) did much the same thing by examining the published literature in organization studies in different countries over time to determine which management models were dominating managerial discourse and thought. If we are concerned with the regulative pillar of corporate institutions, then we may need to pay close attention to the formal means of corporate governance, such as regulations, property rights, and enforcement procedures that define the fiduciary responsibility of managers to stockholders and workers, and the relationships among firms, banks, suppliers, and consumers (e.g., Campbell and Lindberg 1990; Doremus et al. 1998; Roe 1994). If we are concerned with the normative pillar of corporate institutions, then we need to examine what managers, workers, and other actors believe are the socially appropriate ways to make corporate decisions and treat members of the firm (Dore 1983; Streeck 1997).

The second consideration in specifying dimensions concerns the perspectives of the researcher and the people who occupy the institutions that the researcher is studying. This is the issue of *salience*. As is well known (e.g., Weber 1978, 4–22), researchers often impose their own categories on the phenomenon they observe. These categories include the institutional dimensions that they believe are important. The danger is that researchers may confuse dimensions that are relevant to themselves with those that are salient to the actors they are studying. This could inadvertently obscure important aspects of the institution that might otherwise be discovered. For instance, an anthropologist who lived in Atlanta, Georgia, and then traveled to study an unfamiliar, rural village in Samoa observed in the first few months that not much was happening. From his point of view, the pace of life seemed to be very slow. However, once he had a chance to acclimate to the culture and discover those institutional aspects of it that were important to its people, it became clear that there was actually a lot happening. He had started to pay attention to the things that mattered to the inhabitants of that culture rather than to the things that mattered to him (Shore 2001). In other words, when selecting the dimensions of institutions that we think are important, we should try to ensure that they are salient for the people who actually live with them.

The third consideration affecting the selection of dimensions involves the analyst's *level of analysis*. Institutionalists vary greatly in terms of their favored levels of analysis. Many historical institutionalists focus on nation-states and national economies. Organizational institutionalists focus on the organizational field, itself something that could include a single industry comprised of many business firms, the world polity comprised of many nation-states, or any other set of related organizations. Rational choice institutionalists may focus on a small group of people, such as the U.S. Congress, or a large group of organizations like the international state system. The point here is twofold. First, the dimensions a researcher chooses to examine may be influenced by the level of analysis he or she selects. Second, this affects the sort of theoretical insights the researcher is likely to gain.

For example, in a clever reexamination of his earlier work on the U.S. civil rights movement, Doug McAdam (McAdam and Scott forthcoming) shifted his level of analysis from the nation-state to the world polity. Initially, he had adopted an approach similar to historical institutionalism insofar as he focused on the formal political institutions governing civil rights within the United States. Specifically, he showed how it was not until the civil rights movement was able to put enough pressure on Washington during the late 1950s and 1960s that it was able to win changes in federal law that resulted in better protection of civil rights for minorities. Subsequently, however, he learned from organizational institutionalists, notably John Skrentny (1996, 1998), about the importance of normative institutions associated with the world polity and how these institutions may affect domestic politics. As a result, he began to pay closer attention to the world polity institutions within which the U.S. civil rights movement operated. Following Skrentny, he realized that during the late 1940s and early 1950s, international norms changed and increasingly favored democratic reform worldwide. This normative shift was led by the United States to help stop the international spread of communism after the Second World War. Ironically, however, the change in international norms was a blessing for the U.S. civil rights movement because it brought increasing international pressure on Washington for African Americans to receive equal protection under the law. This made U.S. policymakers more vulnerable on normative grounds to pressure from the civil rights movement and provided an important political opening that went a long way in ensuring the movement's success in changing national civil rights law. In sum, by appropriating insights from a different theoretical perspective, McAdam shifted his attention from one level of analysis to another in a way that had significant analytic payoffs. He gained a greater appreciation for the multidimensional institutional complexities of the situation and, as a result, realized that while institutions remained stable at one level, they were changing at another in ways that had major ramifications for his story.

Identifying the relevant dimensions is especially important insofar as institutional change is a lumpy and uneven process where change in one dimension may lag change in another. Social scientists often forget this, lapsing into a nineteenth-century mind-set that assumes that social institutions and processes are far more integrated than is true (Tilly 1984, 11–13; Orren and Skowronek 1994). Historical institutionalists, for instance, have shown that states consist of many different institutionalized rules of action and systems of meaning that are unlikely to change in unison (Skowronek 1995). Some change faster than others. And the resulting lags explain why institutional change may be a slower, more incremental, and evolutionary process than observers believe (North 1990).[4]

For instance, the rapid collapse of communist regimes in Eastern Europe beginning in 1989 involved a swift and radical change in economic discourse where the official rhetoric of communism, including advocacy for centralized state planning and ownership, was abandoned in favor of a neoliberal rhetoric that emphasized the desirability of privatization, liberalization of trade, and the unleashing of market forces in all walks of economic life. By many accounts this was a truly revolutionary shift. Regardless of this normative shift, however, more formal institutional arrangements, such as rules mandating tripartite bargaining among unions, enterprises, and state officials, lingered for many years and changed much more gradually. Furthermore, the cognitive orientation of intellectuals and even some politicians started changing slowly and much earlier insofar as they began to advocate "market socialism" during the late 1960s and 1970s—which illustrates the mixing of elements of market competition into the command economy in an effort to reinvigorate flagging economic performance (Kornai 1992, part 3). In other words, although the normative pillar of postcommunist societies changed rapidly and dramati-

---

[4] I am not suggesting that lags are necessarily resolved over time or that their resolution necessarily results in a unified, coherent set of institutional dimensions. Institutions may consist *normally* of dimensions that contradict or conflict with each other in important ways (Friedland and Alford 1991; Orren and Skowronek 1994). The implications of this point are explored later in this chapter.

cally around 1989, it was preceded by a slow change in the cultural-cognitive pillar and followed by a slow change in the regulative pillar. Viewed in this way, an episode of apparently discontinuous and revolutionary institutional change was actually much more continuous and evolutionary (Campbell and Pedersen 1996; see also Stark 1996). Hence, if we want to determine which pattern of institutional change best characterizes a particular empirical episode, we need to identify and examine over time all the relevant institutional dimensions. The fact that organizational, historical, and rational choice institutionalists are beginning to agree that cultural-cognitive, normative, and regulative dimensions are all important should be cause for optimism in this regard (e.g., Guillén 1994a; Knight and North 1997; Rueschemeyer and Skocpol 1996b).

All of this is important if we want to determine how much institutional change has occurred in a particular setting and which pattern of change best characterizes it. As discussed earlier, which dimensions we choose to track is an open question, depending on the researchers theoretical orientation, issues of salience, and level of analysis. We might want to track changes in different aspects of the written law, the norms that guide behavior, the logics that actors subscribe to, or other institutional dimensions that we deem important. But the point is that once we identify the key dimensions, we can track them over time and determine what the pattern of change has been (e.g., Haveman and Rao 1997; Rao et al. 2000, 241–42). If they all change suddenly, after having been rather stable for a long time, and if long-term stability returns across the board, then we have an example of punctuated equilibrium or revolutionary change. If relatively few change, or if one changes first, then another, and so on, over a long period of time, then we have an example of more evolutionary, or incremental, change. In other words, patterns of change can be differentiated according to how many dimensions change and how fast they do so.

This was precisely the approach Edgar Kiser and Joshua Kane (2001) took to determine whether or not state bureaucratization in Europe corresponded to a pattern of punctuated equilibrium associated with political revolution, or to a more evolutionary pattern. Focusing on the state's capacity to tax in early modern England and France, they found that indirect taxation, such as excise taxes and customs duties, bureaucratized earlier than direct taxation, like income taxes. They also discovered not only that bureaucracy arrived in bits and pieces, rather than unified and fully formed, but that the process began before each country's democratic revolution and ended more than a century afterward. Thus, in contrast to many theories that suggested that democratic revolutions trigger a sudden shift from patrimonial to bureaucratic state institutions, Kiser and Kane showed that in these two cases the process was, upon closer inspection, much more evolutionary than revolutionary.

But an important question remains. How do we decide how long to track our institutional dimensions?

Specifying Time Frames

To determine the pattern of institutional change that has occurred we need to specify the time frame over which we examine the institutional dimensions in question. By time frame I mean duration—the amount of time elapsed for a given event or series of events to occur.[5] Scholars have spent much effort thinking about how time ought to be treated in social science research. They have recognized that the sequencing of events is important in determining how institutional change occurs. They have seen that critical events or turning points may differentiate among historical periods that exhibit fundamentally different social processes and thus require historically specific causal accounts. They have argued that institutions affect how people think about and are constrained by time and that research methods ought to take all of this into consideration. Researchers have even examined how the experience of time and the critical events that are said to separate institutionally distinct time periods are socially constructed and subjectively experienced by the actors involved.[6]

Among institutionalists, the issue of time frames has become increasingly important because we are more concerned than we were previously with the analysis of processes of institutional change. Initially, the focus was mostly on institutional effects, that is, on how institutions affected a variety of outcomes like policy-making, organizational development and efficiency, and the like, over a relatively brief time period. As attention shifted to how the institutions themselves changed, the issue of time be-

---

[5] The concept of a time frame, a methodological concept, should not be confused with theoretical concepts that refer to the ability and willingness of strategic actors to consider the consequences of their actions over longer or shorter periods of time. Notably, much discussion has been given to the issue of discount rates, especially by rational choice institutionalists who seek to incorporate variation in actors' temporal perspectives into explanations of institutional change (e.g., Axelrod 1984, 183; Knight 1992, 129–35; Levi 1988, 32–33).

[6] On the importance of the sequencing of events, see Haydu (1998), Pierson (2000a), and Quadagno and Knapp (1992). On critical events or turning points, see Abbott (1988, 1992, 1997), Griffin (1992), and Kiser and Linton (2002). On how institutions constrain and otherwise affect people's thought about time, see Tilly (1994). On research methods that take time seriously, see Griffin and Isaac (1992), Isaac (1997), and Isaac and Griffin (1989). On how time and critical events are socially constructed and subjectively experienced, see Hay (2001) and McAdam and Sewell (2001, 100–101). For an extended discussion of these and related issues regarding the treatment of time in social science research, see Abbott (2001).

came more salient for institutionalists (Scott 2001, 107–8). Notably, institutionalists recognized that their causal models may vary over time with changes in institutional context (e.g., Bartley and Schneiberg 2002; Isaac and Griffin 1989; Thornton and Ocasio 1999).

Surprisingly, however, institutionalists and others have virtually ignored the issue of how we should specify the time frame over which we track institutions in our efforts to determine how much institutional change has occurred and what pattern it has taken. This is a serious void in the social sciences because some changes take time to unfold—sometimes a long time (Lieberson and Lynn 2002, 13–14). Notably, in an important book that explains how to construct better historical analyses of social change, Charles Tilly (1984, 14) remarked that studies of social change "should be historical in limiting their scope to an era bounded by the playing out of certain well-defined processes, and in recognizing from the outset that time matters." In other words, specifying the appropriate time frame is tantamount to specifying one of the most important scope conditions in our work—a key move for institutionalists insofar as we are interested in developing middle-range theory. Yet Tilly was silent on how researchers ought to determine what these temporal bounds are in their work. Ironically, historical institutionalists, who are the most explicitly concerned of all institutionalists with incorporating history and time into the analysis of institutions, provide few clues as to how we should determine the appropriate time frame for analysis (e.g., Mahoney 2000a, 537; Orren and Skowronek 1994, 329–30; Pierson and Skocpol 2000).

The fact that scholars have neglected this issue does not mean that it is either trivial or easily resolved. Whereas some time frames, such as those associated with war, might be more easily identified by beginning and end points (e.g., declarations of war, ceremonies of surrender), the time frame for others is more difficult to mark. But caution is advised even in the apparently easy cases like war. Some wars are fairly easy to bracket temporally. Japan's war with the United States is clearly marked by the attack on Pearl Harbor in 1941, Congress' declaration of war, and the ceremonies of surrender in 1945. However, not all wars are so clear-cut. The United States' war on Iraq to oust Saddam Hussein might appear to have started in 2002 at the moment when U.S. missiles began to fall on Baghdad. But we might argue reasonably that it actually began sometime earlier when the United States first began to insert covert forces into that country—and it is not entirely clear when those operations began. Similarly, in 2003 once the Bush administration declared victory and an end to major military action, fighting still continued as U.S. forces engaged in various policing and clean-up operations against discrete pockets of resistance throughout the country, and casualties continued to mount. Just like earthquakes, apparently cataclysmic events are bounded by foreshocks and aftershocks. The analyst's problem is to decide whether these matter insofar as they bear on the origins of institutional change and the stabilization or destabilization of the aftermath. Nevertheless, the important point is that when we study institutional change, lack of attention to the issue of time frame may result in empirical findings that incorrectly specify the boundaries, turning points, or critical events that separate different institutional moments (Aminzade 1992, 459–61). In turn, these specification errors can cause us to miss important empirical and theoretical insights (e.g., Blyth 2002, 263; Hoefer 1996, 78).

Consider one of the central arguments of organizational institutionalism. Within organizations many institutional innovations are essentially a matter of formal myth and ceremony, designed more to legitimize or obscure current organizational practices than to achieve real substantive change in how an organization operates. This is often because new rules are not implemented, new procedures are decoupled from old ones, or inspection and evaluation of new practices is avoided (Meyer and Rowan 1977).

For example, a university or corporation may adopt a set of rules regarding affirmative action simply as a token gesture signaling formal compliance with legislative edicts and without intending that the new rules will really have much effect on hiring or promotion outcomes. In this sense, the new rules are no more than symbolic window dressing over the same old organizational practices. However, this may change over time. Employees in other parts of the organization may eventually view the new rules as a resource to be used to press managers on affirmative action issues. Furthermore, people who are hired to staff the affirmative action office may in fact take their jobs seriously and use their positions to work for real change in how the organization operates. Indeed, this sort of thing happens often when governments make seemingly modest and token legislative concessions to advocacy groups, such as environmental or human rights organizations, but then are pressed to live up to these concessions later, grant further accommodations, and eventually change their behavior in truly substantive ways that are consistent with their initially symbolic gestures (Risse and Sikkink 1999). In sum, symbolic change at one moment may eventually precipitate much more substantive change at another (Edelman 1990, 1436–37; Forbes and Jermier 2002, 208; Guthrie 1999, xii; Hoffman 1997; Oakes et al. 1998). Apparently minor events may have extremely important consequences later on (Abbott 1988; Meyer et al. 1990, 104). The time frame matters.

Conversely, events that seem important in the short run may have only minor consequences in the long run. The European Union has passed numerous directives regulating labor markets, the environment, product standards, and financial transactions that member states are supposed to transpose into national law and then enforce. Thus, it would seem that passage of a new directive would constitute an important event in the institutional evolution of the European Union project. However, in many cases, national legislatures failed to generate the political consensus needed to draft laws that transposed these directives, or refused to create new administrative structures, change standard operating procedures, and allocate resources to the task at hand—especially when the directives were at odds with the nation's current policies and practices (Duina 1999). Indeed, studies of policy implementation have long recognized that even when radically new policy is passed by legislatures it may get so diluted during implementation that years later it turns out to have been much less consequential than expected initially (Pressman and Wildavsky 1979). Again, the time frame matters.

Specifying the appropriate time frame for observation requires that we identify the temporal parameters of social processes and outcomes that have their own internal temporal rhythms. From the analyst's point of view the question is, how long should the time frame under investigation be in order to determine whether change has occurred, how profound the change has been, and which pattern (evolutionary, punctuated equilibrium, etc.) best characterizes it?

The selection of an appropriate time frame is tricky for several reasons. First, different social processes have different rhythms. That is, some transpire faster than others. Capitalist institutions, for example, may take centuries to emerge whereas democratic political institutions may take much less time. Of course some dimensions of an institution may change at different speeds, as was the case in Eastern Europe. In addition, the rhythms of a social process may vary historically. For instance, the tempo of capitalist development has varied across countries depending on whether the country in question industrialized earlier or later than its competitors (Gerschenkron 1962). Some scholars have argued that other processes of social change, such as the diffusion of organizational patterns and culture, or the flow of capital and other resources, have sped up during the late twentieth century due to advances in telecommunications and transportation (Harvey 1989). So, presumably, have the institutional changes that they affect. In sum, what constitutes the appropriate time frame for analysis depends on the historical specificity of the phenomenon in question; it cannot be prescribed a priori for all social phenomena (Aminzade 1992, 476). This means that the choice of a time frame must be informed in part by *historical hindsight*.[7]

---

[7] A corollary to this discussion is that not only the time frame but also the *scale* on which it is measured should be selected based on a consideration of the phenomenon and its historical context. A scale of centuries may be appropriate for the analysis of the development of

Second, selection of a time frame should also be informed by our *theoretical orientation*, hunches, and hypotheses (e.g., Pierson 2000c; Stinchcombe 1968, 118). Let me return to McAdam's work on the U.S. civil rights movement. By adopting the theoretical lens of organizational institutionalism, as deployed by Skrentny, to analyze the movement and its effects on political institutions, he was sensitized to the possibility that a change in international norms may have had an important effect on the civil rights institutions in the United States. Looking for such a change caused him to extend his analytic time frame backward to the onset of the Cold War, during the 1940s—a temporal orientation substantially longer than the one he had used for his initial work on the movement, which covered only the late 1950s and 1960s. As noted above, he learned that as the Cold War rhetoric of the United States heated up after the Second World War, the community of nations pressed for African Americans to be granted equal and fair treatment under U.S. law. This institutional shift created important opportunities for civil rights activists to exploit. This case demonstrates not only that our theoretical orientations affect the time frames we select, but that they may do so in ways that affect our empirical insights. Of course, and more generally, the appropriate time frame will also depend on whether we suspect, for whatever theoretical reasons, that institutional change is being driven by long-term historical processes like a demographic transition or industrialization, medium-term processes like political protest cycles, or short-term processes like an unfolding corporate scandal, stock market crash, or terrorist attack (McAdam and Sewell 2001).

Third, because different versions of institutional analysis are inclined toward different *levels of analysis*, they also tend to favor different time frames. As Andrew Abbott (2001, 173–77) argued, change is likely to show up in a macro-level variable more slowly than it does among its micro-level constituents.[8] Notably, rational choice institutionalists tend to assume that relatively short time frames are sufficient because their focus generally is on how the choices of individuals and strategic actors at the micro-level drive social change, rather than on macro-level forces, such as structural tensions or contradictions (Moe 1987; Pierson 2000c; Orren and Skowronek 1994). Certainly, some rational choice institutionalists have tried to apply their frameworks (e.g., game theory, agency the-

---

capitalism (e.g., Maddison 1982), a scale of decades may suffice for an examination of the emergence of different types of capitalist institutions (e.g., Campbell et al. 1991), and a scale of years may be adequate for an analysis of changes from one form of a capitalist firm to another (e.g., Chandler 1977).

[8] Abbott makes this point on both theoretical and mathematical grounds. See Van de Ven and Grazman (1999) for a discussion of the relationship among levels of analysis, rates of change, and theories of evolution and punctuated equilibrium.

ory) to long historical processes, such as the development of military conscription systems, or the divergence of French and English absolutism (Bates et al. 1998). But even sympathetic critics charge that because rational choice theory is based on assumptions about methodological individualism, its microfoundations are not well suited to the analysis of such long-term historical developments, especially those that transpire at high levels of aggregation, such as at the level of states or social classes, or that span generations (Elster 2000). Nevertheless, we should recognize that the relationship between level of analysis and time frame is important and that our selection of a time frame can blind us to outcomes and processes that might otherwise become clear. Generally speaking, change often takes longer to manifest at higher levels of analysis.

Fourth, *pragmatic methodological considerations*, such as the availability of good data, may limit the time frame over which we study institutional change. Scott and his colleagues (Scott et al. 2000, 9, 22) wanted to study institutional change in five organizational populations in the San Francisco Bay Area health care industry. They recognized that studies of organizational populations are more persuasive and the available analytic techniques are more powerful if the time frame selected includes the early period during which the first organizations in the population were founded. Moreover, they knew that such studies often examine periods ranging from 100 to 200 years in order to capture the full trajectory of a population's development. However, they limited their research to the fifty-year period beginning in 1945, even though only two of their five populations had been founded during this period. In part, this was due to the absence of systematic data on some of these populations prior to 1945. But they also wanted to examine changes associated with the most significant event in their study, the 1965 passage of Medicare and Medicaid laws. To do so, they wanted to go back far enough to include a period of relative stability and felt that 1945 was far enough. In this case, then, although they were guided partly by practical concerns in selecting their time frame, they believed that this was a reasonable compromise because they also knew that the period in question was one that had experienced fundamental institutional changes in health care delivery, financing, and decision making, and so historical hindsight was also involved.[9]

Finally, *critical events* may mark the appropriate time frame for analysis. For instance, the beginning and ending of electoral, budget, legislative, or other important cycles may delineate time frames that are useful for studying change in political institutions. Additionally, the onset of an exogenous shock, such as war or depression as well as its resolution, may

---

[9] Personal communication with Richard Scott, October 2002.

help researchers define the appropriate time frame for analysis. The great dilemma here is that it is not always clear how to define important critical events. As suggested above, sometimes events, such as the passage of a new law, can end up having surprisingly little effect on anything and thus not be particularly helpful as a temporal marker (e.g., Scott et al. 2000, 188–94). Conversely, events that appear initially to be rather insignificant can end up having dramatic effects later (e.g., Mahoney 2000a, 527). For these and other reasons, scholars have warned that identifying important critical events or turning points in history is not always an easy task and may require substantial methodological prowess (e.g., Issac 1997; Issac and Griffin 1989).

To review briefly, when studying patterns of institutional change, scholars need to do two things. First, we must identify the important institutional dimensions we want to track. Second, we must identify the appropriate time frame over which we will examine the institutional dimensions we have selected. There appear to be no absolute rules about how to pick the right time frame, but we certainly need to recognize that selecting the appropriate one requires paying attention to the historical specificity of the phenomenon in question (i.e., the processes, cases, and contexts involved), our theoretical perspective, the level of analysis, methodological considerations regarding the availability of data of sufficient quality and comparability over time and across cases, and the presence of critical events. As a rule of thumb, it is probably better to select a longer time frame than a shorter one, if possible, to ensure that the analysis captures all the variation and important processes that may have occurred (Pierson and Skocpol 2000; Van de Ven and Poole 1995, 530–31). How can all of this be done to adjudicate among contending patterns of institutional change?

The discussion that follows shows that the approach I am advocating can be used fruitfully in both qualitative and quantitative research. The distinction between qualitative and quantitative work may seem trite, but in this case it is important and serves a useful purpose. I use it to show that the arguments I have raised earlier are applicable regardless of the researcher's most basic methodological inclinations.[10]

---

[10] Indeed, I suspect that my arguments are useful across a wide range of methodologies. For instance, there has been much debate recently about the relative advantages and disadvantages of "variance" and "process" approaches to institutional analysis (e.g., Abbott 2001, chap. 5; Scott 2001, 92–95). The variance approach is based on traditional multivariate analysis; the process approach is based on the analysis of a series of events and attends more closely to how the sequencing and timing of events affects change. Scholars who concur with me that institutional change should be studied by observing the arrangement of a set of institutional dimensions over time have also suggested that it can be analyzed fruitfully with either a variance or process approach (Van de Ven and Hargrave forthcoming).

TRACKING INSTITUTIONAL CHANGE QUALITATIVELY

Some researchers have disaggregated key institutional dimensions using qualitative data and tracked them over time to make important refinements in our understanding of patterns of institutional change. For example, working from a historical institutionalist position, Peter Hall (1992, 1993) explained the shift in British macroeconomic policy-making from Keynesianism during the 1960s to monetarism during the late 1970s. He argued that this represented a paradigm shift and a clear example of punctuated equilibrium, marked by the ascendence to power of Thatcher and the Conservative Party.

Hall's work is also important because he was one of the first historical institutionalists to recognize that the more-or-less taken-for-granted cognitive and normative dimensions of policy-making institutions are important. For him, a policy paradigm is an interpretive framework within which policymakers customarily work. In this regard, it is similar to Fligstein's (1990) conceptions of corporate control and Guillén's (1994a) models of corporate management discussed earlier. To paraphrase Fligstein, Hall's paradigm is a conception of political control. Specifically, it is a set of ideas and standards that specify three things. First are the *instruments*, such as fiscal or monetary policy, that policymakers deem appropriate to use. Second are the *settings* of these instruments, such as higher or lower tax and interest rates, that policymakers view as acceptable and select to achieve certain policy goals. Third are the policy *goals* themselves, such as minimizing unemployment or fighting inflation, that policymakers assume to be important. For Hall, these three things constitute essential dimensions of macroeconomic policy-making institutions.

He argued that adjustments in instruments and especially the settings of these instruments are normal changes that occur incrementally within an existing policy paradigm. However, a change in goals is rare and more fundamental because it comprises a wholesale shift in policymakers' perceptions and understandings of the problems they confront and the solutions available. In turn, this entails significant shifts in assumptions regarding the instruments and settings that they prefer and believe to be appropriate. As a result, paradigm shifts constitute a new policy-making logic that involves important changes in all three institutional dimensions of macroeconomic policy-making. They stem from the accumulation of empirical anomalies not easily reconciled within the current paradigm and policy failures, both of which trigger debate among proponents of the prevailing and competing paradigms. Paradigm shifts are institutionalized when supporters of the new paradigm gain control over the policy-making process and reorient its goals, organization, and standard operating procedures. Once in place, policy-making under the new paradigm proceeds much as it did before, that is, through normal incremental changes in the settings of policy instruments and the instruments themselves.

Hall examined British macroeconomic policy from the early 1970s through the early 1980s—a time frame selected, presumably, because he knew through extensive historical research (Hall 1986) that it was long enough to capture a period of initially normal policy-making, a paradigm shift, and then a return to normalcy under a new paradigm. Specifically, during the early 1970s the Labor government was committed to setting conventional macroeconomic instruments according to long-standing Keynesian assumptions that favored low unemployment as the chief policy goal. So, in response to recession in 1974, the government increased public spending in typical Keynesian fashion. However, unemployment persisted and inflation increased—an anomaly for the Keynesian paradigm that caused the government to engage in various ad hoc policy experiments that involved deploying new policy instruments, notably incomes policies to restrain inflationary wage increases. But this action eroded a key tenet of Keynesianism, that government should not intervene directly in the affairs of individual economic actors, and proved to be rather ineffective anyway. Keynesianism lost credibility in the public eye, and intense public debate about economic issues erupted in the media and financial circles. As the search for a new paradigm developed, monetarism emerged as the principal challenger. The Conservative Party embraced it because it could be used as a coherent challenge to the Labor government, a vehicle to unify its conservative base, and a rationale for a number of policy maneuvers that it had long favored, such as tax and spending cuts. When the Conservative Party won the election in 1979, Thatcher moved monetarists into key policy-making positions and promoted civil servants that were sympathetic to it. Most important, reducing inflation replaced minimizing unemployment as the chief policy-making goal; preference for monetary instruments took precedence over fiscal instruments; and assumptions changed about where both instruments should be set as the government tightened monetary policy, and cut taxes and spending.

Hall's argument has been criticized for overemphasizing the stability or equilibrium that prevailed during periods of normal policy-making. That is, where he saw a revolutionary shift, others saw a somewhat more evolutionary one. Nevertheless, the debate focused on how much change did or did not occur in the three institutional dimensions he highlighted. As noted earlier, recognition that the Labor government engaged in timid monetarist experiments during the 1970s has led some scholars to argue that these periods of normalcy are best characterized as exhibiting evolutionary rather than equilibrium qualities (Hay 2001). In retrospect, Hall

(1992, 103) might concur but also suggest that Labor's monetarist ventures were more accidental than intentional, as his critics have charged. However, what is important for us is that this debate is only possible because there is agreement on the institutional dimensions that should be tracked, the time frame in question, and the fact that change must be measured along several dimensions to determine how continuous or discontinuous it actually was.

The fact that there is disagreement about how much change occurred along these dimensions illustrates a potential problem with qualitative analyses of institutional change, even those in which there is agreement on the institutional dimensions and time frames involved. That is, the degree of change along the dimensions in question may still be subject to historical interpretation and thus disagreement among observers. Sometimes, quantitative approaches can help resolve these sorts of measurement problems and provide clear information on when change occurred and at what rate.

TRACKING INSTITUTIONAL CHANGE QUANTITATIVELY

To illustrate the advantages of quantitative approaches, consider tax policy.[11] Scholars often differentiate among policy paradigms in the realm of taxation on the basis of qualitative characteristics, such as the economic growth or budgetary priorities upon which policymakers base a set of tax policies (e.g., Martin 1991; Stein 1990). This is similar to Hall's notion that paradigms can be distinguished according to policy goals. However, the problem is that because of the fluidity of these priorities over time, it has been hard sometimes for researchers to identify through qualitative research when paradigm shifts occur in taxation. For example, there has been considerable debate about whether the famous Kennedy-Johnson tax cut in 1964 represented a fundamental shift in economic policy thinking and a pivotal shift toward Keynesianism in the United States, or a move that was more symbolic than substantive (Martin 1991, 16–17; Stein 1996, 196–201). This is not to say that quantitative approaches are necessarily superior to qualitative ones. But sometimes using quantitative measures can add a degree of precision and thus clarity to what has happened.

Nevertheless, problems may remain even after we specify more precise, quantitative criteria for differentiating among paradigms if we fail to dis-

---

[11] Portions of this section appeared originally in "Identifying Shifts in Policy Regimes: Cluster and Interrupted Time-Series Analyses of U.S. Income Taxes," *Social Science History* 25 (2001):37–65, which I coauthored with Michael Allen.

aggregate policy paradigms into their key dimensions. This is frequently the case in statistical analyses of time-series data because scholars often focus on changes in a single outcome variable, such as fluctuations in average tax rates or tax progressivity when they are looking for shifting tax policy paradigms (e.g., Allen and Campbell 1994; Campbell and Allen 1994), or in strike rates when they are looking for shifting labor-management paradigms (e.g., Isaac and Griffin 1989). Those who adopt a single indicator may, for instance, detect paradigm shifts where others with multiple indicators may not. This is what happened in the debate, noted earlier, over whether Reagan-era welfare reforms constituted a fundamental institutional change in the United States. Again, we are reminded that when trying to identify institutional shifts it is important to specify all the important dimensions that are involved and observe them over an appropriate time frame.

This is what Michael Allen and I did in an effort to identify institutional shifts in U.S. income tax policy (Campbell and Allen 2001). We used quantitative techniques to examine the history of the individual income tax in the United States at the federal level from 1916 through 1986. We wanted to examine the entire history of the modern income tax, which was enacted in 1913, but were limited to a somewhat shorter period because comprehensive data on the individual income taxes paid by constant income groups were not available for the years before 1916 or those after 1986. Still, we were satisfied with this compromise because we knew from previous historical studies that during this period important policy changes had occurred in how taxes were collected. We were also interested in whether war, recession, and other theoretically important factors might have been associated with shifts in income taxation and that this time frame encompassed important occurrences of these phenomena. As a result, historical, theoretical, and pragmatic methodological considerations dictated that we focus on this seventy-year time frame.

We examined three of the most important dimensions of income tax policy and systematically tracked changes in them over this period to identify statistically significant shifts in what we called tax regimes, that is, a period during which the income tax exhibited a unique configuration of three institutional dimensions. Specifically, we examined the average effective tax *rate* for moderate income families; tax *progressivity*, the relative income tax burden borne by individuals in different income groups; and tax *coverage*, the proportion of the working-age population required to file income tax returns.[12] Each of these dimensions reflected key institu-

---

[12] The average effective tax rate was calculated as the mean tax paid by individuals with incomes between $25,000 and $50,000 in 1986 dollars. Tax progressivity was calculated as the difference in the effective tax rate paid by families that earned between $25,000 and

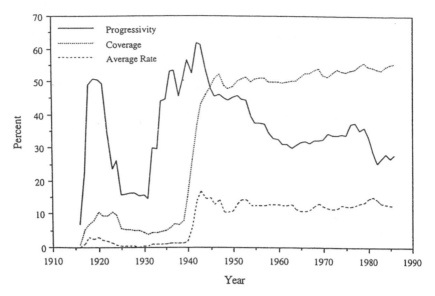

Figure 2.1. Average Tax Rate, Degree of Progressivity, and Coverage of Population of Individual Income Tax, 1916–86.

tionalized rules in the tax code governing income taxation that bore directly on U.S. citizens: the average tax rate represented rules regarding the magnitude of the income tax burden; progressivity represented rules mirroring the redistributive intent and differential impact of the tax on different social classes; and tax coverage represented rules about the percentage of the population actually affected by the tax. Hence, these dimensions were likely salient to much of the population.[13]

Recall that identifying historical turning points can be a tricky business. When we graphed the annual values for each of these dimensions it was difficult to determine visually with any degree of certainty how many regime shifts there had been, or the exact years corresponding to shift points between different paradigms, if indeed there had been dramatic shifts (see figure 2.1). As a result, we turned to a technique known as cluster analy-

---

$50,000 in 1986 dollars and that paid by families with incomes in excess of $1 million in 1986 dollars. Tax coverage was calculated as the proportion of the working-age population (16 years or older) filing income tax returns.

[13] The tax code is extremely complicated due to the proliferation of thousands of tax exemptions and other loopholes, which would be impossible to track in an analysis like this. Hence, we used measures of tax rates, progressivity, and coverage as proxies for the basic content of the tax code.

sis—a data reduction technique that reveals simple patterns of structure in large and complex data matrices (Bailey 1975; Hartigan 1975). In our case, it allowed us to calculate the correlations between years based on the values of our three dimensions of tax policy. In brief, by using this technique we generated a correlation matrix and then partitioned it into two groups of years so that the correlations within each group were relatively high and the correlations between groups were relatively low. In other words, each group comprised a relatively homogeneous cluster. The years before and after 1940–41 were the first two clusters we identified. Once these two clusters were determined, we repeated the process, looking for clusters within the clusters in an iterative fashion. There are no statistical criteria for knowing when to stop partitioning the data, so we needed to examine visually the results and quit partitioning when the clusters seemed to make sense substantively and theoretically. Then, using a technique known as interrupted time-series analysis (Hibbs 1977; McDowall et al. 1980), we determined whether the differences between clusters were statistically significant.[14]

The analysis identified four distinct types of clusters or regimes, each statistically unique. They are marked by dotted vertical lines in figure 2.2. Each type is noted by a different letter, A through D. Two of these clusters consisted of continuous time periods, 1941–53 and 1954–86. The other two were discontinuous, each consisting of two separate continuous time periods. One of these clusters comprised the tax years 1916–17 as well as the tax years 1923–33. The other discontinuous cluster comprised the tax years 1918–22 as well as the tax years from 1934–40.

Cluster A was characterized by low average tax rates, low progressivity, and low coverage, and covered the years 1916–17 and 1923–33. We described this tax regime as one of symbolic income taxation because it had only very minimal impact on most citizens. Cluster B, identified by low average tax rates and low coverage, but high progressivity, covered the years 1918–22 and 1934–40. Insofar as these periods corresponded to the large federal budget deficits associated with the First World War and the New Deal, respectively, we described this regime as one of fiscal crisis taxation. Cluster C, distinguished by high average tax rates, high progressivity, and high coverage, bridged the period 1941–53. Because this

---

[14] There are other quantitative techniques that can be used to identify shift points and to periodize data. The main alternative to our approach is time-varying parameters regression patterns, which identify shift points in terms of changes over time in the parameters of the *independent* variables in a regression equation (e.g., Isaac and Griffin 1989; Isaac et al. 1994). We selected our approach because it focuses on changes in the multiple dimensions of the *dependent* variable, in this case the institutional dimensions of tax policy, and, thus, does not require any theoretical assumptions concerning the underlying causes of the dependent variable (Abbott 1997, 1992; Hibbs 1977).

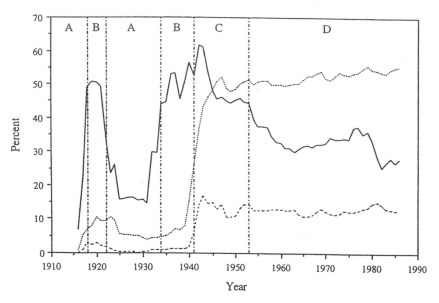

Figure 2.2. Average Tax Rate, Degree of Progressivity, and Coverage of Population by Tax Regime, 1916–86.

period corresponded to the years from the onset of the Second World War to the end of the Korean War we described this regime as one of war-making taxation. Finally, cluster D, typified by high average tax rates and high coverage, but moderate progressivity, encompassed the period from 1954–86, a period marked by tax policies oriented toward achieving macroeconomic stability.

Although our analysis revealed several regime shift points, one could quibble over whether some of these marked the sort of momentous changes that institutionalists have in mind when they distinguish among different patterns of change. The shift from period C to D, for example, involved only a substantial change in one dimension, a decline in tax progressivity. However, most observers would agree that the shift that occurred in 1941 constituted a much more radical change. It was during this period that coverage and average tax rates soared by historical standards and progressivity remained high. It was at this time that the federal government shifted permanently to a revenue system based on a mass income tax and adopted income tax withholding by employers. This shift also denoted the abandonment of conservative fiscal orthodoxy, which had guided tax policy-making since before the Civil War, and the ascendence and eventual institutionalization of Keynesianism as an approach to taxation in particular and macroeconomic management in general (Brownlee 1996). This was precisely the kind of momentous paradigm shift that Hall (1993) described, in which policymakers change not only their assumptions about the preferred policy instruments (e.g., adoption of a permanent mass tax) and the preferred settings of those instruments (e.g., higher rates and progressivity), but also the goals and intellectual macroeconomic models upon which they rely. Broadly speaking, then, our seventy-year time frame could be characterized as one of punctuated equilibrium where the most momentous punctuation occurred in 1941–42, where other more modest shift points were also evident, and where incremental changes (but of no statistical significance) also occurred between shift points.

The tax regimes we identified using these techniques correspond for the most part to those regimes identified by other researchers. However, insofar as there has been debate about whether certain pieces of tax legislation did, in fact, constitute significant regime shifts, quantitative techniques, such as these, are useful because they help adjudicate the evidence. Indeed, we found some surprises. First, scholars have argued that war stimulates major changes in tax institutions (Mann 1988), but we found that this was not always the case. America's entrance into the Second World War was associated with the onset of a new tax regime, but its involvement in the Vietnam War was not. Second, researchers have argued about whether Lyndon Johnson's famous 1964 Revenue Act or Ronald Reagan's 1981 Economic Recovery Tax Act, both of which cut tax rates to bolster the economy, represented radical breaks from the past (Edsall 1984; Stein 1990; Witte 1985). According to our analysis, neither one marked a significant shift in the institutional profile of the nation's tax system. This also reinforces the point that our time frames need to be long enough to encompass not just critical events—such as the enactment of pieces of legislation—but also periods of time both before and after them, in order to see how abrupt and important these events actually are. Surprises like these would have been elusive had we not unpacked the critical institutional dimensions of tax policy and traced them over a fairly long period of time. Moreover, the utility of this approach increases as the number of dimensions under consideration grows. Scholars using conventional qualitative historical techniques are likely to have much more difficulty identifying shifts where four, five, or more dimensions are involved.

Let me be clear. I am not suggesting that quantitative approaches are necessarily better than qualitative ones. Each has its own advantages. One advantage of a qualitative approach, particularly a case study approach that engages in thick description and process tracing, such as Hall's analysis of British macroeconomic policy, is that it can provide a more fine-grained look at the causal mechanisms that either facilitate or inhibit change. This suggests that a multi-method approach may be the most desirable.

A Multi-Method Approach

When researchers combine qualitative and quantitative approaches and give careful consideration to the issues discussed in the previous sections, the results can be insightful and impressive. Recall Scott's (Scott et al. 2000) study of institutional change in the health care industry between 1945 and 1995. This was intended in part to determine the degree to which change had followed an incremental or more punctuated pattern, and so he and his colleagues recognized that they had to disaggregate carefully the theoretically relevant institutional dimensions of the industry and specify the time frame over which they tracked them. With respect to institutional disaggregation, they observed changes in the formal and informal governance structures that regulated the industry, and the normative and cultural-cognitive institutional logics that guided actors' behavior. These dimensions were based largely on Scott's earlier theoretical work—his three institutional pillars. As noted earlier, with respect to time frame, they selected this fifty-year period because it encompassed the fundamental changes that they knew had occurred in how the industry operated, particularly Medicare and Medicaid legislation, and also because it was the longest time frame for which reasonably good data existed on the important dimensions they wanted to examine.

Their investigation was based on quantitative analyses of time-series data of populations and fields of organizations as well as qualitative analyses of the historical development of the wider social and cultural environment and case study data of individual organizations. Hence, they combined several levels of analysis to determine how not only institutional but also other explanations (e.g., strategic, ecological) might account for change in the industry. Results showed that the industry progressed through three distinct institutional eras: the dominance of medical professionals, their associations, and a logic of quality care (1945–65); the dominance of the federal government and a logic of equal access to medical services (1965–82); and the dominance of managerial control, market mechanisms, and a logic of efficient service provision (1982–95).

Their approach shed new light on precisely the sorts of issues that I discussed earlier. First, sometimes events turn out to be much less significant than one might think initially. For instance, a number of legislative changes at the federal level failed to have much effect on how the industry was governed. Conversely, other legislative changes had major effects, such as the passage of Medicare and Medicaid legislation in the mid-1960s, which marked a shift from the era of professional to federal dominance and a fundamental shift in the rules and logic guiding the industry. Second, paying attention to change in only one institutional dimension can be terribly misleading. They reported that focusing only on legislation or formal governance structures would have led them to believe that shifts from one institutional era to the next were rather abrupt. However, changes in the normative and cultural-cognitive elements of institutional logics developed much more gradually and unevenly. For example, a decade prior to the onset of the market-based era, intellectuals in the health policy arena began to articulate in industry publications and professional journals the institutional logic that laid the foundation for this dramatic shift, as codified eventually in legislation in the early 1980s. Thus, while the formal aspects of institutional change may occur abruptly, the informal aspects, notably the cultural-cognitive and normative ones, are more gradual and tend to come first. Third, by demonstrating that institutional eras may contain both primary and secondary logics, their research broached the possibility that the seeds for institutional change may be endogenous to institutions themselves. That is, change may stem from conflicts and contradictions between different but simultaneously occurring institutional logics (Friedland and Alford 1991; Skowronek 1995).

Scott and his colleagues can be challenged for how effectively they disaggregated institutional dimensions. In particular, although they initially differentiated institutional logics from governance structures on the grounds that the former consist of cultural-cognitive elements and the latter consist of regulative and normative ones (Scott et al. 2000, 20–21), they sometimes blurred this distinction by attributing norms to both (pp. 24–25). Thus, their claim that change in governance structures tend to lag change in institutional logics needs to be clarified. Nonetheless, the crucial point is that their insights could be made only by disaggregating institutional dimensions and tracking them over a substantial period of time. The authors explicitly recognized this when they remarked that "identifying a number of different indicators enables us to distinguish among the many factors at work, to determine which changed earlier or later, and which exerted crucial influence" (178).

CONCLUSION

To review, I have argued that if we want to better identify patterns of institutional change to avoid mistaking, for instance, revolutionary for evolutionary change, or vice versa, then we need to unpack the critical dimensions of an institution and track them over time. It is up to the analyst to determine which dimensions are worth studying. This depends on his or her theoretical orientation, level of analysis, and perception of the salience of these dimensions for the people they affect. It is also up to the analyst to select an appropriate time frame across which to track these dimensions—a decision that, again, involves theoretical orientation and level of analysis, but also historical hindsight, pragmatic methodological considerations, and an understanding of critical events. Once these decisions have been made, in order to distinguish among different patterns of institutional change we need to track these dimensions over time and determine how much each one changes. If most, if not all, of them change simultaneously in a given period of time, then change is more punctuated or revolutionary than if only a few change, in which case change is more evolutionary. In this sense, institutional change should not be viewed as a dichotomous variable, but a continuous one; it is a matter of degree and needs to be examined as such. I have also shown that employing this approach can reveal important theoretical and empirical insights about the effects of political revolutions, the transformation of industries, the character of major policy shifts, and more. Overall, then, the fundamental point is that recognizing and defining our institutional dependent variables is a foundational methodological operation of great theoretical consequence if we want to improve our understanding of institutional change.

An additional insight to be gained from this approach concerns the assumption underlying all of the patterns of institutional change that I have discussed. All assume that institutions are relatively stable most of the time, resting in equilibrium or changing only at the margins in incremental, evolutionary ways. Of course, some theorists add that institutions may occasionally experience significant upheaval but that this is relatively rare and that institutions still gravitate toward stability. Studying institutions as bundles of dimensions that can be analytically and empirically disaggregated and traced over time, however, brings this basic dichotomy between stability and instability into question. If it is true that institutions are made up of potentially contradictory and conflicting logics, such as those perhaps associated with formal and informal or symbolic and substantive rules, as some institutionalists maintain (e.g., Friedland and Alford 1991; North 1990; Scott et al. 2000; Skowronek 1995), then it stands to reason that actors may frequently seek to resolve the friction that results by changing at least some dimensions of their institutions on a more-or-less routine basis. If this is so, then institutional order and stability may be *less* typical, and institutional change and instability may be *more* typical than we have suspected, as a few organizational and historical institutionalists have remarked (e.g., Abrahamson and Fairchild 1999,

709; Oakes et al. 1998; Orren and Skowronek 1994, 320–23). Our task, then, in analyzing particular cases and examples is to determine the magnitude of institutional change that occurs across a multidimensional continuum and over a long enough period of time to determine how much stability or instability there actually is. We should not assume that institutional stability or equilibrium is the norm; we should subject that assumption to empirical scrutiny. According to some scholars, our failure to do this has been an obstacle to institutional analysis (Shepsle 1986, 76), but, judging from some of the work discussed in this chapter, it need not be one anymore.

Disaggregating institutional dimensions and tracking them over time also opens up new questions for institutionalists that can lead to more insightful theories and debates. For instance, by differentiating between the formal and informal dimensions of economic institutions, North (1990, 45) began to think about how these dimensions affected each other and, in turn, how their interaction affected institutional change. He argued that different dimensions changed at different speeds in ways that have significant effects on institutional outcomes. More specifically, he surmised that formal dimensions, such as property rights and other official rules that are established, sanctioned, and enforced by the state, change more rapidly than informal dimensions, such as cultural norms and values. This lag, he suggested, creates tensions between formal and informal rules that decision makers must eventually ease by bringing the former into closer alignment with the latter. In other words, the informal dimensions slow down and sometimes partially reverse the transformation of formal ones, especially during war, revolution, or other social upheavals when formal rules often change dramatically (North 1990, 89–91). This was one reason why he believed that change is generally more evolutionary than revolutionary—even in situations that initially appear to be quite revolutionary in terms of formal institutions. Similarly, organizational institutionalists have maintained that formal institutional changes may occur relatively quickly and mask the rigidities of underlying norms and informal practices (e.g., Meyer and Rowan 1977).

Some researchers, however, have found the opposite in their empirical work. For example, in communist Hungary during the 1970s, managers of state enterprises were faced with shortages of important goods and services, such as machinery parts and design work. In response, they began unofficially and informally to encourage their workers to use the enterprise's equipment during their spare time and on the weekends to produce these things and sell them back to the enterprise at a profit. Because these inside subcontracting arrangements operated more efficiently than the enterprises themselves, they proliferated, and economic leaders eventually saw them as a way to improve the overall performance of the economy. Policymakers passed formal legislation in 1982 that officially ratified these heretofore informal, unofficial practices. Hence, formal institutions finally caught up with informal ones (Stark 1986). Such informally organized economic activity both within and between enterprises became widespread throughout the communist bloc, and its development contributed to the formal system's ultimate disintegration (Burawoy and Krotov 1993; Sik 1992). Similarly, Scott and his colleagues (Scott et al. 2000) found that cultural-cognitive and normative changes in the health care industry tended to precede and precipitate formal changes in the industry's formal governance structures. In both cases, rather than *restraining* change, as North theorized, shifts in the informal dimensions of these institutions *facilitated* change.

The Hungarian story also has specific theoretical implications for rational choice theory. As noted earlier, rational choice institutionalists are fond of discussing changes in property rights, especially insofar as these changes affect things like economic performance. The Hungarian case can be understood from this perspective if we unbundle the property rights concept. Property rights regarding the *use* of the means of production and the *appropriation* of benefits from their use were transferred informally from enterprises to workers in ways that improved economic efficiency. Eventually, however, this contributed to the collapse of the system and ultimately to a transformation in *ownership* rights insofar as many of these enterprises were privatized (Campbell 1993b). To my knowledge, rational choice institutionalists have not discussed how changes in one part of a bundle of property rights can lead to changes in another part.

Obviously, all of these debates and insights about sequencing and lags would have been impossible without first thinking about how institutions should be disaggregated into their subcomponents and then considering how each part changes and affects the rest. Historical institutionalists have probably paid the most attention to issues of temporal sequencing, maintaining that the order in which events occur matters a great deal in terms of how they affect outcomes in path-dependent ways (Pierson 2000a, 2000b; Tilly 1984, 14). For instance, cognitive changes in how politicians and others think government should be organized may have dramatically different effects depending on when they happen. If they occur during a war, when politicians are desperately concerned with improving government and economic efficiency, then they may have great transformative effects; if they occur during peace time, when such concerns are less pressing, then they may not (Skowronek 1982). But despite their work on sequencing, even most historical institutionalists have neglected how the sequencing of changes in different dimensions of an institution may affect the overall character of institutional change.

If we want better to identify different patterns of institutional change and avoid mistaking one pattern for another, then specifying important institutional dimensions and mapping them over an appropriate time frame is important. But if we want to explain how these changes occur, then we need to identify the causal forces involved and specify the mechanisms that link causes with effects. Issues of causality and causal mechanisms present institutionalists with another set of problems, to which we now turn.

Chapter 3

THE PROBLEM OF MECHANISMS

THE LAST CHAPTER discussed how to identify different types of institutional change when they occur, specifically evolutionary and revolutionary change. This chapter discusses the mechanisms that cause it. In particular, this chapter focuses on the causal concepts of path dependence and diffusion, which institutionalists invoke frequently to account for change. It explains how we might better specify the mechanisms of path dependence and diffusion to improve our understanding of evolutionary and revolutionary change. This discussion is indicative of a more general problem for institutionalists—the failure to specify adequately the mechanisms underlying some of our favorite causal concepts.

Institutionalists, like all social scientists, rely heavily on causal concepts in our work. Causal concepts signify dynamics of action and change. They imply underlying causal processes.[1] For instance, we often argue that institutions evolve in "path-dependent" ways. We claim that institutions "enable," "empower," and "constitute" actors, by which we mean that institutions help to guide action. Many of us also maintain that institutional practices are "enacted" in ways that result in their "diffusion" among organizational fields. And virtually all of us talk about how social action is "embedded" in institutions in ways that "constrain" actors and the possibilities for change.

The problem for institutionalists is that although these concepts are central to our causal arguments, they often remain vague and mysterious. In other words, the mechanisms whereby institutions enable, empower, constitute, constrain, and exert path-dependent and other effects are poorly specified. Critics have charged that this has undermined the quality of institutionalists' work (Hirsch 1997; Hirsch and Lounsbury 1997). Poorly specified causal concepts can operate only as heuristic devices; they cannot carry an argument alone (e.g., Bendor et al. 2001, 188; DiMaggio 1988, 10; Skocpol 1984, 17). Indeed, it is all too common in the social

---

[1] Of course, not all concepts imply causality. Many are simply ways to categorize social phenomena. So, for Karl Marx, while the concept of social class categorized a group of individuals, the causal concept of class struggle denoted a force for change in the world. Similarly, for Max Weber, while the concept of bureaucracy categorized a type of organization, the causal concept of rationalization signaled a process by which bureaucracies came into existence and were institutionalized. This chapter focuses entirely on causal concepts.

sciences for causal mechanisms to be left implicit in empirical analyses. Unless institutionalists carefully tease out the mechanisms underlying their causal concepts, our theoretical and empirical arguments will be incomplete and unconvincing, particularly insofar as arguments about evolutionary and revolutionary change are concerned.[2]

By *mechanism* I mean simply the processes that account for causal relationships among variables. According to Jon Elster (1989, 3), mechanisms are the nuts, bolts, cogs, and wheels that link causes with effects. The specification of causal mechanisms involves more than just establishing correlations among variables. The identification of a correlation may establish *that* a relationship exists between variables, but unless we understand the underlying mechanisms that cause it, we will not know *how* one variable affects another (Hedström and Swedberg 1998b). Mechanisms, then, are the workhorses of explanation (McAdam et al. 2001, 30). So, for example, if we determine that countries in which policy-making is organized through corporatist institutions are less likely to have higher taxes and more welfare spending than countries where policy-making is organized in other ways, then we may have revealed an interesting relationship between institutions and policy outcomes, but we still do not know how this effect obtains. This requires that we specify through additional empirical research, or at least theoretical argument, the causal mechanism that is responsible, such as showing that business leaders in corporatist countries are willing to support higher levels of social spending by paying higher taxes in order to enable government to maintain a stable political climate in which to do business (e.g., Garrett 1998a).

Because identifying mechanisms enables us to understand the details of causal processes, it reduces the risk of lapsing into either erroneous functionalist accounts in which institutional outcomes are explained by their consequences (Pierson and Skocpol 2000), or spurious accounts that mistake correlations among variables for causal relationships (Elster 1998a; Mahoney 2000b; Sørensen 1998). The latter is an especially thorny problem when we are trying to sort out causal relationships among many variables but have only a relatively small number of cases with which to work (Scharpf 1997, 16). Identifying mechanisms also provides a way to develop middle-range theory. Because most institutionalists recognize the institutional specificity of human behavior and find that institutions change over time, many of us aspire to middle-range theory (Campbell and Pedersen 2001a, 13–14). On the one hand, we are skeptical about the possibility of uncovering universal laws of human behavior that hold across all times

[2] For further discussion of the neglect of mechanisms in the social sciences and the problems that result, see Elster (1989), Hedström and Swedberg (1998a), Lieberson and Lynn (2002), McAdam et al. (2001, 24–28), and Reskin (2003).

and places. On the other hand, we do not want to settle for atheoretical descriptive narratives. Although no social mechanism is likely to operate in every situation, some mechanisms may operate in several situations, so their specification enables us to generalize beyond atheoretical descriptions but without making indefensible claims about universal laws (Stinchcombe 1998; see also Elster 1998a; Merton 1967). For instance, Doug McAdam, Sidney Tarrow, and Charles Tilly (2001, 25–34) identified three basic types of mechanisms that drove several examples of contentious politics like social movements and political revolutions. Their intent was not to develop a general theory of contentious politics, but, more modestly, to develop middle-range theory that specified the mechanisms that operated most frequently across their wide-ranging set of cases.

I am not claiming that institutionalists have always ignored the mechanisms that underlie their important causal concepts. Rational choice institutionalists, for instance, have gone to great lengths trying to specify causal mechanisms (e.g., Knight 1998; Knight and Sened 1998b; Nee 1998, 8–12). Nevertheless, insofar as they equate mechanisms with the imputed motives of actors, skeptics charge that rational choice theory has not specified causal mechanisms at all because motives are mental states, not causal processes (Reskin 2003). Regardless of their position on this issue, even rational choice institutionalists acknowledge that in important instances the mechanisms underlying some of their most prized causal concepts, such as path dependence, are often underspecified (Knight 1998, 97; Nee 2001; North 1998, 21–22). The same is true for other types of institutional analysis.

There are many social mechanisms in the world and it is not my intention in this chapter to try to identify or even classify all of them.[3] Instead, I want to focus on how we might begin to think more clearly about the mechanisms that underlie some of the causal concepts that institutionalists use most frequently. In particular, I examine the concepts of path dependence and diffusion. These are concepts upon which institutionalists rely heavily to account for institutional change. Along the way, I show that better specification of the mechanisms underlying these two concepts also helps clarify some of the processes underlying the other causal concepts noted at the beginning of this chapter.

I begin by discussing the concept of path dependence, a concept that institutionalists are fond of using to explain evolutionary change. I show that the relationship between path dependence and evolution is confusing precisely because we often fail to specify fully the mechanisms underlying

---

[3] For efforts at classification, see Campbell (forthcoming), Campbell and Pedersen (2001b), Hedström and Swedberg (1998a), McAdam et al. (2001). In addition to those mechanisms examined in this chapter, I discuss others in chapters 4 and 5.

the concept of path dependence. Second, I demonstrate that *bricolage*, the process whereby actors recombine locally available institutional principles and practices in ways that yield change, provides important insights into the mechanisms involved in path-dependent evolutionary change. Third, I argue that the reasons why actors create one bricolage instead of another, and why one bricolage is more evolutionary or revolutionary than another, are, in part, the institutional and social locations of institutional entrepreneurs who engage in bricolage and the various constraints they face. Fourth, I examine the concept of diffusion, another impetus for institutional change, and suggest that an important part of the diffusion process is generally neglected by institutionalists—the process whereby imported principles and practices are implemented locally. Fifth, to correct this omission, I explain that one of the most important mechanisms entailed in diffusion is the process of *translation*. Translation resembles bricolage but involves the combination of locally available principles and practices with new ones originating elsewhere. Thus, translation is a potentially important source of revolutionary change. As such, this chapter begins with an emphasis on evolutionary change and ends with an emphasis on more revolutionary change. It will become clear, however, that the basic mechanisms of bricolage and translation are relevant to both. I conclude with a brief discussion about whether the need for a specification of causal mechanisms requires that institutionalists embrace methodological individualism and, in turn, rational choice institutionalism—a paradigm in which causal mechanisms are ultimately reduced to individual actors bent on satisfying their preferences.

Path Dependence

How can we account for evolutionary change? Recall from chapter 2 that change is evolutionary if only a few of the relevant dimensions of an institution change from one moment to another such that today's institutional arrangements differ from but still resemble those of yesterday. Institutionalists typically attribute evolutionary change to a process known as *path dependence*. When institutionalists talk about path dependence they refer to a process whereby contingent events or decisions result in the establishment of institutions that persist over long periods of time and constrain the range of actors' future options, including those that may be more efficient or effective in the long run (e.g., Nelson 1994a, 132; North 1990, 93–95; Pierson 2000b; Powell 1991, 192; Roe 1996; see also Stinchcombe 1968, 101–18).

For instance, Doug Guthrie (1999) argued that as capitalism emerged in China, some firms continued as they had prior to market reform to

offer workers non-wage benefits like housing as a result of the path dependence of institutions, systems, and structures. He argued, "Once a given
structure is set in place in an organization, that structure becomes an
inextricable part of the organization; similarly, once a given cluster of
benefits is associated with employment in an organization, these benefits
become tied to the workplace" (85). Given these and other path-dependent effects that he discussed, the emergence of capitalist institutions in
China was a more evolutionary process than some might expect.

The path dependence concept is ubiquitous. It has also been used, for
example, by organizational institutionalists to characterize the development of economic institutions in postcommunist Europe (Stark and Bruzst
1998). It has been used by historical institutionalists to explain welfare
reform, the outcomes of political revolutions, the persistence of different
types of capitalism, and many policy developments (Mahoney 2000a;
Pierson 2000b; Thelen 1999). It has been used by rational choice institutionalists to explain the evolution of welfare states and national economies (Korpi 2001; North 1990).[4]

The difficulty is that the mechanisms whereby path-dependent effects
occur are often poorly specified, if not completely neglected. Let us return
to Guthrie's (1999) analysis of the emergence of capitalism in China. He
surmised briefly that housing benefits may have persisted in Chinese firms
as they shifted toward capitalism because employees came to expect these
benefits under the old system, and firms owned the real estate upon which
this housing was, presumably, located. But his discussion was speculative,
and important questions remained unanswered. How did employee expectations translate into company policy? Why did they not change with the
shift to capitalism, especially when other expectations were dashed by this
shift? Why did firms necessarily want to provide housing for their workers
simply because they owned this real estate? Implicit, perhaps, was the notion that because employees had grown accustomed to these benefits,
which may have been among the most important of all to them, they would
strike if the benefits were withdrawn. Or perhaps managers saw the continued provision of housing as a means to compensate workers for wages
that were lower than prevailing market rates. In any case, much remained
to be explained about just how these path-dependent processes worked
and why this aspect of the Chinese transition from communism to capitalism exhibited more evolutionary than revolutionary features.[5]

---

[4] Scholars who maintain that institutional and policy legacies constrain change in evolutionary ways make very similar arguments, even though they substitute the concept of legacies for the concept of path dependence (e.g., Berman 1998; Dobbin 1994; Elster et al. 1998;
Guillén 2001a; Heclo 1974; Steinmo et al. 1992; Skocpol 1992; Weir 1992; Ziegler 1997).

[5] Elsewhere, Guthrie did a better job of identifying the causal mechanisms that contributed to path-dependent outcomes, as when he showed that because managers often felt a

As noted in chapter 1, some scholars have admitted that the path dependence concept is used often without a clear specification of the causal mechanisms involved (Knight 1998, 97; North 1998, 21–22; Thelen 1999). In an effort to improve the situation for historical institutionalists, Paul Pierson (1993, 2000a, 2000b, 2000c) argued that path dependence occurs in politics as a result of several feedback mechanisms through which actors gain increasing returns for behaving in ways that are consistent with their past actions. As a result, institutions and the behavior associated with them become "locked in" to a particular path of historical development. First, political institutions have large start-up costs, and so once they are established actors are not likely to seek to change them, especially if they perceive that the chances of other actors doing so are increasingly slim, given the costs involved. Second, sometimes politicians deliberately build institutions in ways that make them difficult to dismantle. They may, for instance, impose procedural obstacles to prevent others from later changing the institutions that they create. Hence, framers of the U.S. Constitution stipulated that subsequent changes to the Constitution would require not only congressional approval, as does normal legislation, but also ratification by three quarters of the states—a provision that contributed, for example, to the defeat of the Equal Rights Amendment in the 1970s (Mansbridge 1986). Third, once a particular policy style or decision-making approach has been institutionalized, actors accumulate knowledge about how it works. The more familiar and comfortable they become with it, the more hesitant they are to deviate from it. Fourth, beneficiaries of legislative or institutional largess reinforce institutional behavior that will continue to provide them with benefits. Notably, senior citizens organize to reelect politicians who support old-age pensions and oppose those who favor cutting their benefits and programs. Pierson is indebted to economic historians and rational choice theorists who have argued that these sorts of mechanisms lock in actors to a particular path of economic or technological development (e.g., Arthur 1994; David 1985; North 1990). Despite his insights, however, there are still problems with the concept of path dependence.

Institutionalists often use the concept of path dependence to account for institutional evolution, arguing that change is evolutionary as long as these sorts of path dependence mechanisms operate (e.g., Peters 1999, 65; Pierson 2000a, 84; Roe 1996). For instance, Douglass North (1990, chaps. 1, 8) maintained that economic institutions that are locked in feedback and constrain actors' choices in ways that generally permit only incremental changes at the margins. These changes accumulate over time, altering the

---

sense of loyalty to workers who had worked for a firm for many years, they did not force these workers into short-term labor contracts (1999, 97).

institutional framework of the economy in an evolutionary fashion. The problem is that once we specify the mechanisms involved in path dependence—mechanisms that are all about political, economic, and institutional lock-in—it becomes clear that this concept, at least as specified in the literature, is far better suited to explaining the *persistence* of institutions than it is to explaining their *transformation* (e.g., Pierson 2000b, 265; Thelen 1999, 2000a, 2000b). In this sense, path dependence arguments are often very deterministic (Haydu 1998; see also Roe 1996, 665).[6] For instance, this deterministic bias is pronounced in the literature on social policy that describes policy institutions as resistant to reform due to sunk costs and ingrained popular expectations (Hemerijck and Zeitlin 2002). My point is not that arguments about path dependence are necessarily incompatible with arguments about evolutionary change, but that the mechanisms of path-dependent evolutionary change need to be better specified.

Institutionalists have tried to theorize change mechanisms in arguments about path dependence by introducing the concept of *critical junctures*— that is, major shocks and crises that disrupt the status quo and trigger fundamental institutional changes of the sort identified in the punctuated equilibrium models discussed in chapter 2 (Haydu 1998; Thelen 1999). Events like wars and energy crises are good examples of critical junctures insofar as the transformation of political institutions is concerned (e.g., Ikenberry 1988, 233). But there are at least two problems with this approach. First, shocks and crises of the sort that constitute critical junctures explain why major, revolutionary changes occur, but not why more incremental and evolutionary change happens (Thelen 2000a, 2000b).[7] Second, the critical junctures approach tends to focus our attention on the key events that start episodes of change, but not on the search process

---

[6] This problem can be traced back to the foundational work on path dependence. In a classic statement of the path dependence argument, Paul David (1985) showed that although several keyboard layouts are available for typewriters, the QWERTY arrangement (so named for the arrangement of the top, left-hand key row) remains the standard even though it is not the most efficient in terms of typing speed. Why? Because once it was institutionalized as the industry standard, the costs associated with switching, such as retraining typists, became so great that it was effectively locked in. Although David claimed that evolutionary change occurs through path-dependent processes, his evidence was really about stasis. Insofar as most contemporary path dependence theorists rely on David's approach, it is not surprising that they suffer from the same problem. See, for example, Roe's work on the evolution of corporate governance (Bebchuk and Roe 1999; Roe 1999, 1996).

[7] A related problem is that the critical junctures approach generally assumes that the impetus for institutional change comes in the form of an exogenous shock. There is little recognition that the internal inconsistencies and contradictions of an institutional arrangement may also spawn crises that result in its transformation (Haydu 1998; Schneiberg 1999). This is a surprising oversight insofar as institutionalists note that institutions are riddled with contradictory logics that often spark change (e.g., DiMaggio 1988, 16; Friedland and Alford 1991; Orren and Skowronek 1994; Skowronek 1995).

that follows whereby actors figure out what evolutionary or revolutionary changes to make in their institutions (Campbell and Lindberg 1991). How, then, can path dependence arguments be used for explaining change, particularly evolutionary change? For this we need to identify a different set of mechanisms.

BRICOLAGE

To begin with, institutions provide a repertoire of already existing institutional principles and practices that actors can use to innovate. The key is to recognize that actors often craft new institutional solutions by recombining elements in their repertoire through an innovative process of *bricolage* whereby new institutions differ from but resemble old ones (Douglas 1986, 66–68; Levi-Strauss 1966, 16–33; see also Veblen [1914] 1964, 50–51). Scholars have described this sort of process in passing but without articulating its evolutionary implications (e.g., Clemens 1997; Emirbayer and Mische 1998; Friedland and Alford 1991, 254–56; Riker 1998, 121; Stark 1996; but see also Haveman and Rao 1997). Insofar as institutions consist of technical and symbolic principles and practices (March and Olsen 1989), we can conceive of at least two types of bricolage.

Much institutional change is undertaken to achieve various substantive goals. Insofar as economic institutions are concerned, these goals include such things as reducing transaction costs, increasing market share, managing labor relations problems, improving product quality, and so on—considerations held dear by rational choice institutionalists. *Substantive bricolage* involves the recombination of already existing institutional principles and practices to address these sorts of problems and thus follows a logic of instrumentality (March and Olsen 1989). For instance, Taiwanese entrepreneurs built hierarchically organized conglomerates after the Second World War by combining the institutional principles of large multidivisional business firms that had already started to develop in Taiwan with the institutional principles of family honor, which had persisted there for centuries. As owners of private firms began to recognize during the 1950s that survival and growth depended on building larger and more far-flung corporations, they also realized that managing these conglomerates would become increasingly difficult, in particular due to principal-agent monitoring problems. They branched out into new and unrelated lines of business by extending the multidivisional form, but they placed close family members (i.e., siblings, sons, daughters, and in-laws) in top divisional posts to ensure that the operations were run by people whom they could trust (Lin 1995). In short, two well-established institutional principles were combined to solve a critical managerial dilemma.

Institutional change also involves the recombination of symbolic principles and practices through a process of *symbolic bricolage*. In this sense bricolage may involve the logic of appropriateness that organizational institutionalists emphasize (March and Olsen 1989). This is particularly important insofar as the solutions that actors devise must be acceptable and legitimate within the broad social environment. Social scientists have recognized that in order for new institutions to take hold they must be framed with combinations of existing cultural symbols that are consistent with the dominant normative and cognitive institutions. The utilization of symbolic language, rhetorical devices, lofty and culturally accepted principles, and analogies to what is believed to be the natural world are central to this framing exercise (e.g., Douglas 1986; Snow et al. 1986; Swidler 1986). A case in point was the rapid industrialization of the South Korean economy after the Second World War—a period that was marked by the creation of massive conglomerate firms that were run with a strong, hierarchical, and often authoritarian hand. To legitimize these practices to employees, directors deployed various symbolic elements of traditional South Korean culture. They argued, for instance, that the firm was like the hierarchically organized family. Employees owed the firm their allegiance because it provided for their livelihood, just as sons owed allegiance to their fathers. Directors also drew on the country's strong nationalist ideology, rooted in a long history of political and economic struggles against more powerful countries like Japan and the United States, to convince workers that their acquiescence to the firm's policies was tantamount to supporting the national interest (Janelli 1993). In sum, directors were bricoleurs combining bits and pieces of Korean culture in innovative ways that created symbolic support for their managerial and organizational approach.[8]

Of course, both substantive and symbolic elements may be involved in a bricolage (e.g., Guillén 1994b). The point, however, is that through bricolage institutions evolve in a path-dependent way. The process is path dependent because the range of actors' choices for innovation are more or less fixed by the set of institutional principles and practices at their disposal. The process is evolutionary because by recombining elements from the set of already existing institutional principles and practices, the new institutions that actors build resemble the old ones by virtue of their containing many elements from the past. Similarly, medieval artisans built an array of structures ranging in size from small huts to massive cathe-

---

[8] Economists tend to forget that institutional innovations require symbolic framing (Douglas 1986, 46; Hodgson 1988, 156). Even the process of market creation requires framing (Fligstein and Mara-Drita 1996). So does the process of organizational innovation (Creed et al. 2000a, 2002b).

drals by combining in different ways the wood, nails, stone, mortar, and glass that were available to them. But because these materials—rather than steel and cement—were the resources at hand, it was impossible for them to imagine, let alone build, an edifice as tall as a skyscraper. The nature of architecture evolved during this era through recombinations of these resources, but within limits established by this resource set. Not until fundamentally new materials were developed did the architectural possibilities expand and more revolutionary structures appear. The fact that access to *new* elements increases the chances for revolutionary rather than just evolutionary combinations is an important issue to which we will return when we discuss diffusion and translation.

In chapter 2, I argued that the degree to which change is evolutionary or revolutionary depends on how many dimensions of an institution change over a given period of time. Bricolage is a process that alters these dimensions (e.g., Dolowitz and Marsh 1996, 350–51). To illustrate the point, let me apply Scott's (2001) three-fold distinction of institutional dimensions, introduced in chapter 2, to the cases of communist Poland and Hungary. The Polish and Hungarian economies really began evolving toward capitalism in the late 1960s and 1970s as the cultural-cognitive dimension of their institutions began to change. In both countries, this dimension changed as ruling elites began to suspect that some elements of the market needed to be incorporated into the communist system in order to improve economic performance. This was reflected in a new discursive bricolage whereby Polish elites began to speak of "socialist companies" and "socialist managers" and Hungarian elites began to discuss the concept of "market socialism" (Campbell and Pedersen 1996, 213). It was not until much later that the normative and regulative dimensions of their institutions, such as rules governing property ownership and the appropriate role of the state in the economy, also began to change through bricolage (e.g., Stark 1996). So in the early days as only the cultural-cognitive dimension was altered through bricolage, change was evolutionary. Later, as additional dimensions started to change in this way, change became relatively more revolutionary.

Recognizing that evolutionary change may stem from the mechanism of bricolage offers important benefits beyond clarifying how institutions evolve in path-dependent ways. First, the concept of bricolage focuses our attention on a creative process in which actors make decisions about how to recombine the institutional elements at their disposal. Thus, it helps to infuse our understanding of both path dependence and evolution with a greater sense of agency, something that institutionalists have been criticized for neglecting (Bendor et al. 2001; DiMaggio 1988; Fligstein 2001b, 1997; Hirsch and Lounsbury 1997).

Second, the notion of bricolage helps us understand the paradox of how institutions not only enable, empower, and constitute actors who seek to change institutions, but also constrain the ability of actors to do so. Institutionalists frequently claim that actors are simultaneously enabled and constrained by institutions (e.g., Clemens 1997, 11; Clemens and Cook 1999; Hall 1993, 292; Jepperson 1991; Rutherford 1994, chap. 7; Skrentny 1996, 9). However, our explanations of the mechanisms involved often remain vague and undertheorized. The situation can be improved by recognizing, on the one hand, that institutions enable, empower, and constitute actors by providing them with principles and practices that they can use to modify existing institutional arrangements. By creatively recombining and extending the institutional principles and practices at their disposal, actors can create new ones. In this sense, institutions provide the tool kit or repertoire with which actors modify institutions (Swidler 1986; see also DiMaggio 1997, 268). On the other hand, institutions also constrain the process of change because the number of elements in the tool kit is finite. Hence, as noted earlier, actors are limited in the number of possible innovations they can envision and make.[9]

Third, bricolage is a mechanism that helps fill an important gap in conventional evolutionary theory as developed by social scientists. When biologists talk about evolution they refer typically to two processes: genetic mutation and environmental selection (Nelson 1994a, 116–19). Trying to specify the mechanisms of evolutionary change is the raison d'être for a large body of theory in economics and sociology, which relies heavily on the biological model. Much of this literature contends that actors innovate (i.e., mutate) new institutional forms that they believe will help them resolve their organizational problems, generate more profits, capture greater market share, and otherwise adapt better to their environment. Once created and deployed, some innovations are selected to survive over others either by the invisible hand of market competition, first mover advantages, and the like, or by political and other institutional factors that determine which innovations are acceptable and "fit" the environment (Brunner 1994; Nelson 1994b; Nelson and Winter 1982; North 1990; Rutherford 1994, chap. 5).[10] However, reviews of the literature indicate that while social scientists know a lot about the selection process, they are less knowledgeable about other aspects of institutional and organiza-

[9] For a much different approach to resolving the paradox of simultaneous institutional constraint and empowerment, see Holm (1995).

[10] Without resorting to the language of environmental selection, many institutionalists suggest that for an innovation to take hold in a particular situation it must fit the prevailing institutional rules, norms, and worldviews (e.g., Dobbin 1994; Guillén 1994a; North 1990; Ziegler 1997).

tional evolution (Nelson 1994a; Hannan and Freeman 1989, 20). In particular, they have paid less attention to how the process that *precedes* selection, that is, innovation, contributes to evolution. Thinking about bricolage helps in this regard.[11] After all, mutation in the biological world is a process that involves in part the recombination of genetic material from two organisms in ways that produce a new organism that differs slightly from its parents. Similarly, institutional bricolage is a process involving the recombination of institutional traits. This is a step in the innovation process that occurs before selection. In short, institutional evolution is partly a process of bricolage.[12]

Now, I am not saying that bricolage is the only mechanism that facilitates evolutionary change. In addition to environmental selection, institutionalized search routines within which organizational actors innovate will yield evolutionary effects (Nelson and Winter 1982, 246–62). Furthermore, new institutions may be layered on top of old ones, such as when amendments are added to a constitution or new judicial rulings are fashioned according to long-standing legal precedents. Evolutionary change may also occur when institutions designed for one function are converted to another, such as when the YMCA shifted from being a religious organization concerned with rehabilitating and providing welfare for the urban poor to one providing social and recreational services to the suburban middle class (Zald and Denton 1963). The same thing happened when Lyndon Johnson's Great Society poverty program, originally intended for all poor Americans, was used later in the wake of race riots to channel resources to poor African-American communities (Thelen 2000a, 2000b). Nevertheless, paying attention to the mechanism of bricolage is one way to add content and clarity to the concept of path-dependent evolutionary change.

But an important question remains. Why on some occasions does bricolage lead to more evolutionary change, but on other occasions it leads to more revolutionary change? After all, the implication of my argument so far is that if actors engage in relatively modest recombinations where only

[11] See Haveman and Rao (1997) for an influential study that identifies the importance of both processes in the evolution of the California thrift industry.

[12] In contrast to some evolutionary theorists, I do not want to suggest that evolutionary institutional development necessarily yields more efficient outcomes. Because bricolage is a process that is guided by a logic of appropriateness as well as a logic of instrumentality, the argument presented here does not imply that actors devise solutions that are necessarily more efficient over time. This is a major departure from some theorists who assume that more efficient institutional outcomes evolve as a result of the selection process of market competition (e.g., Chandler 1977), but it is entirely consistent with the basic premise of path dependence arguments—that relatively inefficient practices may become institutionalized (Arthur 1994; David 1985; Mahoney 2000a).

a few things change, then change is evolutionary; if actors engage in relatively radical recombinations where many things change, then change is more revolutionary. To answer this question, we need to turn our attention to the actors involved in the process of bricolage and to the processes of diffusion and translation in which they may engage. The next three sections of this chapter discuss actors, diffusion, and translation.

ACTORS AS ENTREPRENEURS

Key elements in the process of bricolage are creative and innovative people. These are bricoleurs or, following Joseph Schumpeter ([1934] 1983, chap. 2; see also Aldrich 1999, 224; Kingdon 1995, 179–84), entrepreneurs. These are the ones responsible for recombining institutional elements in innovative ways. Understanding their role is important if we want to know, for instance, why in a particular institution-building episode one bricolage is created instead of another. Does it depend on the voluntary whims and creative genius of the entrepreneur, or is there more to be said about it? Despite calls for a theory of institutional entrepreneurs (DiMaggio 1988), only a few institutionalists have paid much attention (e.g., Fligstein 1997, 2001b; Sheingate forthcoming).[13] This is unfortunate because such a theory would help better to specify the process of bricolage. Although an extended discussion of this issue is beyond the scope of this chapter, it is worth considering at least briefly. I submit that understanding the role of the entrepreneur begins not with an assessment of their individual qualities, like talent or charisma, but with an appreciation of their position within a set of social relationships and institutions.

Understanding how social relationships, institutions, and entrepreneurial skill interact can shed light on why one bricolage is made rather than another and, therefore, why some innovations are more evolutionary while others are more revolutionary. The key is to recognize that being located at the borders and interstices of several social networks, organizational fields, or institutions can enhance the probabilities for relatively revolutionary change (Emirbayer and Mische 1998, 1007; Morrill forthcoming; Piore 1995; Rao et al. 2000). Why? Because if leaders have extensive ties to people beyond their immediate social, organizational, or institutional locations, they are more likely to have a broad repertoire with which to work and they are more likely to receive ideas about how to

---

[13] There is a large literature on entrepreneurialism in organization studies that might prove useful to institutionalists concerned with these issues (e.g., Aldrich 1999, chaps. 4, 5; Burton et al. 2002; Sacks 2002). For reviews of this literature, see Thornton (1999) and Thornton and Flynn (forthcoming).

recombine elements in their repertoire, all of which increase the possibilities for creative and revolutionary thinking, innovation, and bricolage. As Howard Aldrich (1999, 81), a student of evolutionary organizational change, has suggested, regardless of their personal qualities, entrepreneurs depend heavily on these locations. Those who occupy impoverished locations lacking a diversity of connections are more likely to find themselves cut off from knowledge about feasible variations on existing practices and critical resources with which to innovate than those who occupy locations with more diverse connections.

To illustrate the point, consider the development and institutionalization of organizing strategies in the labor movement. Marshall Ganz (2000) showed that labor activists trying to organize migrant farm workers in California to win collective bargaining agreements were most successful when, in addition to having strong ties to their own constituents, they had at least weak ties to others like local civic and cultural organizations and churches. Ties to other constituencies provided them with a broader repertoire of experience upon which to draw. In turn, this helped them form broad-based coalitions (i.e., combinations) of political allies. Organizers from the United Farm Workers (UFW) enjoyed these ties, but those from the AFL-CIO did not. As a result, the UFW developed a much more innovative, revolutionary, and, as it turned out, successful organizing strategy, whereas the AFL-CIO simply followed the same strategy with a few minor modifications that had worked for them for decades in other industries like steel and automobiles. It failed with agricultural workers. Researchers have made similar arguments about how institutional and structural location affected the innovative capacities and success of entrepreneurs in the U.S. civil rights movement (Morris 2000, 450), the women's movement (Mansbridge 1986), the New York City garment industry (Uzzi 1996), and the legal dispute resolution profession (Morrill forthcoming). To reiterate, the point is that entrepreneurs with more diverse social, organizational, and institutional connections tend to have more expansive repertoires with which to work. In turn, the broader their repertoire, the more likely they are to create a bricolage that is very creative and revolutionary rather than one that is less creative and evolutionary (Aldrich 1999, 81–85).

Of course, all of this occurs within a broader institutional milieu that can have additional effects on how creative entrepreneurs are likely to be. Again, following Scott's three-fold distinction, if an entrepreneur's institutional location limits the range of innovations that can be imagined cognitively, as I just suggested, then it may also limit the range of innovations that will be normatively appropriate or legitimate. For instance, prior to passage of the Nineteenth Amendment, women's groups in the United States were more likely to win suffrage rights at the level of state government if they argued that women would use these rights to protect children, homes, and families—that is, if they fit their demands for institutional change into the prevailing normative context regarding women's appropriate roles in society (McCammon et al. 2001). Similarly, the entrepreneur's location vis-à-vis regulative institutions will limit the range of innovations he or she is likely to pursue. In particular, the ability of entrepreneurs to reorganize forms of economic governance in business has long been contingent on their ability to convince the courts and regulatory agencies that these innovations fit existing law (Campbell and Lindberg 1990). In other words, the more entrepreneurs can demonstrate that their innovations fit the prevailing institutional situation, the greater will be their capacity for innovation and the greater will be the likelihood that their innovations will stick. This implies that having to fit innovations to existing institutional arrangements tends to constrain the degree to which innovations will be more revolutionary than evolutionary—a path-dependent effect noted earlier.

However, access to tangible resources, like money and political clout, is also important. If entrepreneurs don't have access to these resources, then their innovative ideas, no matter how brilliant, will often fail to take hold and become institutionalized (Aldrich 1999, 76).[14] For instance, during the late nineteenth century Thomas Edison wanted to institutionalize his concept of centralized electricity power generation. However, his ability to do so depended on his ability to shift from a network of American financiers, led by J. P. Morgan, who favored a decentralized approach, to a network of European financiers who supported his idea of central station power generation (McGuire et al. 1993). Similarly, nineteenth-century merchants and industrialists in the United States were able to create huge corporate organizations because they had the resources needed to win legal and legislative battles that reduced local business regulation, limited personal liability in the event of bankruptcy, and swept away other political and institutional obstacles to the growth of these enormous organizations (Perrow 2002). Had Edison not been able to free himself from the Morgan group and had nineteenth-century entrepreneurs not been able to change the law, a different set of innovations would likely have taken hold.

[14] An important part of obtaining resources involves the ability of entrepreneurs to develop trust with those from whom they require resources. They must cultivate an image of their innovation as something that naturally should be taken for granted, and an image of themselves as risk-oriented but responsible. The more they do this and secure legitimacy and support from those around them, the more likely they will be to make innovations that are sharp departures from the past and, thus, represent truly revolutionary changes. Their ability to generate trust also increases the chances that they can expand their network and institutional locations, increase the breadth of their repertoires, and improve their access to resources. For further discussion, see Aldrich (2000; 1999, 87).

Thus, while entrepreneurs' social, organizational, and institutional locations affect their capacity for creative innovation, they face institutional and resource constraints that affect their capacity to make their innovations stick. Recognizing all of this is important because without an understanding of these constraints and how they limit the range of creative opportunities available to entrepreneurs, we could assume incorrectly that entrepreneurs can create whatever innovation and bricolage they please and that innovation, no matter how evolutionary or revolutionary, is simply a matter of their individual cleverness.

I do not mean to imply that mine is the last word on the mechanism of bricolage. Indeed, there is still much to learn about why entrepreneurs make one bricolage instead of another and, in turn, how the process of bricolage affects the degree to which institutional change is more evolutionary or revolutionary. Most important, I have argued that, all else being equal, institutional change is more likely to be revolutionary if entrepreneurs are located in positions that afford them an expansive repertoire of principles and practices that they can use for bricolage. It follows that the introduction of *new* elements into the repertoire also increases the chances that institutional change will be more revolutionary, particularly if these new elements are much different from those already in place. Just as the possibilities for architectural change were revolutionized by the introduction of steel and cement, so too are the possibilities for institutional change if new principles and practices are introduced into the entrepreneur's repertoire. But understanding where these new elements come from and what happens when they arrive requires further discussion and raises questions about diffusion, another important causal concept for institutional analysis.

DIFFUSION

Institutionalists use the concept of *diffusion* to refer to the spread of institutional principles or practices with little modification through a population of actors (David and Foray 1994; Strang and Meyer 1993). The concept's use is especially widespread among organizational institutionalists who argue that diffusion leads to isomorphic or homogenous outcomes in populations of organizations (Mizruchi and Fein 1999; Strang and Soule 1998). Representative of this genre is the work of John Meyer and his colleagues (e.g., Thomas et al. 1987), who studied the diffusion of many elements of modern world culture through the population of nation-states. Diffusion, they argued, results in the homogenization of political institutions across states. For instance, they showed that the diffusion of a modern ideology of childhood as a distinct stage in the life cycle precipitated the gradual worldwide development of constitutional provisions for the education of children and the regulation of child labor (Boli and Meyer 1987). From this and other studies, they concluded that the practices of nation-states are enactments of broad-based cultural prescriptions operating at the global level (Meyer et al. 1987, 32). By using the concept of enactment they invoked a metaphor from the theater whereby action occurs when performers enact scripts given to them by others.

Meyer's work has been criticized for not specifying the mechanisms by which world culture actually impacted the institutional structure and practices of nation-states and other organizations. That is, it was not clear what mechanisms caused nation-states to enact the principles associated with modern world culture (Boli and Thomas 1999b, 2). This is surprising insofar as researchers have identified a number of factors that are associated with the diffusion of practices through other fields of organizations (e.g., David and Foray 1994; Haveman 1993; Tolbert and Zucker 1983; for reviews, see Strang and Soule 1998 and Wejnert 2002). In an effort to address their critics, world culture theorists have tried recently to specify the mechanisms whereby world culture diffuses to nation-states through the activities of international nongovernmental organizations and other transnational actors like the United Nations (Boli and Thomas 1999a; Katzenstein 1996b; Meyer et al. 1997b). This is an important step forward, although one that is still subject to criticism (e.g., Finnemore 1996; Keck and Sikkink 1998, 33–35, 214; Risse and Sikkink 1999, 4). However, my concern here is different.

The discussion of diffusion generally ignores what happens when an institutional principle or practice arrives at an organization's doorstep and is prepared by that organization for adoption. Here the story often ends and it is assumed that the principle or practice is simply adopted uncritically and in toto (Lounsbury 2001, 29–30). Indeed, sometimes this assumption is explicit (e.g., Eyestone 1977, 442). We are left, then, with a black box in which the mechanisms whereby new principles and practices are actually put into use and institutionalized on a case-by-case basis are left unspecified. In this sense, diffusion appears to be a mindless mechanical transfer of information from one place to another (Rao et al. 2003; Haveman 2000, 477). As a result, many of us tend to assume that diffusion results in homogeneous or isomorphic outcomes where all the organizations in a field gradually adopt identical practices and converge with respect to their form and function (DiMaggio and Powell 1983; Mizruchi and Fein 1999). This is not just a problem for those studying diffusion at the international level. It is also common among researchers examining diffusion among political and economic organizations at lower levels of analysis, such as the spread of a corporate strategy across a national population of firms or the propagation of a particular policy across

U.S. state governments (e.g., Dobbin et al. 1993; Edelman 1990; Greve 1995; Rao and Sivakumar 1999).

Let me provide another illustration. Meyer and colleagues (1997b) argued that the development of a global scientific discourse, embracing the concept of a world ecosystem, caused many national governments to establish environmental ministries during the late twentieth century. To use the language from Meyer's earlier work, the new scientific discourse was enacted by national governments. The problem is that their argument omitted any discussion of the national-level political processes that were responsible for this enactment and institution building. Hence, they assumed apparently that these ministries were all basically the same. Similarly, Meyer's earlier work on the diffusion of constitutional provisions for childhood assumed that such provisions were enacted uniformly across countries. However, institutional diffusion is a process with several moments or stages. Enactment is one of them in which new institutional principles are put into practice within an already existing institutional context (Barley and Tolbert 1997). Yet it is precisely the concept of enactment that requires explanation. As discussed in the next section, some recent work has begun to take enactment into account, but for the most part it appears that this is not the case. In two recent comprehensive reviews of diffusion studies there is virtually no mention of what this process might look like (Strang and Soule 1998; Wejnert 2002).[15] What are the mechanisms of enactment? How do organizations enact scripts, concepts, principles, and practices that they receive from their surrounding environment? And how does this affect the degree to which change is evolutionary or revolutionary?

TRANSLATION AND ENACTMENT

Historical institutionalists and some organizational theorists have sought recently through the use of fine-grained case studies to examine how institutional diffusion occurs (e.g., Dobbin 1992; Duina 1999; Guillén 1994a; Marjoribanks 2000; Vogel 1996). Case studies are more amenable to identifying the mechanisms involved, particularly mechanisms of enactment, than the quantitative approaches favored by many organizational institutionalists, including Meyer and colleagues, who use large data sets with dozens or even hundreds of cases to track institutional change over

[15] Much of the discussion in this literature is about the conditions under which organizations adopt new practices, or not, and how organizations interpret the institutional pressures around them in ways that lead them to adopt an innovation, or not (see also Scott 2001, 169–80).

time. Indeed, in at least one empirical study of this sort, Meyer and his colleagues (Meyer et al. 1997b, 645) have admitted that although his approach may be sufficient for determining the degree to which diffusion and homogenization occur among nation-states, it is less well equipped to identify the causal sequences and processes involved. Case studies have shown that the concept of diffusion is undertheorized because diffusion studies fail typically to recognize that when institutional principles and practices travel from one site to another, the recipients implement or enact them in different ways, and to greater or lesser extent, depending on their local social and institutional context. More specifically, new ideas are combined with already existing institutional practices and, therefore, are *translated* into local practice in varying degrees and in ways that involve a process very similar to bricolage. The difference is that translation involves the combination of *new* externally given elements received through diffusion as well as old locally given ones inherited from the past (e.g., Czarniawska and Sevon 1996; Czarniawska and Joerges 1996; Lillrank 1995). Bricolage typically refers to the recombination only of old locally given ones.

The point is that there are important mechanisms involved in the final steps of diffusion that many of us have neglected. Understanding these mechanisms sheds further light on the processes responsible for evolutionary and revolutionary change. The more new ideas, principles, and practices diffuse to a given locale and are translated fully into practice, the more likely it is that change will tend to be more revolutionary than evolutionary. Of course, as implied in the earlier discussion of entrepreneurs, the introduction of new elements is more likely in the first place for entrepreneurs who are located at the interstices of social networks, organizational fields, and institutions. But once they arrive, several things affect how they are translated into practice.

First, some researchers have shown how the process of translation is constrained by the local institutional context. Institutional entrepreneurs must blend new ideas into local practice (Hironaka and Schofer 2002). This tends to ensure that even implementation of a new idea rarely constitutes a total break with past practice. For instance, Yasemin Soysal (1994) showed how the global diffusion of a new postnational model of citizenship was translated into practice in locally distinct ways in Europe during the late twentieth century. Postnational citizenship is the idea that all residents within a nation-state, regardless of their historical or cultural ties to that state, ought to be guaranteed certain basic rights, notably the right to participate in the authority structures and public life of the polity and the right to have access to basic services, such as welfare, health care, and education. How this was done varied according to local political institutions. In Sweden, a country favoring corporatist institutions, guest workers and other immigrants are treated by the state like other corporate groups. The state helps organize immigrants in associations that represent their interests at national-level negotiations over policy, budgets, and the like, just as it helps organize associations that represent the interests of labor, business, and other groups. In France, a country where the central state ensures directly the protection of citizens, the state spends much money supporting social and cultural activities, housing, education, job training, and so on specifically for immigrants. In Switzerland, a liberal country in the sense that the market is trusted to provide for its inhabitants, the federal government has little direct involvement in immigrant affairs per se, but provides significant resources for social workers, occupational training, and other services, primarily at the local level, to help everyone, including immigrants, obtain what they need by participating in the labor market. Thus, the principles of postnational citizenship were translated into Swedish, French, and Swiss practices in very different ways in order to fit them with local institutions. In other words, the new citizenship idea was translated into local contexts by combining it with already-existing institutional practices. To be sure, the result was a substantial and significant institutional change, but not a complete revolutionary departure from past practice. More generally, this suggests that the process of translation is subject to the same institutional constraints noted earlier in the discussion of the process of bricolage.

Institutionalists have also begun to recognize that political mobilization affects the translation process. Marc Schneiberg and Tim Bartley (2001) found that the manner in which fire insurance regulation was translated into practice at the level of state government in the United States depended in part upon the nature of interest group politics in each state. Elsewhere I have shown that a neoliberal model of fiscal reform was diffused from the West to postcommunist Poland, Hungary, and the Czech Republic after 1989 but was translated into practice differently and in varying degrees in each country, depending on the institutional clout of labor unions and political parties (Campbell 2001). Michael Lounsbury (2001) studied the diffusion of recycling programs across American university campuses and found that some campuses created new programs with full-time recycling managers while others folded recycling into already existing staff duties on a part-time basis. The difference was due in part to the presence, or absence, of well-organized environmental activists on campus. We might call them institutional entrepreneurs. Universities that had well-organized activists advocating recycling were more likely to adopt full-time programs than those that did not. Overall, then, the greater the level of general political support for the new principle or practice, the more likely it will be translated into practice in toto and without much modification.

Organizational characteristics may also be important for translation. In addition to the politics associated with interest groups and social movements, other scholars have drawn on the policy implementation literature to argue that organizations that are exposed to new principles and practices through diffusion are more likely to translate them into practice substantively rather than just symbolically if leaders inside the organization are sympathetic and ideologically committed to the new practice. Substantive translation is also more likely if the organization itself has the financial, administrative, and other implementation capacities necessary to support the new practice (Zald et al. 2002; see also Greenwood and Hinings 1996; Hironaka and Schofer 2002; Westney 1987).

In sum, the degree to which diffusing ideas are translated or not into local practice and, therefore, the extent to which they precipitate change depend on local institutional contexts, power struggles, leadership support, and implementation capacities. This is all demonstrated by Marie-Laure Djelic's (1998) analysis of the diffusion of the American model of industrial production to France, West Germany, and Italy after the Second World War. The American model involved several dimensions, including large hierarchically organized multidivisional firms, oligopolistic markets, and dispersed patterns of ownership. Shifting to the American model required corresponding changes in legal institutions, such as laws of incorporation, antitrust law, and limited liability law, respectively. No European country completely abandoned all of their old, nationally unique production systems and legal institutions, and so there were important differences in outcomes. Briefly, France and West Germany experienced relatively radical shifts on these dimensions toward the American model, but change in Italy was much more modest. Particularly in the northern region, Italian production continued to be based largely on small- and medium-size family-owned firms linked through cooperative networks. Why? First, Italy had weaker cross-national ties to the United States through which the diffusion of ideas could flow, and so Italian political leaders at the national level were less supportive and accommodating of the American model than leaders in other European countries. Second, governments at the local level, particularly Christian democratic and communist ones, opposed the American model because it threatened their political interests. The American model threatened to eradicate the Christian Democrats' petty-bourgeois electoral base and create large-scale capitalist firms, which were anathema to the communists. Third, local governments had the administrative capacities to block implementation of the American model, such as by offering tax breaks and infrastructural supports only to small- and medium-size firms, not to large ones. This created incentives for owners not to expand, vertically integrate, or otherwise transform their operations (see also Weiss 1988). As a result, compared to France and West Germany, in Italy the translation of various organizational and legal aspects of the American model into practice was much less complete, the original institutional context was preserved the most, and a more modest, evolutionary transformation occurred.

The fact that diffusion involves an important translation step has serious implications for those institutionalists who claim that diffusion leads to homogeneous or isomorphic outcomes. Even if we observe that states or other organizations are voluntarily copying a new institutional practice, once we recognize that translation is involved as part of the diffusion process, we are compelled to adopt a much more refined appreciation for what is happening. We are also sensitized to the strong possibility that the principles and practices that have diffused and are being enacted will be transformed, modified, and otherwise altered as they are translated into local practice. As a result, we should be more circumspect in making claims about the isomorphic outcomes of diffusion than many of us have been in the past. This is especially true insofar as institutional change involves power struggles (Fligstein 2001b; Knight 1992; Schneiberg 2002). Power struggles are one reason why, for instance, when members of the European Union agree to adopt new directives from Brussels and translate them into national law there is often much variation in what the new national laws actually look like and how they are implemented from one country to the next. Depending on the prevailing organization and institutional arrangement of political forces, directives may be translated and implemented much as the European Union intended, or in only the most symbolic and superficial ways (Duina 1999). There is a substantial literature on cross-national policy transfer that makes precisely this point and that might provide inspiration for those of us who are interested in the relationship between diffusion and translation (e.g., Dolowitz 2000; Dolowitz and Marsh 2000, 1996; Stone 1999). This literature also reminds us that even when new ideas diffuse and are translated into practice, they are not always successful in part because they may not have been translated in ways that fit comfortably with local institutions.[16]

---

[16] In all fairness, it is worth noting that interest in the diffusion of uniform organizational practices was sparked in large part by DiMaggio and Powell's (1983) classic article on the subject of institutional isomorphism. This was an effort to account for homogeneity, not diversity, within organizational fields. It was not an effort to understand how different organizations might tailor a common organizational principle or practice to their own unique situations. Much research by organizational institutionalists has been based on the approach of this article (Mizruchi and Fein 1999). As a result, it should not be surprising that so little attention has been paid to how translation occurs and why it might yield more heterogenous outcomes than scholars generally assume.

Several additional points are in order. First, translation is a process that can involve many institutional logics of action. By logic of action I mean the motivation and calculus that actors use to guide their behavior. For instance, actors may try to adapt new practices in ways that fulfill their political and economic self-interests. They may also try to adapt new practices in ways designed to accommodate cognitive understandings and discourses about how institutions ought to be organized. According to Soysal (1994), this was another important reason why European governments devised dramatically different ways to translate the postnational citizenship principle into institutional practice—they needed to fit it to local political discourse. And actors may try to adapt new practices in ways that help them maintain their normative identities. When organized labor's rights and benefits came under attack during the 1980s and 1990s as neoliberalism diffused globally, unions most vigorously resisted those elements of the neoliberal model that threatened their organizational identities. (Recall that neoliberalism is a macroeconomic model that calls, in part, for greater reliance on market forces rather than institutional agreements to govern economic activity.) Hence, Italian unions fought to preserve automatic cost-of-living increases, Swedish unions fought to preserve national wage bargaining, and German unions fought to preserve co-determination legislation.[17] Why? Because these had long been core parts of their identities (Locke and Thelen 1995). That different logics of action can be involved in translation is an especially important lesson for those organizational institutionalists and others who tend to assume that diffusion results from the cognitive process of imitation or mimesis when, in fact, it can involve a wider variety of logics that need to be disentangled theoretically as well as empirically (Mizruchi and Fein 1999). Furthermore, insofar as different institutionalist paradigms tend to focus on different logics of action (e.g., Suchman 1997), the fact that several logics can operate in translation suggests that institutionalists from all paradigms ought to find the notion of translation appealing and worth pursuing further in their research.

Second, a closer specification of the mechanisms underlying the diffusion concept is important not just so that we can be more precise theoretically, but because if we recognize these mechanisms our empirical research can improve (Mizruchi and Fein 1999). This point is illustrated by the development of a paper by David Strang and Ellen Bradburn (2001) on the diffusion of enabling legislation for health maintenance organizations

---

[17] Co-determination laws ensure that labor shares some decision-making power with management in non-wage related issues, such as the introduction of new technology into the production process and the reorganization of production (e.g., Rogers and Streeck 1994).

(HMOs) across state governments in the United States. Their paper employed sophisticated quantitative analyses to identify the conditions that affected this institutional diffusion. It was part of a larger group project that examined institutional change. When the authors first presented their results to the other project participants they were criticized for failing to recognize that it might be the case that HMO legislation did not diffuse as a monolithic whole across these states. Instead, it might have been translated into practice differently in different places depending on the constellation of local interests and institutions. As a result, Strang and Bradburn decided to explore whether state governments translated parts of the general HMO model into practice in unique ways. In the end, they found evidence for both homogenous diffusion and heterogeneous translation, depending on which parts of the legislation they tracked. Thus, by recognizing that institutional innovations may involve change along different dimensions, and that diffusion may be a more complex process than they assumed initially, their empirical results changed and the quality of their analysis improved.

Finally, if the notion of translation is a useful way to specify more carefully some of the mechanisms underlying diffusion, and if some institutional elements are more likely to diffuse unchanged than others, then important questions follow. When is translation likely to go smoothly and when is it likely to be contested? When is translation likely to lead to substantive rather than just symbolic change? What are the conditions under which translation, once it occurs, is more likely to yield successful results or not? What sorts of institutional elements are more likely to be translated with important modifications and what elements are more likely to diffuse unchanged? Some of the work done by Schneiberg and Bartley, Lounsbury, Djelic, and others discussed earlier begins to address these questions. We might also speculate, for example, that an important factor here is the degree to which institutional elements are clearly identifiable and unambiguous to potential adopters. For instance, federal laws that govern business practices but that are specified in relatively ambiguous ways, such as U.S. civil rights legislation, enable firms to interpret the law with wide latitude. As a result, firms may translate the law into their compliance procedures in different ways depending on the interests of managers (Edelman 1992). Perhaps those practices most likely to be translated are those that already accord best with the adopter's existing institutional expectations, especially cultural-cognitive ones (DiMaggio 1997; Strang 1990), or when they are technically straightforward and not politically sensitive (Strang and Bradburn 2001). Even so, maybe actors are more likely to translate new ideas into practice when they perceive that the costs of doing so are relatively low (North 1990). In any case, much more work is required to address these issues.

CONCLUSION

Let me review and bring the most important parts of my argument together. Institutionalists need to be more precise in specifying the mechanisms underlying the concepts that we invoke to explain social phenomena like institutional change. Otherwise, gaps will remain in our explanations. I have made no effort to catalogue or discuss all the mechanisms in operation. But those that I have discussed, bricolage and translation, go a long way toward helping us better unpack the processes that are involved in some of our most important causal concepts about evolutionary and revolutionary change—the concepts of path dependence and diffusion.

I have also suggested that although we need to learn more about how the mechanisms of bricolage and translation operate, there are some basic propositions worth further investigation. Concerning bricolage, whether institutional entrepreneurs make one bricolage rather than another in any given situation depends on *an inherited repertoire of principles and practices*. A broader repertoire increases the chances, although does not guarantee, that institutional change will be relatively more revolutionary than evolutionary. Additionally, more revolutionary change is likely when entrepreneurs are *located at the interstices of social networks, organizational fields, and institutions*. The reason is that entrepreneurs at these locations are more likely to have a broad repertoire with which to work and because they are more likely to receive ideas about how to recombine elements creatively in their repertoire. Concerning translation, *the more that new principles and practices diffuse from elsewhere and are translated fully into local practice*, the greater the chance for revolutionary rather than just evolutionary change. Again, entrepreneurs who are located at the interstices of networks and institutions are more likely to be exposed to new principles and practices in the first place.

Furthermore, regardless of whether we are talking about bricolage or translation, or about evolutionary or revolutionary innovations, additional factors are involved that help determine how much institutional change occurs. The chances that innovations will actually take hold increase with (1) the capacity of entrepreneurs to fit their innovations into the local institutional context, (2) their ability to mobilize political support from interest groups as well as organizational and institutional leaders, (3) the availability of adequate financial, administrative, and other implementation capacities to support their innovations, and (4) whatever additional political, economic, or other resources entrepreneurs may need to get the job done, notably those required to ease the institutional constraints that they face. But remember that fitting innovations to the local institutional context tends to constrain truly revolutionary change. It is also difficult to avoid unless entrepreneurs can sidestep or otherwise circumvent these constraints, as occurred, notably, in the cases of Thomas Edison and the nineteenth-century merchants and industrialists discussed earlier. However, I suspect that such circumvention is rare. This last point is important because it underscores the theoretically conservative nature of my argument. Specifically, I suspect that institutional change tends generally to be more evolutionary than revolutionary not only because innovations rarely start from scratch, that is, because they involve at least some recombination of already existing elements, but also because they are usually tailored to blend with local institutions rather than replace them entirely. I am not claiming that truly revolutionary institutional change is impossible, but I suspect that it is probably rarer than most of us assume.

Among all of the causal concepts that institutionalists use, perhaps the most common is the notion of embeddedness. Many institutionalists have claimed that actors are embedded in institutions in ways that constrain and enable them (e.g., Evans 1995; Guillén 2001a, 13; Guthrie 1999, 3; Streeck 1997). Insofar as institutional change is concerned, some of the ways in which this happens should be clear from the preceding discussion. As suggested above, the institutions in which actors are embedded constrain them insofar as they limit the range of innovations they can envision and create. Institutions also constrain them insofar as they provide a well-established context into which new principles and practices must be translated when they diffuse from other locations. However, institutions also enable actors by providing them with principles, practices, scripts, and resources with which to craft innovative solutions to their problems. By clearly specifying these mechanisms, the concept of institutional embeddedness can be elaborated in ways that contribute to the development, on the one hand, of theories of action, agency, and change and, on the other hand, theories of constraint, structure, and stability—an important consideration now that institutionalists recognize that our theories need to account for both sets of causal factors (Clemens and Cook 1999; Greenwood and Hinings 1996; Holm 1995; Thelen 2000b).

Theorists such as Peter Hedström and Richard Swedberg (1998a, 12–13) have argued that the quest for social mechanisms necessarily leads to a specification of actors and their motivations at a micro-level. They suggest that this requires a weak version of methodological individualism in the sense that what links macro-level conditions to outcomes are individuals (or groups of individuals) acting at the micro-level in response to their social and institutional situations and to each other. The strong version of methodological individualism holds that individuals should be pictured abstractly in isolation from these situations. Certainly, the absence of micro-level theorizing has been a problem for organizational and, at least occasionally, historical institutionalists (DiMaggio 1997, 1988). Paul Hirsch (1997; Hirsch and Lounsbury 1997), for example, argued that by neglecting an account of actors and action, organizational institutionalists end up with excessively deterministic stories in which actors appear to be institutional dopes responding blindly and in knee-jerk fashion to the institutionally given scripts, schema, rules, and regulations that surround them (see also Fligstein 2001b).

There is much debate about whether micro-level analysis and methodological individualism is necessary to specify all causal mechanisms in social science research. But even scholars like McAdam and his colleagues (2001, 24–27) and Geoffrey Hodgson (1994, 62), who insist that not all mechanisms can be reduced to the principles of methodological individualism, agree that the weak version of methodological individualism may be useful at least sometimes. That is, there are some mechanisms whose explanation requires a micro-level account. The question, then, for many institutionalists is whether in these instances rational choice theory is required in order to specify social mechanisms. After all, rational choice institutionalists have long embraced methodological individualism arguing that any account of how institutions are built or affect social behavior requires a micro-level account of actors as causal agents. Jack Knight's (1992, 2001) work is representative insofar as he shows that actors build political institutions through complex bargaining games in which they struggle to assure acceptable distributional outcomes for themselves. Although many rational choice approaches assume that actors operate in response to their self-interest, Knight accepts a more open-minded view that all we really need to assume is that people act intentionally toward some goal, which may or may not have to do with their self-interest (Knight 1992, 17). Others concur (Boudon 1998; Ingram and Clay 2000, 529).

Recognition of this possibility creates analytic space for other institutionalist approaches as well. It is possible—even likely—that actors operate according to several logics of action, depending on the institutional and social circumstances in which they find themselves (Boudon 1998). For example, Paul DiMaggio and Walter Powell (1983) argued that three logics may be involved in diffusion. Actors may adopt the institutional practice of others because they believe that it is in their material interests to do so in order to obtain resources from their environment. They may adopt because they believe that it is the appropriate or legitimate way to operate. And they may adopt because they face much uncertainty, do not really know what to do, and so simply do what those around them are doing in the hope that it will improve their situation. The difficult trick is determining which of these logics is operating in a given empirical situation (Hedström 1998; Mizruchi and Fein 1999).

The point is that a turn toward micro-level analysis and perhaps even weak-form methodological individualism as a way to specify causal mechanisms does not necessarily preclude the utility of any of the three institutionalist paradigms I have been discussing. Indeed, although rational choice institutionalism may have been more attentive than the others in trying to specify micro-level mechanisms, there is no reason why those of us operating in the other institutionalist paradigms cannot also make important strides in that direction. Organizational institutionalists, for instance, have suggested recently that cognitive psychology or symbolic interactionism may provide a micro-foundation for their brand of institutional analysis (DiMaggio 1997, 271; Fligstein 2001b). Moreover, some rational choice theorists have tried to incorporate a cognitive analysis into their understanding of change mechanisms and have argued that it has been a serious omission from their paradigm (e.g., Jones 1999; Knight and North 1997; North 1998). Concern with broadening our understanding of change mechanisms has led many institutionalists to begin grappling with the question of how norms, cognitive structures, and other kinds of ideas affect institutional change. This subject is addressed in the next chapter.

Chapter 4

THE PROBLEM OF IDEAS

MANY INSTITUTIONALISTS have become preoccupied recently with figuring out how normative and cognitive ideas affect institutional change. This chapter assesses their progress and offers some suggestions about how we can better understand these things.[1] It also argues that ideas can both constrain and facilitate institutional change. Sometimes ideas constrain change in ways that channel it along evolutionary tracks or block it completely. Sometimes ideas facilitate change in ways that may even cause it to switch to more revolutionary tracks, a point that Max Weber ([1915] 1958, 280) made nearly a century ago. The degree to which ideas do one or the other depends on which types of ideas carry the most weight in specific decision-making episodes.

Scholars have criticized interest-based or realist theories of organizations, politics, political economy, international relations, and economics for neglecting how ideas—such as worldviews, norms, identities, values, intellectual paradigms, culture, and other beliefs—affect decision making and institutional change.[2] (By "decision making" I mean decisions that affect policies and institutions in either the public or private sector.) Now, even some of the most stalwart defenders of the interest-based approach, rational choice theorists, have conceded that ideas like norms and cognitive structures matter. Notably, Douglass North (1990, chap. 5) acknowledged that an important part of institutional change involves actors trying to interpret the world around them through ideologies, norms, and values, which help them to identify their interests in the first place (see also Knight and North 1997; Ostrom 1990, 33–35). In other words, what actors *believe* may be just as important as what they *want* (Vanberg and Buchanan 1989, 51). Nevertheless, North lamented that institutionalists do not have a good theory that helps explain the effects of ideas on institutional change.

---

[1] Portions of this chapter appeared originally in "Institutional Analysis and the Role of Ideas in Political Economy," *Theory and Society* 27 (1998): 377–409, © Kluwer Academic Publishers, with kind permission from Kluwer Academic Publishers.

[2] For criticisms of interest based theories of organizations, see DiMaggio and Powell (1991); for politics, see Dobbin (1994, chap. 1) and March and Olsen (1989); for comparative political economy, see Thelen and Steinmo (1992); for international relations, see Katzenstein (1996a), Rohrlich (1987), and Wendt (1992); for economics, see Fligstein (2001a).

Much of the literature on ideas has taken the form of an attack on rational choice theory by historical and organizational institutionalists. As concern about the importance of ideas developed, a distinction was soon drawn between ideas, broadly construed, and interests, which were viewed as an individual's concern with improving his or her well-being. Moreover, interests were often assumed to be objectively given by virtue of the individual's political, economic, and social situation, whereas ideas were said to be subjective social constructions.

In my view, this is wrong. Interests are a particular type of idea among many. Actors have both interests and other types of ideas; both affect their behavior. Moreover, interests, like other types of ideas, are socially constructed in the sense that they are based on the individual or group's interpretation of their situation (e.g., Hattam 1993; Lukes 1974). In fact, there is convincing evidence that self-interest as an important motivation in the Western world is a historically specific social construction that emerged only after the concept of the individual gained privileged position over the concept of the community (Hirschman 1977). That said, for ease of presentation, I use the term "ideas" to refer to ideas other than interests.

Despite the recent diligent efforts of institutionalists to incorporate ideas into their analyses of decision making and institutional change, scholars have leveled criticisms at this work (e.g., Berman 2001; Blyth 1997, 1998; Campbell 2002; Jacobsen 1995; Yee 1996).[3] These can be boiled down to five important questions that remain unanswered—or at best only partially answered—by institutionalists. This chapter shows how institutionalists have tried to address these questions, how more progress can be made, and where further work is required. Unless satisfactory answers can be found, those of us who try to account for the effects of ideas on institutional change will not be able to persuade the skeptics that ideas are really all that important.

To begin with, critics have charged that institutionalists define ideas too vaguely and that without sharper definitions, attempts to argue for the importance of ideas are futile. Second, even when definitions are fairly clear, it is not always apparent who the carriers of ideas are. That is, although institutionalists often argue that ideas have effects in that they

[3] Organizational and historical institutionalists have done the most to bring ideas back into institutional analysis. Rational choice theory has paid some attention to ideas, particularly how norms and identities emerge and constrain behavior (e.g., Knight and Ensminger 1998; Laitin 1998; North 1990, chap. 5), but they have generally been much more concerned with the effects of *information* than *ideas* on decision making. Much of this work is in game theory and explores how incomplete, biased, and asymmetric information affects political behavior (e.g., Austen-Smith 1990; Austen-Smith and Riker 1987, 1990; Bendor et al. 1987; Calvert 1985; Lupia 1992).

set limits or constraints on decision making and institutional change—
or enable, facilitate, and constitute decision making and institutional
change—it is not always clear which actors are responsible for introducing, shaping, or institutionalizing ideas in ways that produce these effects.
As a result, in many cases our theories about ideas are excessively structural and need a greater sense of agency. Third, following on the discussion in chapter 3, institutionalists need to specify more carefully how ideas
affect decision making and institutional change, and, conversely, how institutions affect ideas. We need to identify the causal mechanisms that
account for how these effects occur if we want to improve our understanding of institutional change. Fourth, institutionalists pay only scant attention to the conditions under which ideas are most likely to affect institutional change—a situation that makes it difficult for us to generate good
theories about when ideas matter most. Finally, much institutional analysis seeks to determine the degree to which ideas other than interests affect
outcomes. Critics charge that the methods employed in such research are
often suspect, and, as a result, claims that ideas matter are not convincing.
In sum, there are five questions that institutional analysis must answer
about ideas. These questions constitute the structure of this chapter:

1. What are ideas? How should we *define* them?
2. Who are the *actors* that are responsible for making ideas matter
   and what are their roles?
3. How do ideas affect institutional change, and, conversely, how do
   institutions affect ideas? What are the *causal mechanisms* involved?
4. Under what *conditions* are ideas most likely to affect institutional
   change?
5. What is the appropriate *methodology* for determining whether
   ideas matter for institutional change?

Let me make one clarification before continuing. Some of the literature
on ideas, particularly from historical institutionalists, is concerned with
how ideas like norms and cognitive schema affect public policy. At first
blush, policy-making and institutional change might not seem to be too
closely related. In fact, they are. Policy-making is generally about writing
or changing rules, regulations, and laws. Sometimes it is about developing
or changing informal procedures and practices that eventually become so
taken-for-granted as to be assumed appropriate and legitimate. Recall
from chapter 1 that this is how many institutionalists define institutions
in the first place. Thus, policy-making is often a process of institution
building and institutional change. Even though the literature on ideas that
focuses on policy-making does not always talk about institutions per se,
we will see that it has important and direct implications for our understanding of institutional change.

What Are Ideas? How Should We Define Them?

Institutionalists mean many different things when they talk about ideas. This makes the literature on ideas confusing. To bring some clarity to the discussion, we can use two conceptual distinctions to identify different types of ideas and their effects. First, ideas can be underlying and often taken-for-granted assumptions residing in the *background* of decision-making debates. In this regard, ideas are institutions in the sense generally intended by organizational institutionalists. However, ideas can also be concepts and theories located in the *foreground* of these debates, where they are explicitly articulated by decision-making elites. Background assumptions can be visible to actors yet taken for granted in the relatively mild sense that they remain largely accepted and unquestioned, almost as principles of faith, whereas ideas in the foreground are routinely contested as a normal part of any decision-making debate.[4] Second, ideas can be either *cognitive* or *normative*. At the cognitive level ideas are descriptions and theoretical analyses that specify cause-and-effect relationships, whereas at the normative level ideas consist of values, attitudes, and identities. In this sense, cognitive ideas are outcome oriented, but normative ideas are not (Rueschemeyer and Skocpol 1996b, 300).[5] As figure 4.1 illustrates, by combining these distinctions we can identify four types of ideas: paradigms, public sentiments, programs, and frames. It is important to recognize that this typology does not differentiate types of ideas by their function or effects. However, as discussed in the next paragraphs, each type of idea does exert unique effects on decision making and institutional change. In particular, because background ideas are often so taken for granted, they tend to constrain change. Because foreground ideas are contested and often used to challenge the status quo, they tend to facilitate or enable change.

---

[4] Some background assumptions may be located at deeper, more taken-for-granted levels than others. For example, Western economists, steeped in the neoclassical tradition, generally assume that supply and demand tend to balance out in the long run and that the long run may range anywhere from a few months to a year or more. During recessions the question of how long we should wait before trying to facilitate market balancing with fiscal, monetary, or other policies brings to the surface assumptions about how long it takes for markets to restore their own equilibrium. However, economists and policymakers rarely question the deeper assumption that markets can balance themselves eventually, let alone the even deeper assumption that market actors respond primarily to the forces of supply and demand.

[5] For further discussion of this distinction, particularly regarding why norms are not outcome oriented, see Elster (1989, chap. 12). My use of the term "cognitive" is different from others who have used it simply to refer to actors' subjective perceptions of their environments (e.g., McAdam et al. 2001, 26). For me, subjective perceptions may involve both cognitive and normative ideas, that is, ideas that are outcome and non-outcome oriented, respectively.

	Concepts and Theories in the Foreground of the Debate	Underlying Assumptions in the Background of the Debate
	Programs	*Paradigms*
Cognitive (Outcome oriented)	Ideas as elite prescriptions that enable politicians, corporate leaders, and other decision makers to chart a clear and specific course of action. Goldstein's road maps & focal points Blyth's weapons	Ideas as elite assumptions that constrain the cognitive range of useful programs available to politicians, corporate leaders, and other decision makers. Fligstein's conceptions of control Esping-Andersen's family models Jones' cognitive architecture
	Frames	*Public Sentiments*
Normative (Non-outcome oriented)	Ideas as symbols and concepts that enable decision makers to legitimize programs to their constituents. Schmidt's communicative discourses Fligstein and Mara-Drita's frames	Ideas as public assumptions that constrain the normative range of legitimate programs available to decision makers. Dobbin's national cultures Levi's perceptions of fairness Hattam's class identities

Figure 4.1. Types of Ideas and Their Effects on Policy-Making.

Paradigms

Paradigms are cognitive background assumptions that constrain decision making and institutional change by limiting the range of alternatives that decision-making elites are likely to perceive as useful and worth considering.[6] At a very general level, sociologists and others have argued that the notion of instrumental rationality itself, that is, making decisions based on anticipated consequences for prior goals, is a paradigm so prevalent and taken for granted today in the Western world that we often assume that it is a perfectly natural way to make decisions, even though it is, in fact, a historically specific, socially constructed way of reasoning (Hirschman 1977; Meyer et al. 1987). However, scholars have identified a variety of other, more specific paradigms. As noted in chapter 1, Neil Fligstein

---

[6] Organizational institutionalists have used the term "institutional logic" in much the same way that I am using the term paradigm. See, for instance, Friedland and Alford (1991).

(1990), an organizational institutionalist, argued that managers of U.S. corporations have subscribed to various conceptions of control or taken-for-granted worldviews about how to organize corporate activity. These paradigms constrained the organizational options managers considered when they tried to cope with their firm's problems. So, for example, during the early twentieth century, managers believed that the best way to ensure profitability and competitiveness was through close control of the manufacturing process. They institutionalized this manufacturing conception of control by mass-producing goods through large, vertically integrated firms, refusing to veer from this approach for several decades despite the fluctuating fortunes of their firms. However, beginning in the 1930s the manufacturing conception of control gave way to a sales-and-marketing conception of control where managers believed that the best way to ensure profitability and competitiveness was through product-diversification strategies and, thus, a new organizational form—the multidivisional firm. In sum, as long as a particular conception of control was in place, it constrained managers' organizational options, but when the paradigm shifted, so too did managers' options.

Historical and rational choice institutionalists have made similar arguments about decision making and institutional change more generally. Among the works by historical institutionalists, Peter Hall's (1993) article on macroeconomic policy paradigms, detailed in chapter 2, is the most notable, but there are also other examples. For instance, Gosta Esping-Andersen (1999) showed that assumptions about the structure and functioning of family systems had powerful effects on the development of welfare state institutions. Notably, in Catholic countries in Southern Europe, decision makers took for granted that the traditional nuclear family would perform certain tasks for itself, such as providing child care and elderly care. Decision makers fashioned welfare states accordingly. Hence, they did not provide day care or maternity leave programs because they assumed that families would not need them. Within the rational choice camp, Bryan Jones (1999) suggested that peoples' ability to make rational decisions is limited by their eagerness to ignore available information if it does not fit what he called their cognitive architecture, by which he meant in part their taken-for-granted understandings of how the world works. Finally, Jack Knight and Douglass North (1997), have emphasized as strongly as any rational choice theorists the importance of cognitive paradigms. According to them,

> Mental models directly affect individual choice. . . [T]herefore, individual actors will disagree over what is the rationally appropriate thing to do. . .[T]he implication is that individuals from different backgrounds will interpret the same evidence differently; they may, in consequence, make different choices. (216)

Public Sentiments

Public sentiments are normative background assumptions that constrain decision making and institutional change by limiting the range of programs that decision-making elites are likely to perceive as acceptable and legitimate both to their constituents and themselves. Public opinion, values, norms, identities, and other "collectively shared expectations" (Katzenstein 1996a, 7) are what I have in mind here. Arguments about the importance of public sentiments emphasize culture and are premised on the notion that decision makers are often guided as much by their understanding of what is appropriate behavior as they are by any sort of cost-benefit calculation (March and Olsen 1989; Skrentny 1996, 1998; Smith 1992, 257). For example, Frank Dobbin (1994) wanted to explain why the same industry can be organized very differently in different countries. He studied the development of national railways. He argued that political elites orchestrated the development of the national railway system in France because they believed that it was appropriate for the central state to intervene forcefully into the economy. Hence, France built a centralized rail system. But in the United States, where people believed that the central state should exercise only limited authority in economic matters, private actors and local state regulators were predominantly responsible for organizing railway development. As a result, the Americans built a more decentralized railway system. National political cultures made the difference.

Similar reasoning has also influenced international relations scholars (Finnemore 1996; Katzenstein 1996b). For instance, some have argued that nation-states, particularly small ones, develop military institutions, capacities, and strategies more because their leaders perceive that this is what the community of nations expects modern states to do than because they fulfill some strategic or national security purpose. Indeed, according to these scholars, why else would small countries buy a few fighter jets that do not appreciably augment their defensive capabilities, or why would countries with nuclear or chemical weapons refuse to deploy them in combat, even when the possibility of retaliation is nil, unless they assumed that these were the appropriate things to do given the prevailing international norms (Eyre and Suchman 1996; Price and Tannenwald 1996)?

The fact that public sentiments can constrain the options available to decision makers is graphically illustrated in Margaret Levi's (1997) study of military conscription. Using a rational choice approach, she concluded that the degree to which citizens are willing to consent to serve in the armed forces during war, risk their lives, and, therefore, put their country's interests above their own, depends on the degree to which they perceive that the system is fair. That is, if draftees believe that all citizens are being subject to the draft in an impartial manner, then they tend to consent to the wishes of their leaders. But if they believe that some groups are being treated differently, due perhaps to their class or status position, then there is likely to be much draft evasion and other forms of resistance to conscription. Public sentiments regarding the fairness of the system are key and constrain how effectively political elites can mobilize for war.

Although these examples focus on public-sector decision making, public sentiments can also constrain the options available to decision makers in the private sector. During the 1980s, shareholders, led by large institutional investors, struggled to transform corporate governance in ways that limited the decision-making power of corporate directors. This happened as shareholders began to suspect that directors were acting inappropriately vis-à-vis shareholder interests. According to researchers, the behavior of directors changed eventually because shareholders convinced government to reform the law regulating corporate governance and because the ideological climate within which directors had to operate had become increasingly pro-shareholder (Davis and Thompson 1994).

Recently, scholars have emphasized how important collective identities are in all of this, particularly insofar as they affect how actors perceive their interests as they build institutions (e.g., Padgett 1998; Piore 1995; Wendt 1992). By identities, they mean how actors understand themselves and their roles as defined through self-reflexive interactions with other actors (e.g., Wendt 1992, 397–398).[7] Although identities are often stable and taken for granted, they do sometimes change with important institutional effects (Laitin 1998). For example, Victoria Hattam (1993), analyzed changes in the U.S. labor movement showing that one reason why unions redirected their efforts to advance workers' interests from legislatures and the courts to the shop floor and factory gates was that their identity as a class changed. During the early nineteenth century, they viewed themselves in republican terms as a class that included both workers and other productive economic actors, including manufacturers and industrialists. Hence, they pursued their interests, just as business did, through the legislature and courts, often seeking equal protection under the law. But after the Civil War, unions redefined themselves in more modern terms as representatives of a proletarian class whose interests were diametrically opposed to those of the business community. Thus, they

[7] I view identities as public sentiments, that is, normative rather than cognitive ideas, because they are not outcome oriented and do not specify causal relationships. They are collections of attributes that are associated with normative obligations and expectations. For instance, most senior faculty in academic departments have an identity based on certain professional attributes, such as being tenured and being more experienced in academic matters than their junior faculty colleagues. This identity carries with it certain normative obligations and expectations, including responsibility for mentoring junior faculty and shouldering more departmental and university committee assignments.

confronted capitalists in the factories to advance their interests and shifted their energies from trying to influence one set of institutions, the law, to another set of institutions, formal labor-management agreements. Others have made similar arguments about how union identities affected institutional change during the late twentieth century (Locke and Thelen 1995).

Programs

Programs are in the foreground of decision-making debates. Programs are cognitive concepts and theories that enable or facilitate decision making and institutional change by specifying for decision makers how to solve specific problems. Programs are found in both the public and private sectors and include such things as policy prescriptions and corporate strategies, respectively. As noted earlier, programs are often the key dependent variable for institutionalists. They are important because they determine most directly how institutions change. For instance, Esping-Andersen (1999) sought to explain the conditions under which European countries adopted various welfare programs that led to the creation of welfare state institutions, and Dobbin (1994) sought to explain the conditions under which countries adopted different railway development programs that affected the railroad industry's institutional structure. Nevertheless, institutionalists have done relatively little research to examine how the character of programs per se, as opposed to the forces surrounding them, affect their adoption. Some scholars have noted that decision makers are most likely to embrace programs that are simple and easily understood (Campbell 1998; Woods 1995). Judith Goldstein (1993; Goldstein and Keohane 1993b, 17–20) argued that programs are more likely to be adopted when they provide clear "road maps" that offer convincing directions out of a particular dilemma as well as "focal points" or ideas that have enough appeal to facilitate coalition building and political support. Mark Blyth (1998, 2002) suggested that decision makers are more favorably disposed to programs that constitute "weapons" with which they can struggle to gain power and resources. However, more work is required to understand better why some programs are more appealing than others. In this regard, frames are very important.

Frames

Frames are normative concepts that reside in the foreground of decision-making debates. They enable elites to legitimize their programs and institutional changes to their constituents and occasionally to each other. This is what Vivien Schmidt (2000, 2001) referred to when she explained that national political elites need to develop a communicative discourse to justify or legitimize neoliberal programs to their citizens. She showed that policymakers often justify neoliberalism, that is, a general reduction in state control over the economy, by strategically cloaking it in the language and rhetoric of national public sentiment. For instance, British policymakers successfully legitimized Margaret Thatcher's radical neoliberalism in the 1980s by framing it in terms of the country's long-standing adherence to a limited state and liberal economic principles. On the other hand, French elites could not follow suit, given their country's long history of indicative planning and state intervention, and so resorted to a pro-European integration frame stressing that neoliberalism was a way to embrace the more liberal, open, and market-oriented principles of the European Community that the French already favored. Similarly, Fligstein and Iona Mara-Drita (1996) demonstrated that members of the European Commission who sought to develop a single European market were careful to frame this institutional project in terms deemed appropriate by national governments and business elites. They emphasized how this new institution would involve only new rules of exchange rather than new property rights or governance structures that would threaten national sovereignty and the interests of industrial actors. Indeed, framing has been critically important to the rise of many neoliberal projects during the late twentieth century (Block 1996; Bourdieu 1998).

Framing is also important in business. Organization theorists, for instance, have shown that framing is often crucial to the development of new industry niches, such as micro brewing in the United States. The recent success of micro brewers depended heavily on their ability to convince consumers that their products had a uniquely desirable identity steeped in the traditions of small-scale craft production rather than the mass production techniques that characterized most beers on the market (Carroll and Swaminathan 2000). Indeed, framing is often about establishing discursive oppositions like this, as occurred in France when the characteristics of classical and nouvelle cuisine were juxtaposed by renegade chefs seeking to establish an identity and niche for themselves within their profession (Rao et al. 2003).

Of course, framing is also important when business leaders are trying to affect institutions. During the 1980s, television broadcasters in the United States were threatened with the loss of part of their broadcast transmission spectrum to land-based mobile broadcasters, such as citizen band radio operators. Initially, the National Association of Broadcasters (NAB) pressed the Federal Communications Commission and Congress not to set aside a portion of the broadcast spectrum for land-based users. The NAB argued that this would lead to interference with television signals and distort reception—even though the organization did not really believe that interference was likely to be a serious problem. However, this frame failed to persuade government officials not to revise regulations, and so broadcasters lost part of their spectrum. Later, they changed frames and argued that bandwidth needed to be preserved for the development of high-definition television. This was a new technology, they suggested, that needed to be developed in the United States to maintain the electronics industry's competitive advantage over the Japanese and to preserve jobs in the electronics industry. This frame worked, and the government agreed not to pass another round of regulations cutting further into their spectrum (Dowell et al. 2002). Of course, as this example suggests, frames can be manipulated and they can be used to block institutional change as well as facilitate it.

To review briefly, my point here is twofold. First, although plenty has been written about ideas and their effects on decision making and institutional change, scholars have made little effort to distinguish clearly among different types of ideas. Without such clarity, we will have trouble understanding fully how and when ideas matter. The typology in figure 4.1 helps rectify this problem. Second, paradigms and public sentiments are second-order concepts insofar as they constitute the underlying ideas upon which the first-order concepts, that is, programs and frames, rest, respectively. As such, paradigms and public sentiments are constraints that limit the range of options from which decision makers may choose when trying to solve their political, economic, and organizational problems, and when grappling with institutional change. Conversely, decision makers engage programs and frames more actively and directly at these times. They propose, test, and revise their programs and frames as they try to fit them to the prevailing constraints posed by reigning paradigms and public sentiments. This implies the need to consider more closely the role of actors and agency.

WHO ARE THE ACTORS AND WHAT ARE THEIR IDEATIONAL ROLES?

Ideas do not emerge spontaneously or become influential without actors, and so it is important to situate these actors and theorize their roles vis-à-vis ideas in any account of institutional change (Berman 2001, 235). However, we have paid surprisingly little attention to the issue of actors and agency in much of our work (Christensen et al. 1997; Haas 1992, 27; Thelen and Steinmo 1992, 14).[8] As noted in chapter 1, rational choice

---

[8] Historical institutionalists are less guilty of this error than other institutionalists. For instance, Stephen Skowronek's (1982) early work on U.S. state building showed that academics, economists, and other intellectuals played key roles in providing ideas, particularly new cognitive models of government, that shaped political institution building. Similarly, Theda Skocpol's work on the development of social security in the United States showed

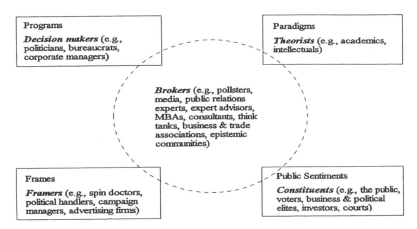

Figure 4.2. Actors and Their Ideational Realms.

theories start from the premise that institutional change is driven by actors pursuing their interests, and so they have a clear place for actors and agency in their analysis, but they pay little attention to the role of ideas. Conversely, organizational institutionalists consider ideas in their analyses, notably taken-for-granted worldviews and cognitive schema, but pay relatively little attention to actors and agency (Hirsch and Lounsbury 1997). The trick is to link the two. How can this be done?

We can proceed by elaborating the key actors who embrace, fabricate, manipulate, and carry the different types of ideas introduced earlier. Some of these actors are the institutional entrepreneurs discussed in chapter 3. After all, institutional entrepreneurs seek to mobilize ideas to affect institutional change (DiMaggio 1988; Fligstein and Mara-Drita 1996; Kingdon 1995, 122–24). But there are also other actors involved. Unfortunately, because most institutionalists have failed to differentiate among types of ideas, we have also neglected that there may be different types of institutional entrepreneurs and other actors operating in different ideational realms. The actors associated with the different types of ideas discussed earlier are represented in figure 4.2 and discussed next.

Decision Makers

To begin with, for ideas to matter at all, high-level public and private decision makers must embrace programs and seek to incorporate them

how academics and social reformers in Wisconsin, Ohio, and other states developed intellectual models that influenced welfare state building first at the state level and later at the national level (e.g., Skocpol and Ikenberry 1995).

into decision making. Thus, decision-making elites are the most proximate carriers of ideas that affect decision making and institutional change. In the political world these elites are key policymakers in the legislative and executive branches of government. In the corporate world they are top corporate managers.

Theorists

Often programs do not originate just among decision makers themselves but also elsewhere in the minds of theorists, such as professional academics and other intellectuals. Generally, theorists operate by deriving specific programs from the underlying paradigms that they help promulgate and sustain in the first place. Occasionally, however, these thinkers may alter paradigms in ways that have huge consequences for the programs that they or others are likely to suggest. For instance, Mauro Guillén (1994a) showed that intellectual-paradigm shifts in business, as reflected in management journals and books, have been associated with the development and institutionalization of new ways to organize and run firms. In the United States the principles of scientific management, theorized by Frederick Winslow Taylor and others in the engineering profession, became the dominant paradigm in the management literature between 1900 and 1930 and contributed to the rise of Fordist production techniques, notably hierarchically organized mass production. More recently, during the 1980s concern arose among academics, business consultants, and other theorists over the inefficiency and inflexibility of large-scale corporate bureaucracies and conglomerates, and a new management paradigm emerged stressing the virtues of decentralization (e.g., Ouchi 1981). This paradigm shift led to the downsizing of management structures in the 1980s and 1990s and the disassembling of many large conglomerates in the United States (e.g., Davis et al. 1994; Harrison 1994). Similarly, during the 1970s a paradigm shift in economic theories of industrial regulation helped facilitate the deregulation of the U.S. airline and trucking industries. In airlines, deregulation was actually led by an economist from Cornell University, Alfred Kahn, who spearheaded this paradigm shift before being appointed chairman of the Civil Aeronautics Board, where he oversaw the industry's deregulation (Derthick and Quirk 1985).

Framers

Of course, for decision makers to embrace them, programs need to be considered acceptable or appropriate as well as intellectually appealing and convincing. That is, they must fit not only with the prevailing cognitive paradigm but also with dominant norms, values, and other public sentiments. This generally requires the presence of people who frame programs in ways that they believe will be acceptable to the relevant constituencies. I am speaking again of institutional entrepreneurs whose success in building and reproducing institutions depends in part on their ability to provide appropriate frames in order to mobilize people (Fligstein 2001b, 106). This is most obvious in the realm of politics where these framers include spin doctors, political handlers, campaign managers, and other operatives, sometimes including political elites themselves. For example, although a variety of programs were floating around during the early 1980s as to how Europe might overcome slow growth, inflation, high unemployment, and other collective problems, the Single Market Project (SMP) emerged as the idea that finally carried the day. In part, this was due to the efforts of key institutional entre- preneurs, such as Heinz Narjes, one of the European Commissioners, and later Jacques Delors, the commission's president, who strategically framed the SMP and its related projects as a way to continue unifying Europe. This was a deliberate effort to frame the SMP in terms vague enough so that actors could read almost anything into it that they liked (Fligstein 1997; Fligstein and Mara-Drita 1996). In the private sector, spin doctors, advertising firms, and other organizations play the role of framers. As noted earlier, the National Association of Broadcasters played an important role as a framer in the struggle to protect its portion of the broadcast spectrum.

That framers use ideas deliberately and strategically is important. Others who discuss actors in order to introduce an element of agency into their analyses argue that actors are merely "carriers" who transmit ideas, or "gatekeepers" who govern the entry of ideas into decision- making arenas (Haas 1992, 27). But framers build frames by creatively blending different ideas through the process of bricolage, discussed in chapter 3. For instance, institutional entrepreneurs who pressed U.S. cor- porations not to discriminate against employees on the basis of sexual preference constructed a frame emphasizing that the issue was about up- holding basic civil rights and that such a program would be good for business. Their frame was a bricolage of basic beliefs about fair play, equal protection under the law, and the notion that treating employees fairly would foster employee commitment to the firm, and, therefore, greater corporate efficiency and profitability (Creed et al. 2002a, 2000b). View- ing actors only as carriers and gatekeepers denies that they also transform and generate new ideas like this in the first place and so misses another important way of infusing the analysis of ideas and institutional change with some agency.

Constituents

The targets of framers are the constituents from whom approval and support must be obtained in order to carry out a program and change institutions. Constituents may be either the general public, as is often the case in politics, or decision-making elites, as was the case when activists tried to force corporate executives to treat all employees equally regardless of sexual preference, and when the television industry tried to cajole federal regulators and Congress to protect its portion of the broadcast spectrum. In U.S. business, Wall Street is often a key constituent insofar as firms need to convince investors that their programs and institutional changes make sense.

In any case, scholars have argued that programs and institutional changes must appear to conform to the public sentiments of constituents. In the European Single Market Project case, these constituents were not only national governments, whose concern was that their sovereignty and national identities be preserved, but also influential business leaders throughout Europe whose perceived interests were of much concern to framers (Fligstein and Mara-Drita 1996). At the national level, framers are keen to couch their programs in rhetoric and symbolism that resonates with the perceived public sentiments of the general electorate, as was the case in France when political elites deployed the pro-European integration frame to justify neoliberalism (Schmidt 2000, 2001, 2002). Similarly, in the private sector, for managers to institutionalize new organizational forms they often must convince the courts, as representatives of the general public, that their innovations are legitimate and socially appropriate (Campbell and Lindberg 1990). Indeed, the history of the modern U.S. corporation involved all sorts of legal battles over its organizational legitimacy and, in particular, whether its various forms violated the principles of market competition (Campbell et al. 1991; Fligstein 1990; Roy 1997). The institutionalization of collective organizations, such as business associations and labor unions, also required the imprimatur of the courts (e.g., Hattam 1993; Schneiberg 1999).

Brokers

The foregoing discussion assumes that for different kinds of ideas to affect decision making and institution building they must be linked, connected, or somehow transported from one ideational realm to another. Again, how this occurs depends heavily on actors, some of whom operate at the intersections of these realms (see the dashed circle in figure 4.2). We might call these people ideational brokers.[9] For instance, pollsters play a key role in identifying and conveying public sentiments to political framers. After all, framers often use the sentiments identified by public opinion polls to frame the programs they favor. Conversely, the media and public relations experts convey well-framed messages back to the public in ways that may affect public sentiments (Moore 1995).

In European politics, political parties often have expert advisors whose job it is to craft programs from the broader paradigms upon which their parties are based. One reason the Swedish Social Democratic Party enjoyed significant and sustained electoral success between the two World Wars, and why it was so quick to embrace Keynesianism, was that key theorists, some of whom had helped establish the party's reformist paradigm, were strategically positioned within the party apparatus in ways that put them into direct contact with the party's decision makers in an advisory capacity. They linked the party's paradigms and programs (Berman 1998). More recently, experts and officials from the OECD, the European Commission, and the German banking community proselytized the virtues of price stability when they met with economic decision makers from European countries and disseminated programs involving European exchange rate and currency reform that were based on the neoclassical economic paradigm (Marcussen 2000; McNamara 1998, chap. 6). In the United States, university-trained professionals, economists, and other intellectuals were brokers advising decision makers on how to develop a more professional bureaucratic state during the early part of the twentieth century (Skowronek 1982).

Corporate consultants act as ideational brokers in the business world, especially when they simultaneously occupy faculty positions in business schools. Consultants are often responsible for starting new managerial programs and paradigms, such as the Quality Control and Total Quality Management, and disseminating them to corporate decision makers through their consultancies and the business press. They also spread them to academic theorists through scholarly publications (Abrahamson and

[9] Even before the advent of organizational institutionalism, organizational analysts recognized the important role that actors play in spanning different organizational realms and conveying ideas among them (e.g., Hirsch 1972; Powell 1985). Of course, existing institutional arrangements may also facilitate this movement of ideas among ideational realms. In business and politics in the United States, institutionalized policy discussion groups, like the Council on Foreign Relations and the Business Council, bring together high-level decision makers from business and government, expert advisers, academics, and representatives from other ideational realms to develop new programs (Domhoff 2002, 81–94). In some European countries these institutions are especially prevalent. In Denmark they are so central to decision making that observers refer to this as a "negotiated economy" (Nielsen and Pedersen 1991; Pedersen 1993).

Fairchild 1999; Davis et al. 1994). High-level managers often play the role of ideational broker themselves insofar as they receive MBAs and other graduate-level degrees from leading business schools, where they learn about different paradigms and then move into executive positions in firms where they devise and implement programs based on them (Fligstein 1990, 282).

In politics, think tanks and policy institutes are especially important brokers because they connect several ideational realms (Allen 1994; Ricci 1993; Stone 1996). Particularly since the early 1970s, think tanks in the United States and Europe have become increasingly interested in simplifying and disseminating the paradigms and programs of other researchers rather than conducting research themselves. They have learned to transmit these ideas to decision makers through pithy policy briefs designed to affect programmatic thinking. And, to influence public sentiments, they transmit these ideas to the public through op-ed pieces and articles in the major newspapers and financial press, and through appearances on television and radio talk shows. In Britain, Sweden, and the United States, conservative think tanks were especially adept at playing these roles in successful efforts to push neoliberalism onto the decision-making agenda and into the public consciousness as solutions to the emergent problems of globalization (Blyth 2002, 1998; Hall 1992, 104–5). Think tanks have also sponsored and occasionally published work by academics that pays close attention to framing programs in ways intended to appeal to both the public and decision makers.

Business and trade associations also operate as ideational brokers. For instance, in the United States during the Great Depression, the American Farm Bureau Federation (AFBF) and similar organizations brokered the flow of different types of ideas about farm relief programs. The AFBF measured public sentiments, notably public opinion, among farmers and conveyed it to decision makers in Washington, and the organization advised decision makers on farm relief programs. Conversely, these organizations also helped decision makers frame programs in ways that would resonate with farmers and fed propaganda and other information back to farmers on behalf of the politicians that they supported (Hansen 1991). Similar functions have been performed by business associations in the United States and Europe during the late twentieth century (e.g., Martin 2000; Swank and Martin 2001).

At the international level, brokering often involves so-called epistemic communities, that is, networks of intellectuals, academics, experts, and government liaisons, as well as international nongovernmental organizations (Boli and Thomas 1999a; Haas 1992). Epistemic communities develop new paradigms and transmit their programmatic implications, often deliberately couched in clever frames, to national decision makers as well as to the citizenry—an activity sometimes referred to as "information politics" (Keck and Sikkink 1998). Networks like these played a pivotal role in disseminating a new national security paradigm during the 1980s that helped trigger important shifts in national defense programs, notably a softening of Soviet policies under Mikhail Gorbachev that helped end the Cold War (Risse-Kappan 1994). They were also responsible in part for the institutionalization of various international agreements and treaties around the world that affected both governments and corporations (e.g., Boli and Thomas 1999a; Meyer et al. 1997b).

One note of caution is in order. The location of different actors in different ideational realms in this discussion is illustrative and requires further thought. It is entirely possible that there is more slippage than I have indicated here. That is, it is possible—even likely—that some of the actors I have located in one ideational realm or another actually operate closer to the interstices of these realms than I have indicated. Nevertheless, the point remains that we should pay close attention to how actors operate in these realms in order to infuse our analyses of institutional change with a greater sense of agency than has previously been the case.

How Do Ideas Affect Institutional Change?

So far, I have argued that institutionalists must more clearly define what we mean by ideas and specify who the actors are that are responsible for mobilizing ideas for institutional change. I have also provided some suggestions for how this might be done. Specifying the actors affiliated with different ideational realms and tracking their activities is one way to help infuse the analysis of ideas with a degree of agency heretofore lacking in much of the institutionalist literature. In other words, actors are important because their activities provide some of the ways by which ideas affect institutional change. But is that all there is to it? No, there are additional ways in which ideas exert effects.

It should be clear by now that programs affect institutional change by virtue of the fact that key decision makers embrace new programs, transport them into decision-making arenas, and implement them in ways that change institutions. In the short term, the effects of programs are direct and obvious insofar as they cause a shift in the decision-making orientation of elites.

In the long term, however, the implementation of programs may lead to long-lasting decision-making and institutional legacies that have more subtle, indirect, and self-reinforcing or path-dependent effects that constrain change later on (Goldstein 1993, chap. 1). First, as discussed in chapter 3, once they are institutionalized, programs generate constituents who defend them if alternatives are suggested later (Pierson 1993). In the United States and Europe, old-age insurance programs developed such strong political constituencies that they were virtually off limits during the 1980s and 1990s for budget cutters and welfare reformers who wanted to change the laws regarding benefits and eligibility (Pierson 1994; Skocpol 2000). Second, institutionalizing programs often entails establishing a particular set of implementation capacities that limit the range of options available to decision makers in the future (Hall 1993). One obstacle to the adoption of European-style industrial policy in the United States when it was debated during the late 1970s and 1980s was that implementing such a program would have required a variety of planning, bargaining, and financing capacities that the government simply did not have, such as French-style planning commissions or state-owned investment banks (Campbell 1998). Similarly, in the private sector, many U.S. corporations long pursued a program of low-cost production, rather than continuous product innovation, as the key to success. As a result, they developed mass production techniques, large vertically integrated firms, and rigid labor contracts as the instruments to achieve this goal. So when market volatility increased during the 1980s and 1990s, and product innovation became necessary, American managers had great difficulty switching programs because they lacked the decentralized and flexible production techniques and cooperative relationships with suppliers, customers, and unions that existed in other countries like Germany and Japan (Best 1990; Piore and Sabel 1984; Streeck 1991). The point is that once a program is adopted it tends to become institutionalized in ways that reinforce and bolster its influence over time.

Paradigms constrain institutional change too, although the mechanisms involved are particularly subtle. In part, the reason is that paradigms are often taken for granted and thus difficult to observe and document. However, one important mechanism by which they exert effects is by structuring discourse. By discourse I mean a system of language, concepts, and rules of logic through which people communicate. If it is true that one's reality is largely a matter of perception and that these perceptions are structured in part through discourse (Berger and Luckman 1967), then it follows that the structure of discourse within a particular paradigm, such as neoclassical economics or scientific management, limits the perceptions of those engaged in it. In other words, if perceptions are limited to what we can articulate, and if only certain ideas are capable of being articulated as a result of the limited availability of concepts, metaphors, symbols, analogies, and linguistic rules in the dominant discourse, then paradigms influence decision making and institutional change by constraining the range of programs that can be imagined and articulated in the first place (Yee 1996). Fred Block (1990, 1996) has shown that economic discourse in the United States is rooted in the paradigmatic language, logic, and metaphors of neoclassical economics, which makes it very difficult for decision makers to conceive of programs that do not fit this rhetoric. Similarly, as noted earlier, Guillén (1994a) and Fligstein (1990) demonstrated that different management paradigms constrained the range of organizational models that corporate managers could envision. In short, paradigms act like "cognitive locks" that restrict decision makers to certain intellectual paths (Blyth 1999, 2002).

Public sentiments constrain institutional change in ways similar to those associated with paradigms. That is, public sentiments both constrain the range of policies and institutions that decision makers believe will be publicly acceptable and affect how collective actors perceive and interpret their interests (Weir 1992). In this sense, public sentiments act like "normative locks" on decision making. For instance, Peter Katzenstein (1993) argued that Japanese and German anti-terrorist programs differ in part because each is embedded in a different set of normative expectations among the public in both countries about how the police ought to operate. In Germany, public sentiment as well as the Constitution dictate that the police may take aggressive action against any organization or individual that is expected to threaten state security. This includes, under certain conditions, arresting people in the absence of suspicion of actual criminal activity. In Japan, norms are much less permissive and the police are much less aggressive.[10]

What are the implications of all this for institutional change? When actors succeed in pressing programs for change into practice this is often heavily mediated by already existing discourse structures—both normative and cognitive—in the sense that actors translate new ideas into practice in ways that remain consistent with the old discourse. For example, when Japanese politicians began shifting toward neoliberalism, a program intended in part to deregulate industry, rather than truly deregulating industries, as occurred in Britain, they simply decentralized the regulatory apparatus and limited the further growth of regulatory budgets. This approach was consistent with their long-standing normative convictions

---

[10] Many researchers who stress that norms constrain decision making and institutional change fail to specify through careful process tracing the causal mechanisms involved (Finnemore 1996, 339; Keck and Sikkink 1998, 33–35). At least among historical institutionalists this may be due simply to the fact that public sentiments, including public opinion as well as the normative positions of decision makers, have been long neglected as important determinants of decision making and institutional change (Burstein 1998, 1991, 332–34; Smith 1992, 257; Weir 1992, 13–14). The reason is that until recently, historical institutionalists have been averse to arguments that invoke notions of political culture, ideology, and the like to explain outcomes (Smith 1995). For an important effort to rectify the situation, see Keck and Sikkink (1998).

that a strong state was appropriate and their cognitive convictions that the economy required much state intervention to achieve maximum economic performance (Vogel 1996). Hence, paradigms and public sentiments rooted in discourse constrained what actors perceived and interpreted to be reasonable and appropriate behavior. As this example demonstrates, barring a shift in paradigms or public sentiments themselves, each tends to channel institutional change in more evolutionary than revolutionary directions.

It is worth mentioning briefly that public sentiments also have effects by providing the raw materials for framers who use these materials for building frames either to press for change or to block it. Through bricolage, various public sentiments are blended together to create frames for programs. Decision makers in Britain were successful in moving neoliberal programs into practice because they framed them in a bricolage of deeply ingrained beliefs in the virtue of free markets, on the one hand, and individualism, on the other. This is also why Prime Minister Thatcher as well as her successors, John Major and Tony Blair, found a globalization frame so attractive. They justified neoliberalism in part on the grounds that globalization, i.e., unbridled free trade and capital flows across borders, was an irresistible fact of modern life that crippled traditional Keynesian expansionary policies but was compatible with deregulation, privatization, and lower social wages (Schmidt 2000).

In sum, different types of ideas affect decision making and institutional change in different ways. Sometimes it is direct and obvious; sometimes it is indirect and subtle. The adoption of new programs often facilitates institutional change, but once new programs become institutionalized, constituencies and implementation capacities tend to develop that constrain in path-dependent ways further programmatic changes. Paradigms and public sentiments also constrain institutional change in path-dependent ways as long as they remain stable themselves. But what about the possibility of reciprocal effects? Do institutions also affect ideas?

How Do Institutions Affect Ideas?

The degree to which ideas affect institutional change depends on how they are embedded in surrounding institutions in the first place. For instance, the formal and informal institutional channels through which carriers of programs gain access, or not, to decision makers mediates the effect that these programs have on decision making and institutions (Hall 1989a; Haas 1992; Rueschemeyer and Skocpol 1996a; Weir 1992). Keynesian programs made a greater impact in Sweden than in the United States during the 1930s in part because Keynesians had greater access to decision-making circles in Sweden than they did in the United States. As a result, Sweden developed a more extensive set of welfare institutions than the United States (Weir and Skocpol 1985). Similarly, neoliberal tax programs had a more dramatic effect in Britain than in the United States during the 1980s because political power is more centralized institutionally in Britain insofar as one party generally controls both parliament and the executive branch, thereby enjoying the luxury of doing more or less what it wants when it is in power. In the United States there are different institutions, one-party rule is much less likely, and so elections generally do not create opportunities for radically new programs to dominate policy-making (Steinmo 1993). In other words, institutions in Britain were more conducive to the penetration and adoption of fundamentally, new programs than they were in the United States. In turn, tax law changed more decisively in Britain than in the United States.

Institutions also mediate the impact of programs at the international level. During the late 1970s, transnational actors bearing new ideas about national security and arms control easily penetrated the U.S. state due to its fragmented, decentralized institutional structure, but, ironically, also failed to form a solid political coalition around these ideas because it was difficult to unite decision makers in such a fragmented and decentralized state. In Germany it was harder for these new ideas to penetrate initially, given the German state's more centralized, corporatist structure, but once they did, the presence of consensus-building institutions facilitated comparatively easy coalition formation (Risse-Kappan 1994).

The impact of programs on decision making and institutional change in business is also affected by surrounding institutions. A case in point is the U.S. computer industry. Annalee Saxenian (1994) showed that during their early years semiconductor, computer, and other companies in the Silicon Valley region in Northern California had authority structures that were rather flat and decentralized, thereby facilitating the rapid flow of new ideas within firms to top corporate managers who could act on them quickly, if they desired. Moreover, these firms enjoyed all sorts of informal connections with each other. Scientists and engineers from different and often competing firms as well as nearby Stanford University routinely consulted with each other and shared ideas. As a result, new and innovative ideas also circulated freely among firms. Frequently, these ideas involved the creation of formal collective agreements, such as joint ventures and research consortia, that institutionalized and made official interfirm collaboration and contributed to the region's phenomenal success as a hot bed of cutting-edge technological development. In contrast, in the Boston, Massachusetts, region electronics and computer firms had steep, centralized authority structures and firms remained much more insulated from each other. Corporate managers were more conservative in their approach to innovation and were more suspicious of their competitors. Ideas did not circulate so easily. In particular, new ideas requiring interfirm cooperation often fell on deaf ears, and, as a result, corporate institutions were less collaborative, technological development was stifled, and the industry languished relative to its Californian counterpart. The point is that institutions act as filters through which programmatic ideas must pass in order to have effects on decision makers and, by extension, institutional change. In this sense, ideas do not float freely (Risse-Kappen 1994).

Institutional arrangements also affect frames. In a very insightful paper, Schmidt (2001) argued that in states where decision making is centralized and insulated from the public, such as France, framing is directed largely toward the general public, who must be convinced that the programs favored by insulated elites are necessary and appropriate. However, in states where decision making is more fragmented and open and where it is more difficult to reach consensus among political elites in the first place, such as the United States or, to a lesser extent, corporatist Germany, framing must be targeted more toward the rather large number of actors involved in decision making—including politicians, political and technocratic elites, opposition parties, and interest group leaders—who construct, debate, and refine programs in the first place. In other words, institutional arrangements determine the degree to which framers must design frames for the public or members of the decision-making community itself.

Similarly, institutions influence paradigms. Institutions in the professions, universities, and vocational training systems, as well as institutions governing their relationships with both the state and business community, affect which paradigms are dominant. For example, Nicholas Ziegler (1997) found that in France elite scientists and engineers, who have been trained at the best public universities and who often work for the central government in top bureaucratic jobs, are responsible for technology innovation programs. Given their elite training and positions, they favor a top-down, state-led approach to technology development that tilts programs in a "mission-oriented" direction favoring dramatic innovations on a large scale. Conversely, in Germany technological expertise and control is located more in the private sector and decision makers are accustomed to facilitating collaboration and knowledge sharing among firms, state agencies, unions, and professions in ways that unite different groups of experts—both elite and nonelite—in "diffusion-oriented" research where more incremental innovations are sought on a less grand scale. In short, the paradigmatic bent of decision makers for mission or diffusion-oriented approaches depends on the institutions through which the production of technical knowledge is organized. Paradigmatic orientations like these are resilient even in the face of shifting political and economic pressures because these institutions change slowly. The same seems to be true for corporations. Indeed, for this reason corporate research and development programs across the advanced capitalist countries have remained remarkably stable and diverse throughout the 1980s and 1990s when one might expect that the pressures of globalization would cause them to converge (Doremus et al. 1998).

Institutions also affect public sentiments. Once established, institutionalized practices, such as solidaristic wage bargaining or insulated technocratic decision making, tend to reinforce certain norms and identities. After a while, through repeated episodes of solidaristic wage bargaining, technocratic decision making, or other practices, actors begin to take these things for granted and assume that this is the appropriate way to behave (Jepperson 1991). Participants come to define their identities in terms of the roles they repeatedly play (Wendt 1992). For instance, Michael Burawoy, although not an institutionalist, showed that when industrial workers encounter institutionalized piece-rate systems on the shop floor, devise elaborate strategies to ensure that they will meet their production quotas, and then deploy these strategies on a daily basis, they are repeatedly defining their roles and identities as workers vis-à-vis management and eventually take for granted that the rules of piece-rate work are normatively acceptable (1979, 81, 93).

Finally, it is important to recognize that fragmentation, conflict, and overlap among institutions often provide important opportunities for ideas to compete in ways that may lead to institutional change. For instance, social scientists often regard the institutional logics associated with bureaucracies and professions as inimical to each other (Blau and Scott 1962, 60–63; Friedson 1994, chap. 8; Gouldner 1954, 22; Kornhauser 1962). Briefly, a bureaucratic logic emphasizes the primacy of hierarchical authority, the subordination of individual autonomy to standardized and simplified rules and procedures, and responsibility and loyalty to the organization. In contrast, a professional logic emphasizes the primacy of professional authority, the encouragement of individual autonomy based on the individual's professional expertise, use of rules and procedures in unique ways appropriate to the complexities of individual cases, and responsibility and loyalty to the profession (Scott 1992, 253–56; Waters 1989). When these two institutional logics meet, they often produce conflict and competition over programmatic and other types of ideas. Often this conflict materializes as struggles between bureaucratic administrators and professionals (Bensen 1973; Parsons 1963; Scott 1966, 265–75; Wilensky 1964). Occasionally, institutions are transformed as a result.

For example, consider the organization first established to regulate the development of the U.S. commercial nuclear energy industry, the Atomic

Energy Commission (AEC). The AEC's legislative mandate stipulated that, on the one hand, the agency facilitate the development and commercial success of nuclear energy and, on the other hand, ensure that nuclear power plants be operated safely. During the 1960s, staff scientists and engineers at the AEC and the national laboratories grew concerned in light of their research and experiments that the emergency cooling systems on commercial reactors were not trustworthy. These systems were intended to prevent catastrophic accidents that could release lethal amounts of radiation into the environment. They recommended to bureaucratic administrators that plant licensing be deferred until further tests could be done and improved safety standards implemented. Administrators refused, tried to suppress the evidence that safety systems were suspect, and ordered their scientists and engineers to be quiet about it. In other words, the AEC became engulfed in a clash between professional and bureaucratic institutional logics. The conflict was leaked to the press and the agency was soon engulfed in a serious legitimation crisis. Congress held public hearings where it became clear that for years the scientists and engineers had been advocating a new program for the AEC, one that favored safety over development, but that the agency's administration had virtually ignored their pleas. Eventually, the crisis was resolved when Congress abolished the AEC and created two new agencies. By law, the Nuclear Regulatory Commission was given responsibility for safety concerns and the Energy Research and Development Administration was given responsibility for development. Thus, conflicting institutional logics created an opportunity for advocates of new safety programs to push their program onto the decision-making agenda and into practice in ways that transformed the political institutions involved (Campbell 1988, chap. 4).

Under What Conditions Are Ideas Most Likely to Affect Institutional Change?

The last two sections discussed some of the causal mechanisms by which ideas affect institutions and institutions affect ideas. Institutionalists have paid much less attention to the conditions under which these effects are more or less likely to occur. This is unfortunate insofar as careful specification of scope conditions is an integral part of theory building (Kiser and Hechter 1998). My focus here is on the conditions under which ideas matter most for institutional change. Needless to say, however, ideas also matter on a routine basis for stabilizing institutions. As we have seen, different types of ideas constrain change in ways that can provide much institutional stability.

Most institutionalists agree that ideas other than interests matter most for institutional change under conditions of great *uncertainty*, that is, when decision makers are faced with unusual or unsettled situations that make it difficult for them to devise clear programs based on their interests, in part because it is not clear what their interests are, given the prevailing uncertainties (Goldstein and Keohane 1993b; Marcussen 2000; McNamara 1998). In the extreme, actors perceive such situations as *crises*. Fligstein and Mara-Drita (1996), for example, argued that the initial impetus to the Single Market Project occurred because European decision makers believed that the stagflation of the 1970s and 1980s had reached crisis proportions. Similarly, Fligstein's (1990) work on U.S. corporations showed that new conceptions of control were likely to emerge and affect corporate governance as well as regulatory law when managers faced political or economic crises. Indeed, crises often trigger institutional shifts in economic governance (Campbell et al. 1991).

What constitutes a crisis is, of course, an important *definitional* issue for institutional analysis that cannot be taken for granted. In other words, crises are not entirely self-evident; decision makers must define them as such in order to begin searching for new ideas to guide decision making and institution building. Indeed, decision makers facing common sets of problems may interpret and define them in remarkably different ways. Although Britain and Denmark experienced recession, inflation, low productivity growth, and unemployment during the 1970s and 1980s, decision makers interpreted things differently in each country. The British defined inflation as the paramount problem and therefore pursued monetarist ideas, while the Danes saw unemployment, labor market rigidities, and poor technology innovation as critical and so embarked on a series of industrial policy adjustments (Hay 2001; Kjaer and Pedersen 2001). The difference was due to institutional variations. The Danes had a long tradition of social democratic corporatism and, as a result, decision makers across the political spectrum took for granted that managing unemployment should be a top priority (e.g., Pedersen 1993). The British had no such tradition and, therefore, no assumptions, particularly within the Conservative Party, about the importance of minimizing unemployment. Furthermore, conservative governments in Britain enjoyed a set of electoral institutions that protected them from the wrath of voters most affected by unemployment. Specifically, given Britain's first-past-the-post electoral system and the fact that unemployment was concentrated in manufacturing regions that had long been solid Labor Party strongholds anyway, the Conservative Party could endure high levels of unemployment and concentrate on controlling inflation with little concern for the electoral repercussions of these policies (King and Wood 1999).

How actors perceive and define situations in different ways is something that we need to address more carefully. We often assert that these perceptions matter but do not fully explain where they come from or how actors construct them. For instance, North (1990) accepted that ideas, such as social norms, influence decision making under conditions of uncertainty and that these kinds of ideas are more likely to have effects when actors perceive that the costs of normative action are lower than those of interest-based action, but he said nothing about how actors arrive at these perceptions. Similarly, as discussed earlier, Hattam (1993) attributed a shift in strategy in the U.S. labor movement to a shift in the class identity of workers. Although this shift in perception and identity explained much in Hattam's analysis, she said very little about why this important perceptual shift occurred in the first place (but see Babb 1996).

Poor understanding of the perceptual process is one reason why many institutionalists, including some rational choice theorists, have turned recently to cognitive and social psychology for insights (e.g., DiMaggio 1997; Fligstein 2001b; Jepperson et al. 1996; Knight and North 1997; Zerubavel 1997). In this regard, a particularly promising theoretical avenue emphasizes how patterns of interaction affect how actors perceive and define their situations (e.g., Fligstein 2001b; Piore 1995). Eleanor Ostrom's (1990, chap. 5) research on the collective action problems of natural resource management provides convincing evidence that interaction patterns affect perception. Among other things, she found that rice farmers in Sri Lanka who depended on communal irrigation systems to sustain their crops had been unable for decades to devise effective institutions for rationing water when it was scarce. This was largely because farmers defined their problems and interests in individualistic terms, and so it made sense for them to take as much water as possible for their own paddies with little regard for the effects that this would have on neighboring farmers or the irrigation system as a whole. Thus, upstream irrigators benefitted systematically over downstream irrigators, and the overall level of agricultural production suffered accordingly. However, in the early 1980s the state sent community organizers into the villages to encourage local farmers to discuss collectively their irrigation needs and problems among themselves. This change in interaction gradually enabled farmers to perceive their interests in more collective than individualistic terms. In turn, they developed a sense of trust toward each other and devised new institutions for managing the irrigation system more effectively and fairly. Similar perceptual transformations have occurred in advanced industrial countries. For instance, in the United States the state of Pennsylvania encouraged corporations and unions to brainstorm collectively for solutions to the problem of industrial decline during the 1980s. This effort resulted in less hostile interaction, the formation of a new collective identity, and a variety of innovative programs for revitalizing the economy (Sabel 1993).

The important lesson is that patterns of interaction affect how actors perceive their situations. Changes in these patterns can cause changes in the paradigms and public sentiments with which actors interpret the world around them. In turn, this enables them to recognize, reexamine, and ultimately reinterpret their previously taken-for-granted assumptions about their problems and interests. Indeed, variation in interaction helps to explain why actors whose objective economic situations are the same may hold much different views of their political and economic interests. For example, U.S. corporations responded differently to skyrocketing health care costs during the 1990s depending on the degree to which they were isolated from each other and from decision makers in Washington. Research indicates that after controlling for sales, profits, capital intensity, and other economic factors, corporations that had been consulting regularly with each other and with policymakers in various formal and informal networks were significantly more supportive of health care reform than corporations that did not participate in these interactive networks (Martin 2000, chap. 3).

Even when a crisis is perceived and the possibility opens up for new ideas to affect decision making, there are no guarantees that new programs will take hold and yield institutional change. Certainly, all sorts of interest-based struggles and institutional constraints are involved that mediate the odds of this happening. Additionally, however, some analysts have suggested that new programs can exert effects only when actors perceive that they offer *effective alternatives* to the status quo, that is, when there is some sort of proof that they will make things better. For instance, Kathleen McNamara (1998) argued that the European Monetary Union (EMU) project proceeded in part because European decision makers perceived that the monetarist theory upon which the EMU was to be based worked. Germany's success with a pragmatic version of monetary policy that emphasized a strong and stable currency provided the evidence. Conversely, one reason why German industrialists have resisted dismantling centralized wage bargaining and other corporatist labor market institutions in the face of global pressures for greater labor market flexibility is that they understand that there are certain benefits associated with the current system, including peaceful and cooperative labor-management relations at the plant level due to the separation of wage bargaining from local co-determination processes. But an equally important explanation is that they do not perceive an alternative model that might work better (Thelen and Kume 1999; Thelen 2000c).

The key to establishing that new programs provide effective alternatives is to link them to material conditions in ways that give them weight and credibility. For instance, state-level rate regulation laws for the fire insurance industry were passed in the United States only after advocates clearly established that the absence of such law had contributed to a variety of rate wars and insurance company bankruptcies during the late 1800s and that these and other sorts of market failures could be avoided through regulation (Schneiberg 1999). Similarly, during the 1980s and 1990s business consultants and others managed to convince U.S. corporations that they needed to disassemble their conglomerate structures and downsize only after these consultants demonstrated convincingly that corporate diversification increased company value and profitability. To do so, one consulting firm developed its "chop shop" valuation model that determined exactly how much more a conglomerate would be worth if it were broken up (Davis et al. 1994, 554).

Eventually, to provide a basis for the generation of more systematic hypotheses and thus more rigorous theory building we will have to think more carefully about how these and other scope conditions affect the degree to which ideas influence institutional change. This may involve a nested approach that acknowledges the factors that I have detailed in this section as well as others addressed earlier in this chapter (see also Kingdon 1995, chap. 1; Marcussen 2000, chap. 1; Woods 1995). For instance, given the perception of significant problems, uncertainties, or crises for which decision makers seek a remedy, alternative programs must be *available* to them in the first place. If such an idea exists, then it must also be *credible* to them in the sense that it fits their dominant paradigm. If it does, then they must believe that it is *effective* insofar as it promises a reasonable solution to a decision-making problem—a perception that is enhanced to the extent that the idea is packaged in simple enough terms for decision makers to understand; provides clear guidelines for action; and, based on their view of empirical evidence, known cases, and links to material conditions, appears to be an idea that will actually work if implemented. If decision makers perceive that an idea is effective in this sense, then they must also deem it *legitimate*. That is, they must believe that it resonates with prevailing public sentiments. If it does not, then it must be framed so as to improve this resonance. In other words, it is the cumulative effects of different types of ideas and perceptions that influence whether or not a new program carries the day and transforms institutions.[11] Of course, other factors, including the pursuit of interests, may also be important. The issue is that if institutionalists want to convince skeptics that ideas other than interests matter for institutional change,

---

[11] For a similar view, see Sarah Babb (1996), who argues that credibility, effectiveness, and legitimacy all depend to an important degree on how problems and solutions are framed.

then we need to develop and test arguments like these. This requires that researchers also deploy appropriate methodologies to demonstrate that these sorts of arguments have real explanatory power.

What Methodologies Are Available to Determine Whether Ideas Matter?

Institutionalists have used several methodologies for analyzing the effects of ideas other than interests on institutional change (Berman 2001; Blyth 1997, 1998; Yee 1996). An exhaustive review of them all is well beyond the scope of this chapter and has been provided by others (e.g., Schneiberg and Clemens forthcoming). But let me make a few general observations. To begin with, many of us have engaged in detailed *process tracing*. This approach tends to be extremely descriptive and often focuses on explaining how ideas have affected decision making and institutional change in a single case (e.g., Kjaer and Pedersen 2001; Hall 1992; Hay 2001). To be sure, process tracing is useful in showing how ideas affect outcomes and in generating hypotheses for further study (Berman 2001, 243). By using this technique we can tell plausible stories about how, for instance, programs must fit into existing cognitive and normative constraints, and that if they don't, then they are not likely to be effective. But without comparison cases or tests of competing explanations from broader theoretical debates about the determinants of decision making, these stories lack enough analytic punch to appeal to skeptics who are concerned with generalizing beyond single cases and who prefer a more positivist approach.[12]

Of course, some scholars have been particularly concerned with testing explicitly whether ideas like paradigms and public sentiments motivate decision making and institutional change more than interests do. Their work suffers from other methodological problems. For instance, Judith Goldstein (1993; see also Blyth 1999) utilized a *deductive counterfactual* method to determine the degree to which ideas, notably new economic theories, affected U.S. trade policies historically more than the pursuit of interests by political and business elites. She began by deducing the policies that actors would pursue if they simply followed their structurally given

[12] Although many scholars advocate that the analysis of ideas necessitates research that is qualitative, descriptive, and historical in nature, and that involves much detailed process tracing (Haas 1992; Stråth 1990, 7), this does not have to be so. If clean hypotheses could be generated, quantitative analysis is possible—even analysis that tests the conditions under which ideas, such as cognitive paradigms and values, matter more or less than interests (e.g., Anthony et al. 1994; McDonough 1997; Strang and Bradburn 2001). For a detailed review of both quantitative and qualitative approaches, see Schneiberg and Clemens (forthcoming).

interests, and she used this as her null hypothesis. Then she compared actual policy outcomes against this deduced counterfactual and argued that the difference between the counterfactual prediction and real policy outcome, if there was such a difference, reflected the degree to which ideas other than interests determined outcomes (see also Kelman 1988; Moore 1988). Deducing the interests of actors with reasonable confidence is, however, a very tricky business, particularly insofar as actors may have contradictory long- and short-term interests (Lukes 1974). More important, as noted earlier in the discussion of Hattam's (1993) work on U.S. labor union strategy, some institutionalists maintain that what motivates actors in this regard is their subjective understanding of their interests—understandings that may diverge significantly from their objective interests as deduced by researchers and other observers (Gaventa 1980).

Rather than trying to figure out how actors ought to act if they were following their interests, another approach is for researchers to let the actors speak for themselves. Dobbin (1994) maintained in his comparative railway study that national principles regarding the desirable relationship between state and economy rather than the material interests of business and political elites determined railroad policy and development. He based his argument on an analysis of the public pronouncements, speeches, and official congressional and parliamentary proceedings recorded at the time. In this way, he constructed what I would call a *simple inductive counterfactual*—an empirically based account of actors' interests and preferences against which he could compare actual policy outcomes to determine the degree to which their interests, on the one hand, or paradigmatic beliefs and public sentiments, on the other hand, determined these outcomes. However, people may say one thing publicly but another privately to shield their true motives—both interest-based and normative—from public scrutiny and otherwise legitimize their behavior (Elster 1989, 117; Kowert and Legro 1996, 485; Kuran 1995; Scott 1990). Recall, for instance, how television broadcasters used frames publicly to advance their interests in preserving their broadcast spectrum even though they did not necessarily believe these frames themselves. Although Dobbin recognized that politicians may be committed to taken-for-granted paradigms and sentiments, by focusing on public testimonies he neglected to investigate the possibility that they may also engage in much more self-conscious framing exercises to conceal ulterior motives including self-interest. As a result, Dobbin's use of the simple inductive counterfactual made it difficult to tell whether or not interests were at work in his empirical cases. Because his methodology was not sensitive to the full array of ideas, especially frames, and how they might have affected railroad decision making he failed to provide the sort of critical test that might have resolved the issue.

A better test would have been to compare the public pronouncements against more private documents, such as personal diaries and correspondence, where actors may be less likely to conceal their true motives if these differ from those that they express publicly. Using this more *complex inductive counterfactual* would have created an opportunity to determine the degree to which the private thoughts of actors matched their public declarations, whether or not framing had occurred to conceal ulterior motives, and to what extent self-interests were involved.[13] Of course, the possibility of using this approach depends on the availability of private documents or personal interviews with key actors if they are still alive.

Sheri Berman (1998) has developed one of the most carefully articulated methodologies for determining the relative impacts of interests or other types of ideas. She showed how Social Democrats in Sweden and Germany adopted reformist or revolutionary Marxist paradigms, respectively, in the nineteenth century and how they created a series of institutional and intellectual legacies that shaped Social Democratic Party and national politics during the period between the two world wars. She argued that to convince us that ideas other than self-interests determined policy and institutional outcomes, researchers must establish empirically, through detailed process-tracing, that there were real differences between the ideas held by different actors and that these ideas implied different policy choices; that some of these ideas correlated positively with policy outcomes; that the relevant ideas predated the outcomes in question; and that these ideas cannot be reduced to some other observable variable. Furthermore, researchers must identify the actors who carried the important ideas into the decision-making fray and show that these ideas were eventually institutionalized, thereby taking on a life of their own beyond these actors. Finally, and perhaps most important, she stipulated that researchers must demonstrate that actors who bore similar ideas made similar choices over time even as the environment changed, or, conversely, that actors with different ideas made different decisions even when placed in similar environments (see also Rohrlich

---

[13] See Scharpf (1997, 63) for a dissenting view. See Schneiberg and Clemens (forthcoming) for an excellent discussion of the relative advantages and disadvantages associated with using both public and private transcripts in studies of institutional change. Some rational choice theorists have suggested another approach to this problem. The idea is to conduct detailed textual analyses of decision-making debates in order to map the causal arguments presented by participants and then determine whether there are inconsistencies in the logic of these arguments that violate the principle of transitivity. If there are, then they say that we can conclude that actors are behaving strategically and trying to frame their arguments in ways that conceal their true motives (Anthony et al. 1994). However, if inconsistent logic may also stem simply from the intricacies of complex decision-making debate, then we are still left wondering what is going on.

1987, 71). Not until all of this is established, she claimed, can we be sure that ideas other than interests had significant effects on decision making and institution building.

Berman's method may be an effective methodology for showing how ideas other than interests have path-dependent effects and ensure programmatic and institutional *stability*. However, her approach does little to help us understand how ideas affect *change*, cause shifts from one path to another, and disrupt programmatic and institutional equilibria. Certainly explaining stability is important, but so is explaining change. Indeed, they are two sides of the same analytic coin.

Some of the work discussed is better suited to analyzing change, such as McNamara's (1998) argument about how crisis and the availability of an alternative model, German monetarism, led to a change in thinking and in institutions governing European exchange rates, or Fligstein and Mara-Drita's analysis of crisis, frames, and the rise of the European Single Market Project. However, the trick is to devise theories that can account for both change *and* stability in a given case over time or among different cases (Kowert and Legro 1996, 488–90). Mark Blyth's (1998, 1999, 2002) analysis of the shift toward neoliberalism in Swedish macroeconomic and welfare policy is an important step in the right direction. As we shall explore more fully in the next chapter, he argued that decision makers from all political parties found it difficult to abandon Keynesian programs when economic crisis hit in the 1970s and 1980s. Only after conservative politicians and business leaders began mobilizing alternative programs, closely associated with the basic assumptions of the neoclassical economic paradigm, and framed them in strategic ways did they begin to push policy off the received path and initiate institutional changes. In sum, he used an analysis of several types of ideas to account for both stability and change in this historical episode.[14]

Blyth's work suggests that methodological difficulties may stem in part from the other problems that I discussed earlier. These include poor understandings of what we mean by ideas, who the actors are that are pivotal in carrying and mobilizing ideas, how ideas affect decision making, and the conditions under which we expect different types of ideas to matter for institutional change. Most obviously, until we differentiate among different types of ideas, it will be impossible to devise methodologies appropriate to determining how ideas can affect both institutional stability and change.

---

[14] An approach similar to Blyth's was offered in a much different context by Abrahamson and Fairchild (1999), who discussed the rise and fall of managerial fads in the corporate world.

Conclusion

This chapter does not provide a full-blown theory of ideas for institutional analysis. More modestly, it raises several questions for which institutionalists must provide answers if we want to argue successfully that ideas matter for institutional change. Unless convincing answers can be found, then it is unlikely that those of us who claim that ideas other than interests matter can sway the critics and skeptics who suspect that they do not.

Finally, we must remember that much of the work on how ideas matter begins with the question of whether ideas *or* interests matter the most. This is often the wrong way to think about it. Actors often have both interests and other types of ideas. Both often affect their behavior. And both tend to work together in complex ways in most episodes of institutional change. As a result, a more fruitful approach, although one that may certainly be more complicated, is to ask what the relationships are between interests and other types of ideas. Some institutionalists, for instance, now maintain that the two are linked insofar as normative structures affect the identities of actors in ways that influence how they perceive their interests and thus the programs and institutional arrangements they prefer (e.g., Hattam 1993; Locke and Thelen 1995; Jepperson et al. 1996). Other institutionalists try to show how an interest-based rational actor model can be combined with an idea-based social constructionist model to provide insights into the processes whereby new programs are spread (e.g., Keck and Sikkink 1998; Risse et al. 1999). In any case, it is this complexity that is most intriguing but also the most difficult to untangle analytically and the toughest to demonstrate empirically.

Chapter 5

THE PROBLEM OF GLOBALIZATION

ACCORDING TO THE OLD CLICHE, the proof is in the pudding. If the arguments developed in the preceding chapters about the nature of institutional change, causal mechanisms, and ideas have value, then they ought to help us better understand important social phenomena in the world around us. To demonstrate the utility of these arguments, this chapter examines the phenomenon of globalization and its impact on national political and economic institutions. In particular, I pay close attention to the institutions associated with national taxation.

I argue, contrary to much conventional wisdom, that globalization has not precipitated the sort of dramatic institutional changes in taxation and other policy areas that are often attributed to it. Instead, the effects of globalization on key institutions have been much more modest and evolutionary. This chapter shows that this misunderstanding could have been avoided if observers had taken institutional analysis into account in ways elaborated earlier in this book.

However, it is not my intention to mount a full-blown attack on the conventional wisdom regarding globalization. That would require another book.[1] Instead, my purpose here is to show that by using the lessons about institutional analysis developed in chapters 2, 3, and 4, we can develop greater insights into this and, by implication, other important real-world phenomena.

The significance of globalization is hard to exaggerate. It is almost impossible to open a newspaper today and not see a story about globalization. Moreover, globalization studies have become a major growth industry for social scientists, judging at least by the exponential rise in the number of journal articles and books dedicated to the subject during the past twenty years (Guillén 2001b; Ó Riain 2000). In particular, institutionalists of all stripes have become interested in globalization and its effects on corporate governance, the organization of economic production, welfare policy, nongovernmental organizations, and more.[2] Al-

---

[1] For examples of books critical of the conventional wisdom concerning globalization, see Gilpin (2000), Held et al. (1999), Hirst and Thompson (1996), Rodrik (1997), Rosenberg (2000), and Swank (2002).

[2] For illustrative discussions of globalization and corporate governance, see Davis and Useem (2000), Davis and Marquis (2001), and Doremus et al. (1998); for economic produc-

though the term "globalization" means many things (Waters 1995), scholars often use it to refer to sharp increases since the mid-1970s in trade, production, and capital flows across national borders. In this sense they speak of economic globalization, the empirical focus of this chapter (Sassen 1996).

The conventional wisdom in the globalization literature is represented by the so-called globalization thesis. Social scientists and others have offered two basic arguments that constitute the core of the globalization thesis. First, the pressures of globalization are forcing advanced capitalist *nation-states* to pursue a common set of *neoliberal* programs. Specifically, states are being forced to reduce taxes on firms and investors, cut the spending that these taxes support, especially welfare spending, and deregulate their economies to reduce the costs to firms of doing business. Why? Competition for capital is the key. Dramatic advances during the late twentieth century in transportation, telecommunications, and other technologies—such as overnight air delivery, fiber optics, microwave and satellite communications, and computer micro processing—have vastly improved firms' knowledge of profitable economic opportunities around the world and have increased the speed and effectiveness with which they can pursue them. International capital mobility has increased accordingly. Capital mobility has been facilitated further by the breakdown in 1971 of the Bretton Woods system of fixed exchange rates, the decontrol of capital flows, and trade liberalization both unilaterally and through international agreements, such as the General Agreement on Tariffs and Trade. All of this has increased the threat of capital flight, the tendency for capital to move from one country to another in search of the most profitable business environment. In turn, states must compete more aggressively to attract and retain capital investment within their borders. To do so successfully, they must adopt neoliberal reforms. If states balk, they will suffer rising interest rates, lower rates of economic growth, higher unemployment, and other economic maladies that will eventually force them to adopt these measures anyway (Bauman 1998; Cerny 1997; McKenzie and Lee 1991; Ohmae 1995, 1990). The net effect is that states gradually level the international playing field for capital and converge on a similar set of policies and institutions with which to manage their economies. According to some observers, "taken to its logical extreme, the notion of

---

tion, see Berger and Dore (1996), Guillén (2001a), and Keohane and Milner (1996); for welfare states, see Fligstein (2001a, chap. 9) and Stephens et al. (1999); for nongovernmental organizations, see Boli and Thomas (1999a). Note that these authors represent all three rational choice paradigms: Davis and colleagues, Fligstein, Guillén, and Boli and Thomas represent organizational institutionalism; Doremus et al., Stephens et al., and Berger and Dore represent historical institutionalism; and Keohane and Milner represent rational choice institutionalism.

leveling the playing field implies that nations should become homogeneous in all major respects" (Tanzi 1995, xvii).[3]

In this view states are becoming more vulnerable to the influence of business and are experiencing a decline in their capacity to manage their economies through the traditional taxation, spending, and regulatory policies that marked the post–Second World War era of Keynesianism (Cerny 1997; Giddens 2000; Greider 1997; Guéhenno 1995; Jessop 1997; McKenzie and Lee 1991; Reich 1991; Strange 1997). The implication of this argument for national political institutions is grim. According to Saskia Sassen (1996, 1998, chap. 10), a prominent globalization theorist, globalization has caused states to suffer a reduction and destabilization in the institutions in charge of regulating the economy and, therefore, a decline in state sovereignty. She argues that although institutional state capacities have not been obliterated, they "have been reconstituted and partly displaced onto other institutional arenas outside the state and outside the framework of nationalized territory" (Sassen 1996, 29).[4]

The second basic argument of the globalization thesis is that globalization is transforming *national economies*. Again, large corporations have become geographically footloose, abandoning whatever allegiance they may have had to their country of origin and eagerly seeking to shift capital and operations from one country to another depending on which one offers the greatest profit potential (Greider 1997; Ohmae 1990). As a result, firms, like states, are developing increasingly common institutional structures and strategies (Guéhenno 1995, 64). For instance, firms have developed more decentralized and networked organizational forms that transcend national borders, such as interfirm alliances, joint ventures, outsourcing agreements, and commodity chains (e.g., Gereffi 1994, 217–22; Gulati and Gargiulo 1999; Powell 1987). They are doing so to respond more effectively and flexibly to the volatile and unpredictable demands

---

[3] Others maintain that the rise of international political organizations, such as the United Nations and other nongovernmental organizations, is leading to the diffusion of common political culture and practices among nation-states—another argument about global convergence but one that stresses political rather than economic causes and does not suggest that the convergence is necessarily neoliberal in outcome (Boli and Thomas 1999a; Keck and Sikkink 1998; Meyer et al. 1997a, 1997b).

[4] When I have discussed these ideas with colleagues, some of them have dismissed their importance and argued that we should not take them seriously. While I believe that this part of the globalization thesis is wrong, I believe that the argument itself is important and should not be dismissed out of hand. First, it continues to enjoy a respectable place in academic debate (e.g., Genschel 2002). Second, politicians frequently invoke the argument to justify a variety of policy moves (e.g., Schmidt 2002, part 3). Third, international agencies, such as the OECD (2000b), continue to lament the threat of capital flight and urge countries collectively to address it. In short, while we may doubt the validity of the argument, we still need to take it seriously because it is influential in important academic and policy circles.

of an increasingly global marketplace (Harrison 1994). Furthermore, as equity markets become integrated internationally, and especially as the number of foreign listings on U.S. stock markets soars, states adopt corporate governance systems that are similar to the U.S. model, and so firms experience strong incentives to follow the standards of practice set by American institutional investors. The result is convergence on the U.S. model of corporate governance and finance (Levine and Zervos 1998; for a review, see Davis and Useem 2000). Finally, the organizational and political strength of organized labor is being undermined as unions grant concessions to employers to convince them not to move production and jobs overseas (Harrison 1994; Jacoby 1995). As a result, the corporatist institutions and the bargaining between centralized labor unions and employers' associations that characterized many West European countries after the Second World War are being weakened, and more neoliberal, American-style institutions are replacing them (Lash and Urry 1987).

All of this is important for institutional analysis for two reasons. First, at an empirical level, globalization theorists conclude that economic globalization is leading to a world in which national political and economic institutions are becoming homogenized across countries. Moreover, these institutions matter less and less as important determinants of political economic performance (Guéhenno 1995, chap. 4, 6). This is because they are being incapacitated and hollowed out by globalization. According to Anthony Giddens (2000, 36–37),

> Everywhere we look we see institutions that appear the same as they used to be from the outside, and carry the same names, but inside have become quite different. . . . They are what I call "shell institutions." They are institutions that have become inadequate to the tasks they are called upon to perform.

Institutionalists should be skeptical of these ideas insofar as they recognize that institutional change is often a path-dependent process whereby institutions retain many of their important capacities even as they change. They should also be skeptical insofar as they understand that not all countries respond in the same way to common external pressures. This skepticism should be greatest among historical and rational choice institutionalists, especially those who pay close attention to how national institutions remain robust even in the face of serious international shocks and how they shape responses to these shocks in nationally specific ways (e.g., Gourevitch 1986; Hall 1986; Keohane and Milner 1996). Organizational institutionalists, who focus on how organizations in a field tend to adopt common—that is, isomorphic—forms and practices, might be more inclined to concur with the notion that globalization leads to a common response across countries (e.g., Meyer et al. 1997a, 1997b). However, at least some organizational institutionalists would probably argue that the distinctive character of each nation's institutions shapes their responses to common problems in ways that yield different outcomes across countries (e.g., Dobbin 1994; Fligstein 2001a, chap. 9; Soysal 1994). Finally, some institutionalists would surely point out that, rather than hollowing out national institutions, globalization might lead to the fortification and strengthening of national institutions, particularly in countries that are most vulnerable to globalization pressures and that would want to provide services and other protections for citizens who might be adversely affected by the vicissitudes and risks associated with international capital mobility (e.g., Cameron 1978; Garrett 1998a; Katzenstein 1985; see also Rodrik 1996, 1997). Even those organizational institutionalists who accept the isomorphism premise have argued that the development of international pressures has led to the building up, not the breaking down or hollowing out, of national institutions (e.g., Boli and Thomas 1999a).[5]

Second, at a theoretical level, the globalization thesis is important for institutional analysis because it implies that globalization threatens the relevance of much conventional social theory, particularly the classic theoretical traditions of Karl Marx, Emile Durkheim, Max Weber, Karl Polanyi, and, by extension, the various forms of institutional analysis that derive from them and upon which this book has focused. This is because most social theories still take *national* societies and cultures as their unit of analysis when, according to globalization theory, the appropriate unit of analysis has now shifted to the *global* level. Critics of globalization theory object to this. If taken seriously, they argue, globalization theory leads to the abandonment of an important set of theoretical tools that could in fact help us better understand the phenomenon of globalization itself. Worse still, globalization theory trivializes many social science theories insofar as major political, economic, and cultural changes are attributed simply to the effects of increased capital mobility without regard to the far more complex processes that these theories articulate (Rosenberg 2000, chap. 1).[6] This is why globalization is a problem for institu-

---

[5] Many institutionalists might also object to the implicit assumption underlying much globalization theory that increased capital mobility and economic integration have been uniform everywhere. In fact, these things have been far from uniform. International trade and capital flows have increased among some countries, particularly those in the northern hemisphere, much more than others. Thus, globalization pressures are different for different countries, and so institutional responses will also likely be different (e.g., Fligstein 2001a, chap. 9; Glatzer and Rueschemeyer 2002; Mann and Riley 2002).

[6] This should be troubling even for organizational institutionalists who focus on changes in the world culture. Why? Because, in contrast to globalization theory, they emphasize the causal impact of political and cultural forces rather than transnational capital flows (e.g., Boli and Thomas 1999a).

tional analysis. If scholars accept that globalization threatens the relevance of institutional analysis for understanding societies during the late twentieth and early twenty-first centuries, then they are likely to stop trying to improve institutional analysis and, instead, turn toward alternative analytic approaches.

To avoid trivialization and being relegated to the theoretical dustbin, it is incumbent on institutional analysis to demonstrate its utility in an age of globalization. In this chapter I do just that, arguing that institutional analysis is essential for understanding globalization. Because the debates about globalization have focused primarily on its implications for nation-states (Giddens 2000, 37) this is where I focus most attention, although I also occasionally discuss its implications for national economies. More specifically, I show that globalization is not leading to the homogenization of nation-states. I suggest, as have others, that divergence remains the rule rather than the exception because national institutions, which vary across countries, mediate the degree to which global pressures affect decision making by states and private actors in ways that militate against convergence (e.g., Berger 1996; Garrett 1998a, 1998b; Garrett and Lange 1996; Kitschelt et al. 1999; Milner and Keohane 1996; Wade 1996).[7] By "mediate" I mean that institutions create incentives and constraints for action that affect the degree to which actors adapt to globalization pressures by transforming current institutions, policies, and practices. In other words, institutions mediate globalization in ways that do not always lead inexorably toward wholesale neoliberal reform. I show that if we take seriously the lessons of previous chapters, we get a much different and substantially more accurate picture of how globalization affects nation-states than the one presented by most globalization theorists. As a result, rather than having its relevance threatened by globalization, institutional analysis is becoming more important than ever if we want to understand how globalization operates.

I noted in earlier chapters that institutions are complex. Broadly speaking, three dimensions may be in play in any instance of institutional change, including that associated with globalization: a regulative dimension that consists of legal, constitutional, and other formal rules that constrain and regularize behavior; a normative dimension that involves binding expectations about what constitutes appropriate behavior; and a

---

[7] My argument is consistent with the so-called compensation thesis, which states that increased international capital mobility tends to generate pressure not to reduce but to either maintain or increase spending for welfare and other types of social protection—spending that might also militate against reductions in taxation (e.g., Garrett 1998a, 1998b; Glatzer and Rueschemeyer 2002; Rodrik 1996, 1997; Swank 2002). For earlier versions of this argument, developed before the globalization thesis rose to prominence, see Cameron (1978) and Katzenstein (1985).

cognitive dimension that includes taken-for-granted assumptions, scripts, and schema about the way the world works (Scott 2001, chap. 3; see also Boudon 1998; Suchman 1997). Most critics of globalization theory neglect the mediating effects of the normative and cognitive aspects of institutions, privileging instead the regulative aspects (e.g., Berger and Dore 1996; Keohane and Milner 1996). We will see that all three play important roles in mediating how globalization affects nation-states and, therefore, the extent of institutional change. Often all three types of institutions constrain change in ways that lead to much more modest and evolutionary change than globalization theory expects.

I do not mean to suggest in the arguments that follow that institutions were solely responsible for mediating the effects of globalization. Other factors were important too, including a variety of struggles among social movements, social classes, and other groups (e.g., Mittelman 2000, part 3). Indeed, these struggles are also a normal part of decision making and institutional change. Furthermore, demographic factors may have mediated how globalization influenced national-level policy-making. There is much concern in many advanced capitalist countries that as the average age of the population increases, so too does demand for social security, health care, and other social services for the elderly. In turn, this may mitigate pressure for reducing taxes insofar as taxes pay for these services. But, again, because my purpose in this chapter is to demonstrate the utility of the concepts, methods, and arguments developed earlier in this book, the emphasis here is necessarily on institutional rather than other factors.

This chapter is organized around the major themes developed in previous chapters and proceeds as follows. First, I show that the *time frame* with which we view globalization matters a great deal. Contrary to conventional wisdom, globalization is not a recent phenomenon limited only to the late twentieth century. Globalization also occurred at the beginning of the twentieth century. More important, globalization during the earlier part of the century was not associated with the same types of institutional changes that it is said to have caused more recently. National institutions were being built up and fortified, not incapacitated and hollowed out. This raises serious questions about the causal mechanism that lies at the heart of globalization theory, the notion that capital flight leads to the declining importance of national institutions.

Second, globalization theory claims that increased international economic integration has caused changes in the institutional structure of nation-states. In particular, it says that states compete for investment capital by cutting taxes and otherwise reforming their tax institutions. I demonstrate that by carefully specifying the important *institutional dimensions* of taxation in the advanced capitalist countries and tracking changes in them over time, there is very little empirical support for this argument.

At best, tax institutions have evolved only slightly in the direction predicted by globalization theory. There has not been a revolutionary overhaul. Again, this calls globalization theory into question.

Third, I examine some of the regulative *mechanisms* that have mediated the influence of globalization pressures to show why globalization has not had the effects on taxation that globalization theory predicts. I discuss how the institutional arrangement of organized labor, business, and electoral politics constrain the predicted effects of globalization.

Fourth, I explore how the normative and cognitive mechanisms associated with *ideas* have also constrained the influence of globalization on taxation, paying particular attention to tax reform in the United States and Sweden. For each country, I review the neoliberal program associated with tax reform. I argue that its initial rise to prominence was facilitated by the deployment of strategic frames that legitimized it and by its close fit with the prevailing paradigm in professional economics. However, I also show that public sentiments constrained the ability of decision makers to sustain neoliberal tax reform and make it stick.

Fifth, I shift attention away from tax reform and show how neoliberal reform in other institutional areas occurred through the mechanisms of *diffusion* and *translation*, and how these mechanisms mediated in path-dependent ways the impact of globalization on national political institutions. Finally, returning to the issue of time frames, I offer a few remarks about why, for institutional reasons, it is unlikely that globalization theory will be vindicated even if we wait longer.

Organizing the discussion around the themes of time frames, institutional dimensions, mechanisms, ideas, and diffusion and translation may seem a bit ad hoc—at least from the standpoint of developing a critique of the globalization thesis. In fact, there is nothing ad hoc about it. Remember that the primary goal here is not to critique the globalization thesis per se, but to show how various arguments concerning institutional analysis, developed earlier in this book, can be used to better understand important phenomena around us in the world. As a result, the discussion here quite systematically parallels the presentation of themes in previous chapters.

Before proceeding, let me explain why taxation is important and worth such detailed consideration in this chapter. As elaborated below, globalization theory makes strong claims about how globalization reduces taxation. As such, if globalization theory is correct, then we should find clear evidence supporting it in the area of taxation. But beyond that, why should institutionalists care about taxes? First, institutionalists have long been concerned with property rights. Property rights are the rules, that is, the institutions, that define not only who owns the means of production, but also who uses them and who appropriates the benefits from their use

(Bromley 1989, 187–206; Barzel 1989, 2). Property rights constitute an essential part of the institutional membrane that connects the state and economy. They are among the most important institutions in which capitalist economic activity is embedded. As historical, organizational, and rational choice institutionalists have recognized, states regulate both the behavior and organization of firms and other actors within national economies through the manipulation of property rights (Campbell and Lindberg 1990; Fligstein 1990; North 1990). What is important to understand is that taxation is one of the most important forms of property rights. Tax law impinges directly on rights of private property ownership and appropriation by specifying, for instance, how much income may be retained by individuals and organizations. It affects how firms and individuals use their property, such as by influencing investment decisions. And, as a result, it influences national economic organization and performance. Second, institutionalists have long been concerned with the determinants of welfare, regulatory, and other government programs that influence the economy. More recently, they have become interested in how globalization is affecting these programs and, in turn, the organization of firms and economic production in general (e.g., Fligstein 2001a, chap. 9; Guillén 2001a). Because taxes constitute the "life-blood" of the modern state without which it cannot support its regulatory and welfare efforts (Braun 1975, 243), understanding how globalization affects taxation should be of great interest to institutionalists who are concerned with these other issues.

In chapter 2, I argued that institutions are multidimensional entities and that change may vary across these dimensions. Some dimensions may change a lot; others may change a little or not at all. Globalization is said to impact a wide variety of institutions in capitalist societies. In addition to tax institutions, it may also affect the institutions associated with welfare states, labor market regulation, environmental regulation, trade, culture, and so on. As we shall see, taxation is complex enough institutionally to warrant sustained attention in its own right. Nevertheless, some might argue that while globalization has not precipitated the sort of changes in taxation that the theory predicts, the effects of globalization may have been more striking and the theory may have been more applicable in some of these other areas. Perhaps. But, as indicated briefly later in this chapter, there are reasons to be skeptical about this—skepticism that is expressed in a growing literature that examines many of these other areas. Still, my argument may be criticized for only examining one subset of the many institutional dimensions at issue in the debate on globalization. However, remember again that my purpose here is not to launch a comprehensive attack on the globalization thesis that includes a thorough examination of each and every institution that globalization may affect.

Instead, my goal is to illustrate the utility of my earlier arguments about institutional analysis by applying them to a specific, if somewhat narrowly defined, empirical subject.

TIME FRAMES: EXAMINING THE EXTENT OF GLOBALIZATION

In chapter 2, I argued that when studying institutional change it is important to consider the appropriate time frame for analysis. Globalization theory concentrates on the period after the Second World War, particularly after about 1970. Globalization theorists argue that several aspects of economic activity have taken on increasingly international proportions during this time. To begin with, international trade expanded dramatically among the advanced capitalist countries during the past few decades. Between 1960 and 1990 the ratio of merchandise exports to Gross Domestic Product (GDP) increased worldwide from 8 to 13 percent, a significant if not dramatic rise. The ratios were nearly twice as large for many advanced capitalist countries (Crafts 2000, 20). More notable increases occurred in foreign direct investment (FDI), the investments firms make in foreign firms and production facilities, which increased sevenfold between 1975 and 1990, with almost all of the increase occurring after 1982 (Hirst and Thompson 1996, 55). Even more impressive was the increase in international portfolio investment, that is, investment by financial and fiduciary institutions in foreign stocks, bonds, and the like, which grew among OECD countries at rates two and sometimes three times faster than those of FDI between the mid-1980s and mid-1990s (Simmons 1999, 46). Finally, and perhaps most spectacular of all, foreign exchange turnover, the value of foreign currencies traded annually on international currency markets, skyrocketed from $18 trillion in 1979 to $295 trillion in 1995 (Held et al. 1999, 209).

A few clarifications are in order. First, most of the changes just described have been restricted primarily to the so-called triad region of North America, Western Europe, and Japan. For instance, in 1995 roughly 67 percent of world trade was within this region. (e.g., Fligstein 2001a, chap. 9; Hirst and Thompson 1996, 63). Second, there is much variation across advanced countries in how open their economies are and, thus, how vulnerable they might be to the pressures stemming from global trade. For example, between 1960 and 1994, exports and imports as a percentage of GDP increased in the Netherlands from 42 to 50 percent; in France they increased from 14 to 22 percent; and in the United States they increased from 5 to 11 percent (Kenworthy 1997, 9). Many of the smaller OECD economies have been much more open than the larger ones for a long time (Katzenstein 1985). Third, domestic investment remains the norm. FDI remained only a small fraction of total firm investment during this period. Even for firms in smaller, more open economies, which typically have the highest rates of FDI, this amounted to only about 20 percent of total firm investment (Hall 2000). Fourth, domestic investment also remained the norm insofar as stocks and bonds were concerned. Notably, foreign participation in stock markets increased during the 1980s but still remained quite small. Foreign listings on the New York Stock Exchange increased from only 2.5 to 5.4 percent of total listings; on the London Stock Exchange they increased from only 13 to 22 percent; and on the Tokyo Stock Exchange they increased from only 1 to 7 percent (Simmons 1999, 51–56).

Although it is clear from these figures that economic activity has become increasingly globalized during the late twentieth century, if we adopt a longer time frame, then things look a bit different. In particular, if we examine the recent period against the early part of the century, the level of globalization that has occurred during the post-1970 era does not seem quite so extraordinary (Chase-Dunn et al. 2000, 2002; Temin 1999). Although international trade increased substantially in absolute terms during the twentieth century, in relative terms it rose only slightly. From the late 1800s into the beginning of the twentieth century, economic activity was already becoming globalized. By 1914, 14 percent of all world economic activity involved international trade—a figure that remained the century's high water mark until it was surpassed in the mid-1990s, reaching 17 percent in 1996. During the two world wars and the Great Depression of the 1930s, trade declined so much that by 1953 it was only 6 percent of world GDP (Fligstein 2001a, 196; Held et al. 1999, 168–69). Modern concepts of FDI and portfolio investment were developed only in the early 1960s (Hirst and Thompson 1996, 19), but it appears that they likely followed a similar pattern of expansion through the First World War, a pronounced retreat from the 1930s through the 1950s, and then accelerating growth from the 1960s to the present (Crafts 2000, 21). Finally, international capital flows, organized primarily by multinational banks, increased during the late nineteenth and early twentieth centuries, but then dropped precipitously during the interwar period. International financial flows, including investments in bonds, equities, and currencies, recovered fully only with the emergence of the Eurocurrency market, the collapse of the Bretton Woods system, and the oil price shocks of the 1970s (Held et al. 1999, 198–215; Kapstein 1994).

Of course, there were differences between the early and latter parts of the century. The velocity with which capital moves, the diversity of capital flows, and the gross amount of capital that is moving across borders are all much greater now than they were then. The composition of trade has also shifted from being predominantly raw materials and agricultural products to manufactured goods (Held et al. 1999, 220–25; Temin 1999, 84). Nevertheless, by extending the time frame back to the early part of the century we begin to find at least a few hints that there may be problems with the globalization thesis. Specifically, although economic activity was becoming internationalized during the late 1800s through 1914, as it has since 1970, it was not matched during the early period by the declining importance or homogenization of national-level institutions that globalization theory points to during the more recent period. In fact, the opposite occurred.

At the beginning of the twentieth century, West European and Anglo-Saxon states were beginning to experiment with a variety of social programs and welfare state institutions, such as poor relief, pensions, and fledgling social security systems, which took on very different forms in different countries. The Swedes and Danes were starting to develop what became social democratic welfare states based on principles of equity, universal eligibility, generous benefits, full-employment, and maximum revenue income to support it all. The Germans, French, and Italians were beginning to build corporatist welfare states. They were less concerned than the Scandinavians with equity and redistribution and more concerned with preserving basic class and status distinctions. However, they still sought to provide pension, social security, and some other forms of assistance to their citizens rather than rely on the private sector to do so. The United States was embarking on the creation of a residual welfare state, assuming that the private sector should cover most social needs and that the state, therefore, should intervene only to furnish means-tested benefits and modest social insurance programs (Esping-Andersen 1990; Furniss and Tilton 1977). Until the 1930s, these experiments were being conducted in the United States primarily at the subnational level (Skocpol 1992). To finance these nascent programs, but also to provide national defense and the infrastructure required for industrialization, almost every industrializing nation began to turn toward modern systems of taxation at the turn of the century. Income taxes on the wealthy and on corporations were introduced in virtually all of these countries. Although they remained modest by today's standards, tax rates increased quickly and the overall distribution of the tax burden shifted from the lower to the upper classes (Steinmo 1993, 22–23).

Furthermore, during the late nineteenth and early twentieth centuries the economies in these countries were beginning to develop diverse institutional arrangements. Germany was building a system of centralized cartels and vertically integrated firms organized in part by a few large German banks (Kocka 1980). France was organizing its economy around a combination of family-owned firms and large financial holding companies, although it too experimented with cartels, and banks played an important, if more modest, role compared to those in Germany (Gerschenkron 1962; Levy-Leboyer 1980). Britain's economy was cultivating industry-wide holding companies (Hannah 1980). Large, independent corporate enterprises were emerging in the United States (Chandler 1977). And in East Asia, more networked forms of economic activity were being institutionalized, such as the Japanese zaibatsu, which were huge financial and trading cliques that ran the financial, extractive, and commodity markets (Friedman 1988, 38–39; Hamilton and Biggart 1988). States played an increasingly important role in facilitating these institutional developments (Dore et al. 1999). Even in the United States, known for its comparatively laissez-faire approach to state-economy relations, there was increasing state intervention at both the national and subnational level as government provided property rights structures, corporate charters, antitrust legislation, industry regulation, and financial assistance to firms and industries (Lindberg and Campbell 1991; Galambos and Pratt 1988; Keller 1981; Roy 1997).

The point is that the time frame we choose for analyzing globalization and its relationship to institutional change matters a great deal. Extending it backward reveals some surprises. On the one hand, at the beginning and end of the century, the levels of international economic activity were increasing and in important respects were quite similar. Furthermore, this was facilitated at the beginning of the century by dramatic improvements in transportation (railroads and steam ships), communication (telegraph and telephone), and other technological breakthroughs, just as breakthroughs in these areas facilitated international economic activity at the century's end. On the other hand, however, the relationship between globalization and the institutional structure of taxation, welfare states, and the economy seems to have been much different at the beginning of the twentieth century than globalization theorists say it was at the end of the century. Rather than cutting taxes on capital and reducing welfare expenditures at the beginning of the century, many countries were raising taxes on investors and corporations and were starting to build welfare states in ways that resulted in divergence rather than convergence in these political institutions. Moreover, rather than converging on a decentralized form of economic activity, the industrializing countries were creating several different institutional types of capitalism, although each one involved the increased centralization and organization of economic activity (Lash and Urry 1987). In short, by lengthening the time frame, we discover that the relationship between globalization and institutional change was quite different at the beginning and end of the twentieth century.

The association of increasing international economic integration with opposing institutional trends at the beginning and end of the century raises questions about the globalization thesis. If globalization precipitated a shift away from organized capitalism in the late twentieth century, why did it not prevent the development of organized capitalism in the early twentieth century? Why would states facing increased capital mobility, and thus threats of capital flight, cut taxes on capital during the late twentieth century but raise them during the early twentieth century?

Globalization theorists would probably argue that the nature of globalization was different insofar as the velocity, amount, and threat of international capital mobility are all much greater now than they were then, and so the effects of capital mobility would also have been different. Perhaps this is true, but these incongruities also point to the fact that the impact that globalization has on political and economic life is far more complex than globalization theory recognizes. Indeed, many of the institutional changes that occurred during the beginning of the century were driven in part by democratization, pressure from labor movements and left-wing political parties, and the unique institutional legacies within which public and private decision makers operated (e.g., Dore et al. 1999; Esping-Andersen 1990; Lash and Urry 1987). As we will see later, this is an important clue about some of the causal mechanisms beyond capital mobility and the threat of capital flight that affected institutional change during the late twentieth century. But first, we need to determine how much institutional change actually occurred during the late twentieth century. This requires a closer look at some of the important dimensions of institutional change upon which globalization theory dwells. Among the most important is the institution of taxation.

INSTITUTIONAL DIMENSIONS:
EXAMINING THE EFFECTS OF GLOBALIZATION

We can hardly deny that there have been revolutions in telecommunications, transportation, and other technologies since the mid-1970s. And in at least some areas of economic activity—notably the velocity, volume, and composition of capital mobility—there have also been astounding changes during this period as a result of these technological breakthroughs. Globalization theorists contend that this is also having a revolutionary impact on the political institutions of advanced capitalist societies. But how revolutionary have these institutional changes been? As I argued in chapter 2, determining the degree to which institutional change has been revolutionary or evolutionary requires that we carefully specify the important dimensions involved and track them over an appropriate period of time. According to globalization theory, three major institutions have experienced fundamental change insofar as states in advanced capitalist society are concerned: taxation, welfare, and economic regulation.

Each is an institution in the sense that each is organized through a set of rules, regulations, and guidelines established by law. As noted above, a comprehensive analysis of all three of these institutions is beyond the scope of this chapter. My focus here will be only on taxation, a political institution that is itself comprised of several important dimensions.

Given the increasing threat of capital flight, globalization theorists argue that one of the most important competitive strategies available to states to attract and retain capital is to reduce the tax burden on individuals and corporations (McKenzie and Lee 1991). Indeed, according to Vivek Dehejia and Philipp Genschel (1999, 403–4), "many economists argue that the competition for a mobile tax base will lead to a *fiscally ruinous 'race to the bottom,'* where the competing states interactively cut their taxes on capital and other mobile factors to lower levels" (my emphasis). Eventually, this will lead to convergence on low tax rates and an erosion in the ability of national governments to control the making of tax policy (Hallerberg 1996, 324; see also Crafts 2000, 42–43; McKenzie and Lee 1991, 12–14; Steinmo 1993, 29). The OECD is so concerned about this that it warned recently that tax competition will undermine the ability of national governments to maintain their tax bases and, therefore, urged international cooperation to eliminate such harmful tax practices (OECD 2000b).

To support this argument, globalization theorists often point to changes in *marginal tax rates*, the statutory rates imposed on taxpayers by the law.[8] They note that in most advanced capitalist countries governments have significantly reduced marginal tax rates on both individuals and corporations since the mid-1970s (Steinmo 1993, 30). For instance, in the advanced capitalist countries the highest marginal tax rate for corporate income averaged 45 percent in 1981, but dropped to 35 percent by 1995 (Swank and Steinmo 2002). This supports the idea that states are racing to the bottom in response to the increased threat of capital flight.

Marginal rates are only one dimension of a tax regime, however, and they are not the most important one to the extent that few individuals or corporations actually pay marginal tax rates, especially in the higher tax brackets. The reason is that they take advantage of a number of so-called tax expenditures, that is, deductions and other loopholes in the tax code, which effectively reduce the amount of tax they pay. This is why it is more important to examine the *effective tax rate*, which is the percentage of

---

[8] The tax code in most countries is very complicated. It would be an extraordinarily difficult task to analyze all the important changes in tax law per se, especially for several countries. However, tax rates represent the ultimate effect of the tax code and, therefore, provide a convenient overall reflection of the tax law. As such, they offer an indirect way to track changes in the law over time. Hence, throughout this section I will track changes in tax rates, which are readily available, as a proxy for tracking changes in the tax code itself.

reported income or profits actually paid in taxes by individuals or corporations, respectively, after they take advantage of these tax expenditures. Both marginal and effective rates reflect the tax burden for different income groups as specified by the tax code, but effective rates are a better indicator of the full complexity of the law. As a result, the effective tax rate provides a more realistic view of the institutional structure of the tax code than does the marginal rate. In fact, the effective tax rates have not changed much because while governments were cutting marginal rates, they were also scaling back or eliminating investment tax credits, exemptions, and other tax expenditures that had lowered the taxes that individuals and corporations really paid. Some studies report that during the 1980s and 1990s the effective tax rate on capital declined only slightly on average from 38 to 36 percent in the advanced capitalist countries (Swank and Steinmo 2002). Others report that it increased slightly (Genschel 2002). In this regard, there is no clear evidence of a race to the bottom.

Another important dimension of taxation is the overall *level of taxation* imposed by a state's tax law on its society. If globalization theory is correct, then a race to the bottom should precipitate a "fiscally ruinous" decline in the level of revenues that states can collect due to reforms throughout the tax code. Table 5.1 presents total government tax revenues as a percentage of GDP between 1970 and 1998 for eighteen advanced capitalist countries.[9] An examination of the means and medians shows that over this period the average tax burden actually *increased*. The means rose from about 32 percent of GDP to nearly 40 percent of GDP. The medians rose from about 33 percent of GDP to 39 percent of GDP. Furthermore, the corresponding measures of dispersion increased. The standard deviation, associated with the mean, rose during this period from about 6.1 to 7.2, and the interquartile range, associated with the median, increased from 8.1 to 9.9.[10] In this case, the measures of disper-

---

[9] One might worry that for our purposes reporting changes in tax revenues is less desirable than reporting changes in tax rates. After all, changes in revenues are the joint product of rates, which are affected by policy, and economic growth, which is affected both by policy and other factors, such as fluctuations in corporate profitability and individual income. To address this concern, I report tax levels as a percentage of GDP because this approach provides a rough control for expansion or contraction in the economy. If we examined revenues simply in dollar amounts, we would not know if they rose or fell due to expansions or contractions in the economy or changes in the tax code, or some combination of the two.

[10] I report median as well as mean values of central tendency because the median is not affected by countries with extreme values as is the mean. Similarly, I report the interquartile range because, in contrast to the standard deviation, it is a measure of dispersion that is not influenced as much by extreme values in the data. It represents the range of dispersion around the median. It is calculated by subtracting the twenty-fifth percentile of the data from the seventy-fifth percentile and, therefore, encompasses the middle 50 percent of the observations (Pagano and Gauvreau 1993, 41–43).

TABLE 5.1.
Total Tax Revenues in Eighteen OECD Countries (as a percentage of GDP)

	1970	1980	1990	1998
Australia	22.9	27.4	29.3	29.9
Austria	34.9	39.5	40.2	44.4
Belgium	35.7	43.1	43.1	45.9
Canada	31.2	32.0	36.1	37.4
Denmark	40.4	43.9	47.1	49.8
Finland	32.5	36.2	44.7	46.2
France	35.1	40.6	43.0	45.2
Germany	32.9	33.1	32.6	37.0
Ireland	29.9	31.5	33.6	32.2
Italy	26.1	30.3	38.9	42.7
Japan	19.7	25.4	30.9	28.4
Netherlands	37.1	43.4	42.8	41.0
New Zealand	27.4	33.0	38.1	35.2
Norway	34.9	42.7	41.8	43.6
Sweden	39.8	47.1	53.7	52.0
Switzerland	22.5	28.9	30.9	35.1
United Kingdom	37.0	35.3	36.0	37.2
USA	27.7	27.0	26.7	28.9
Mean	31.54	35.58	38.31	39.56
Median	32.70	34.20	38.50	39.20
Standard deviation	6.06	6.73	6.97	7.15
Interquartile range	8.08	11.58	10.10	9.88

Source: OECD (2000a, table 3, pp. 67–68).

sion indicate how close countries tend to cluster around the average tax burden for the group as a whole. Smaller measures of dispersion indicate tighter clustering, that is, convergence, than do larger ones. Thus, not only did the tax burden increase rather than decrease, but there was no convergence toward a common level of taxation among these countries. On both counts the evidence contradicts globalization theory.

One argument that might rescue globalization theory from this contradictory evidence is that there may be convergent tendencies within smaller groups of countries. As suggested earlier, there are different types of capitalism, each with unique political, economic, and institutional arrangements (Hall and Soskice 2001a; Hollingsworth et al. 1994; Hollingsworth and Boyer 1997). Countries of a particular type tend to share common features, such as similar tax regimes. It follows that different types of countries may tend to cope with globalization pressures in different ways. Thus, although convergent tendencies in taxation might not be apparent when all the advanced capitalist countries are examined as a single group, there may be convergent, race-to-the-bottom effects among countries that share important features, such as similar types of welfare states or similar means for coordinating economic activity (e.g., Kitschelt et al. 1999). However, there is no evidence among smaller groups of countries with either similar types of welfare states or similar means for coordinating economic activity to support globalization theory insofar as the level of taxation is concerned. Details of this analysis need not concern us here but are reported in the appendix at the end of the book.

In sum, analyses of tax levels in the advanced capitalist countries provide no support for the notion that globalization is causing states to change their tax laws in ways that result in convergence on lower tax burdens. Therefore, states do not seem to be risking the sort of fiscal ruin that globalization theorists have predicted. However, there is still another institutional dimension of taxation that needs to be explored. It is possible that globalization may have caused changes in the *structure* of national tax regimes without affecting the overall *level* of tax burdens. After all, as suggested in chapter 2, states may change the tax code in ways that shift where the tax burden falls without altering the level of taxation per se. For example, changing the law to shift from progressive income taxes to flat social consumption taxes, such as sales or value-added taxes, may move the burden of taxation from one income group to another without affecting the total amount of revenue the government collects. So it is possible that if states did not converge toward lower levels of taxation due to globalization, perhaps they tended at least to alter their tax laws in ways that shifted the tax burden off investors and corporations and on to others.

To investigate this possibility, table 5.2 examines seventeen advanced capitalist countries for the percentage of total central government revenues collected through three major taxes: income and profit taxes, social security taxes, and taxes on goods and services.[11] Together these three types of taxes comprise the vast majority of government revenues and constitute the foundation of modern tax regimes. They provided on aver-

[11] Although included in the previous table, Japan is omitted in table 5.2 due to missing data.

TABLE 5.2.
Central Government Revenues for Seventeen OECD Countries by Tax Type
(as a percentage of total government revenues)

	Income & Profit Taxes		Social Security Taxes		Taxes on Goods & Services	
	1990	1998	1990	1998	1990	1998
Australia	65.0	68.0	0.0	0.0	21.0	21.0
Austria	19.0	26.0	37.0	40.0	25.0	25.0
Belgium	35.0	37.0	35.0	33.0	24.0	25.0
Canada	51.0	54.0	16.0	19.0	17.0	17.0
Denmark	37.0	36.0	4.0	4.0	41.0	42.0
Finland	31.0	29.0	9.0	10.0	47.0	44.0
France	17.0	20.0	44.0	42.0	28.0	29.0
Germany	16.0	15.0	53.0	48.0	24.0	20.0
Ireland	37.0	42.0	15.0	13.0	38.0	37.0
Italy	37.0	33.0	29.0	31.0	29.0	26.0
Netherlands	31.0	25.0	35.0	41.0	22.0	23.0
New Zealand	53.0	62.0	0.0	0.0	27.0	28.0
Norway	16.0	21.0	24.0	23.0	34.0	38.0
Sweden	18.0	14.0	31.0	34.0	29.0	28.0
Switzerland	15.0	15.0	51.0	51.0	23.0	23.0
United Kingdom	39.0	39.0	17.0	17.0	28.0	31.0
United States	52.0	57.0	35.0	32.0	3.0	3.0
Mean	33.47	34.88	25.59	25.77	27.06	27.06
Median	35.00	33.00	29.00	31.00	27.00	26.00
Standard deviation	15.37	16.98	16.78	16.50	9.85	9.87
Interquartile range	21.00	21.00	20.00	27.00	6.00	8.00

Source: World Bank (2001, table 4.13, pp. 242–44).

age between 86 and 88 percent of all the revenue these governments collected during the 1990s. The rest came from taxes on trade, miscellaneous taxes, and non-tax revenue (World Bank 2001, 242–44). The table presents data from 1990 and 1998, a relatively short period, but one that is appropriate because the sharp increases in foreign direct investment, international portfolio investment, and foreign exchange transactions with which globalization theory is so concerned occurred after 1985, and so their effects, if any, would not likely begin to appear until the 1990s.

Table 5.2 shows that there was very little change in the percentage of revenues received from each type of tax during the 1990s. In particular, we might expect that taxes on income, which include individual and corporate income taxes, profit taxes, and capital gains taxes, would be the form of taxation most likely to be affected by globalization pressures if states want to shift taxes off individual and corporate investors. Yet the evidence for such an argument is not compelling. An examination of the means shows that the percentage of revenues collected through income and profit taxes increased from about 34 to 35 percent of total government revenues. However, the median declined from 35 to 33 percent of total government revenues. Neither the standard deviation nor interquartile range of income taxes declined at all. The mean tax receipts associated with social security taxes was essentially stable and the median increased slightly from 29 to 31 percent of total revenues. The standard deviation barely declined from 16.8 to 16.5, but the interquartile range increased from 20 to 27. The mean tax receipts collected through taxes on goods and services was unchanged while the median declined modestly from 27 to 26 percent of total revenues. The standard deviation was virtually unchanged, and the interquartile range increased from 6 to 8. There is little evidence here that the structure of tax regimes changed in ways that are consistent with globalization theory. In fact, there was little change at all—a finding that is consistent with studies, discussed earlier, that report that the effective tax rates on capital did not change much during this period. The appendix reveals that the same is true if we examine different subgroups of countries.

Of course, globalization theorists might argue that focusing on the full ensemble of income and profit taxes is not precise enough. After all, this category includes not just taxes on investors and corporations, but the rest of the income-earning population as well. However, if we look more closely to determine whether states altered their laws to shift the tax burden at least off of corporations, we find a very similar story. Table 5.3 reports the percentage of government revenues collected from corporate income taxes among eighteen advanced capitalist countries. Between 1975 and 1998, there was no evidence that states fundamentally shifted the tax burden away from corporations—another finding that is consonant with the fact that effective tax rates on capital remained fairly stable. The mean rose from 10.7 to 13.4 percent of government revenues and the median rose from 9.5 to 13.1 percent. Again, the appendix shows that globalization theory fares no better when we examine subgroups of countries.

TABLE 5.3.
Corporate Income Taxes in Eighteen OECD Countries
(as a percentage of total government revenues)

	1975	1985	1998
Australia	15.5	11.5	19.4
Austria	6.9	5.0	6.3
Belgium	10.5	7.9	21.0
Canada	20.9	13.9	15.9
Denmark	3.9	6.0	7.8
Finland	3.4	2.9	9.7
France	10.1	9.4	13.8
Germany	5.2	7.6	5.6
Ireland	6.2	3.9	12.4
Italy	11.3	14.4	12.0
Japan	29.4	30.7	22.3
Netherlands	13.1	13.4	19.0
New Zealand	12.8	8.9	11.5
Norway	3.1	26.7	14.1
Sweden	3.8	5.7	9.9
Switzerland	6.3	5.7	8.4
United Kingdom	8.8	18.2	14.3
USA	21.6	13.6	16.9
Mean	10.71	11.41	13.35
Median	9.45	9.15	13.10
Standard deviation	7.27	7.58	5.00
Interquartile range	7.58	8.05	6.90

Source: OECD (2000a, table 131, p. 202).

To review, when we examine a number of the critical institutional dimensions of national tax regimes in the advanced capitalist countries,
there is precious little support for the notion that globalization precipitated a convergent race to the bottom in taxation, that effective tax rates
on corporations were cut much, that the tax burdens on investors and
corporations were reduced appreciably, or that states faced fiscal ruin.
Only in the relatively inconsequential area of marginal tax rates do we see

much evidence in support of the globalization thesis. In sum, globalization does not seem to have had much effect on national tax institutions.[12]

If the degree to which institutional change is evolutionary or revolutionary can best be determined by examining several dimensions of the institution in question, as I argued in chapter 2, then we must conclude that the institutions of taxation in the advanced capitalist countries have exhibited, at best, only very limited signs of evolutionary change during the globalization era. Certainly there is no clear support for the sort of punctuated equilibrium or punctuated evolution models discussed in chapter 2. This does not mean, however, that these models are wrong or otherwise unsuited to the study of institutional change. After all, national tax regimes constitute only one case where we might expect to find institutional change in the face of globalization pressures. Other cases may reveal more change as well as patterns of change that resonate more closely with these other models. Nevertheless, the more important point is that we can determine how much change occurs, and which model best describes it, only by tracking the relevant institutional dimensions over an appropriate time frame, as I have done here.

But what accounts for the relative lack of change in this case despite such a sharp increase in the globalization of economic activity? Here institutional analysis is particularly useful because it helps specify the mechanisms that mediate the impact of globalization on nation-states.

REGULATIVE MECHANISMS

I explained in chapter 3 that an adequate account of institutional change requires a careful specification of the causal mechanisms involved. I suggested earlier in this chapter that an important clue for understanding the

---

[12] Many of the cases under consideration here are European countries that are subject to fiscal constraints specified in the Maastricht Treaty, an important element in the run-up to the European Monetary Union. Among other things, the Maastricht Treaty stipulates that members will limit government budget deficits to no more than 3 percent of GDP. This is an international, but not global, institutional constraint that might help militate against a race to the bottom in taxation insofar as member states, concerned about their deficits, would be reluctant to cut taxes too much. Hence, one might question whether the cases upon which I have focused are biased in favor of my argument. Certainly the Maastricht constraint is important. But these are also the countries with which proponents of the globalization thesis are generally most concerned. Moreover, there are reasons to suspect that these are the countries that ought to be most susceptible to the globalization pressures emphasized by globalization theory. As noted earlier, about two-thirds of world trade transpired among these advanced capitalist countries during the mid-1990s. And nearly three-quarters of the world's foreign direct investment flowed among them (Held et al. 1999, 249).

causal mechanisms by which globalization affects states is contained in the observation that democratization, political pressures from labor movements and left-wing governments, and national institutional legacies influenced many of the institutional changes that occurred during the early twentieth century. During the late twentieth century, these things mediated the degree to which globalization transformed national political economies. The manner in which this occurred depended in part on how politics were organized through regulative institutions. What follows in this section is a discussion of how the mechanisms associated with regulative institutions mediated the effects of globalization on taxation in the advanced capitalist countries. The next section examines how the mechanisms associated with normative and cognitive institutions did this.

Two things are important here. First, as is well known, regulative institutions affect how political and social actors are organized and maneuver politically. Some countries have laws that facilitate the organization of labor unions and business firms into centralized peak associations with formal standing in the decision-making process. Other countries do not. In turn, centralized labor organizations and business associations with direct access to decision-making arenas tend to have different interests and capacities for influencing legislation than actors who are organized differently (e.g., Rogers and Streeck 1994; Streeck 1991, 1997; Streeck and Schmitter 1985; Western 1997). Hence, the institutions through which social actors are organized affect how they perceive and act on their interests around issues of taxation. Second, the regulative institutions through which electoral politics are organized have similar effects. In particular, actors operating in electoral systems whose laws require proportional representation tend to have different interests as well as electoral and legislative strategies than actors operating in winner-take-all systems. Notably, electoral institutions affect the degree to which politicians and organizations are willing to compromise on issues of taxation. Much has been written about how these institutions and the interests, capacities, and strategies of actors that derive from them have affected taxation during the late twentieth century (e.g., Campbell 1993a), and so I will be brief.

To begin with, several studies report that during the late twentieth century countries where the law enables the labor movement to be centralized and politically strong, such as Sweden and Germany, tend to have persistently higher tax rates than countries where labor is more decentralized and politically weak, such as the United States. Additionally, workers in countries with strong centralized labor movements tend to enjoy the benefits of works councils, state employment services, active labor market policies, employment guarantees, and other welfare programs that workers elsewhere forego (Hicks and Kenworthy 1998; Western 2001). Insofar as the state needs to collect taxes to pay for these benefits, labor has an interest in supporting relatively high taxes and does so in the expectation that this will lead to a higher social wage. Labor's capacity to support these policies is often enhanced in these countries because unions are integrated into the policy-making process through corporatist institutions that provide it with an important voice in decision making. Moreover, when strong centralized labor unions are coupled with strong labor or social democratic governments, as is often the case in these countries, the tax burden on everyone, including business, tends to be higher than elsewhere (Steinmo and Tolbert 1998). This is not to say, however, that leftist governments allied with well-organized labor movements have free rein to do as they please. They still exercise self-restraint recognizing that excessive demands for a very high social wage could drive away capital and, therefore, hurt the labor movement as a whole (Garrett 1998a).

However, business and investors also seem willing to bear heavier tax burdens in countries with corporatist institutions governing labor-management relations and more extensive welfare states. This is because they recognize that it may be in their own interests to do so. Corporatist countries have strong centralized business associations and persistently higher tax rates than elsewhere because capital is willing to help pay for social expenditures that protect workers from the risks associated with an increasingly global economy. Such expenditures help ensure the social peace that business needs to maintain productivity (Garrett 1998a). Indeed, a top priority of business is to reduce uncertainty and stabilize the business environment (Fligstein 2001a; Kolko 1963). Business also supports higher taxes insofar as this enables the state to provide public goods that directly benefit firms, such as a more educated and, therefore, flexible work force, universal pension and health benefits that reduce job shifting across firms, and the like (Kiser and Laing 2001). All of this helps explain why the percentage of total government revenues collected from corporate income taxes increased in the Christian democratic and social democratic countries since 1975 (see appendix, table A.5). After all, most of these countries had corporatist labor market institutions. Business, of course, had to learn that there were long-term benefits to be gained from this sort of social investment. Centralized business associations often play an important role in teaching these sorts of lessons to their members (Streeck 1997; Streeck and Schmitter 1985). This is one reason, for example, why German business associations have defended co-determination policies, the rules guaranteeing various worker rights and input into important managerial decisions (Thelen 2000c). It is also why Scandinavian business associations continue to educate their members on the benefits of substantial welfare spending (Swank and Martin 2001). The point is that for institutional reasons business is less averse to high taxes in some countries than globalization theory recognizes.

In addition to the institutional capacities of important economic actors, electoral institutions exert important effects on tax policy. In majoritarian systems, like Britain and Japan, single parties tend to control the government. The party in power wants to keep taxes low in order not to lose voters and the next election. In systems that tend to result in coalition governments where one party dominates the coalition, as the Social Democratic Party has done in Sweden for most of the twentieth century, the dominant party strikes long-term compromises with its coalition partners to keep the coalition intact. Taxes tend to be higher to pay for the expenditures required to keep coalition members happy. Finally, in systems that tend to produce shifting coalition governments in which no single party dominates the coalition, all parties have incentives to defect and try to gain control of new coalition governments, and so there is little incentive for long-term compromise and, thus, spending and taxes tend to be low (Steinmo and Tolbert 1998).

It is worth mentioning briefly that scholars have made similar arguments about another major aspect of globalization: welfare state reform. Globalization theory claims that globalization exerts downward pressure on welfare spending because welfare programs represent a major financial liability to mobile capital in a competitive global environment and because they are hard to finance due to the downward pressure on taxes associated with capital flight. However, in the seventeen largest OECD countries social welfare transfers, including social security, in-kind benefits, and transfer payments, increased on average from 14 to 18 percent of GDP between 1974 and 1993 (Kenworthy 1997). Although countries that often had social democratic governments spent more than their Christian democratic or liberal counterparts, this trend held for all three types (Stephens et al. 1999). Why? Research suggests that national institutions mediate global pressures for reducing the size of the welfare state (e.g., Esping-Andersen 1999; Pierson 1994; Stephens et al. 1999; Swank 2002). An exhaustive review of the empirical research concluded that the design of political institutions governing the interaction between government and organized economic actors influenced greatly how globalization affected the conduct of public spending in general and welfare policy in particular. Countries with institutions facilitating the collective representation of interests, such as corporatism and consensus democracy, were much less likely to reduce spending than others (Schulze and Ursprung 1999, 345–46).[13]

---

[13] Regulative institutions also help mediate the impact of neoliberalism outside the advanced capitalist countries. For instance, variation in formal institutions governing the political influence of organized labor as well as the structure of electoral politics helps account for how different postcommunist European governments responded during the early 1990s to external pressure for neoliberal reform in fiscal policy (Campbell 2001).

Overall, then, the regulative institutions configuring national politics shaped people's perceptions of their interests and political strategies in different ways in different countries. Because these institutions were rather stable, they tended to stabilize tax regimes and, therefore, the differences among regimes despite whatever global pressures there may have been otherwise for a convergent race to the bottom.

Many institutionalists agree that regulative institutions shape people's perceptions of their interests. I noted in chapter 3 that institutions are said to both constrain and enable action. Taxation is a good example of how political institutions enable action in the sense that these institutions created incentives for labor, business, and politicians that encouraged them to act in certain ways rather than others. Furthermore, insofar as these institutions and their associated incentives were stable, people's action was locked in or constrained from changing. Cognitive and normative institutions, however, were also important in enabling and constraining globalization-era changes in taxation. Put in slightly different terms, ideas other than interests were important. But what ideational mechanisms were at work?

NORMATIVE AND COGNITIVE MECHANISMS

I argued in chapter 4 that ideas involve both normative and cognitive factors.[14] Recall from this chapter that cognitive ideas like *programs* and *paradigms* specify cause-and-effect relationships. Normative ideas like *public sentiments* and *frames* specify what people value as appropriate and legitimate. Researchers often turn to comparative case studies to show how these kinds of ideas influence decision making and institutional change (e.g., Berman 1998; Dobbin 1994; Keck and Sikkink 1998; Soysal 1994). This is the approach that I will take by examining tax reform in the United States and Sweden during the late twentieth century.

Before proceeding, some clarifications are necessary. First, in chapter 4, I discussed several methodological approaches to the analysis of ideas. Several of these, such as the use of counterfactuals, were designed to determine the degree to which ideas other than interests affect decision making and institutional change. Because I have already acknowledged in the previous section that institutionally based interest struggles influenced how globalization affected tax reform during the late twentieth century, the comparative case approach is sufficient for present purposes. After all,

---

[14] Portions of this section appeared originally in "Institutional Analysis and the Role of Ideas in Political Economy," *Theory and Society* 27 (1998): 377–409, © Kluwer Academic Publishers, with kind permission from Kluwer Academic Publishers.

one goal of this chapter is to show that the mechanisms associated with cognitive and normative institutions as well as those associated with regulative institutions mediated the effects of globalization on taxation. Second, the following discussion of ideational mechanisms is more extensive than the previous discussion of regulative mechanisms. This is not because I think that programs, paradigms, public sentiments, and frames were necessarily more important than interests, but because much less has been written about how these sorts of ideas have affected taxation during this period, and so more elaboration is required. Both interests and these other types of ideas mattered a great deal in these two cases (e.g., Bennett and Asard 1995; Blyth 2002).

I pick the United States and Sweden for two reasons. First, they represent two very different types of states and political economies. The United States is a good example of a residual welfare state with low taxes and relatively minimal welfare programs for its citizens. It is also a liberal market economy insofar as the state plays a relatively limited role in facilitating economic development, preferring to let market forces operate rather freely. Sweden is a good example of a social democratic welfare state with high taxes and far more extensive welfare programs. It is also a coordinated market economy insofar as the state plays a more extensive role in facilitating economic development, intervening frequently to prevent or correct market failures (Esping-Andersen 1999; Soskice 1999). Hence, these cases should give us a good view of how globalization affects institutional change in two very different types of advanced capitalist societies.

Second, both countries underwent significant tax reform during the recent globalization era. In the United States there were two major tax cuts: the 1981 Economic Recovery Tax Act, the largest tax cut in U.S. history up to that point, and the 1986 Tax Reform Act. In Sweden the government passed a large tax cut in 1991 that was heralded at the time as the "tax reform of the century." Furthermore, both countries experienced significant globalization pressures during the time when they pursued these tax reforms. FDI from U.S. investors and corporations into other countries increased sharply after 1975. By 1994, FDI emanating from the United States was by far the largest dollar amount of any other country in the world and accounted for 25 percent of total world FDI.[15] Sweden

---

[15] For this reason, it is important to note that the role of the United States in the process of globalization is formidable. As these figures suggest, it enjoyed a hegemonic status economically and, of course, politically into the twenty-first century. And, as noted later, many of the ideas that are central to the international diffusion of neoliberalism emanated from the United States. Still, although U.S. hegemony seems secure for the moment, some might argue that it is on the wane. For instance, while FDI from the United States remains by far the largest in the world, the United States' share as a percentage of total world FDI has been shrinking since 1960 (Held et al. 1999, 247).

also experienced a sharp rise in FDI during this period, was a relatively open economy in terms of trade, and was one of the most heavily taxed countries in the world (Held et al. 1999, 247; Steinmo 1993, 31). It should not be surprising, then, that tax reforms in both countries were driven in part by globalization concerns and called for steep reductions in marginal tax rates. All of this would seem to support globalization theory.

In fact, this evidence is misleading. Tax reform did not occur as an automatic reaction to globalization but as a result of political processes in which ideas played important and complicated roles. To be sure, new tax programs were proposed and framed in ways designed to produce substantial changes in the tax code. Moreover, the credibility and weight of these programs was enhanced by virtue of their fitting the underlying, institutionalized, economic paradigm of their time, neoclassical economics. These programs did not resonate well, however, with important public sentiments, which presented substantial obstacles to change. As a result, decision makers were constrained by institutionalized norms and values in how far they could push tax reform. I suggested in chapter 4 that ideas like these can both enable and constrain institutional change. There is evidence for both effects in these two cases. But, on balance, these sorts of ideas constrained the degree to which tax reform was sustained and institutionalized on a permanent basis in ways that do not support globalization theory. In both countries, tax reform ended up being far more modest and evolutionary than globalization theory would suggest.

The Programs

Recall that programs are cognitive concepts and theories located in the foreground of decision-making debates that facilitate action among elites by specifying how to solve specific problems. Beginning in the 1930s, Keynesianism had become the dominant macroeconomic program in the United States and Sweden (Weir and Skocpol 1985). Although Keynesianism took different forms in different countries (e.g., Hall 1989a; Weir and Skocpol 1985), at its core was the notion that governments needed to intervene into economic affairs to smooth out unacceptably large swings in the business cycle. Otherwise, periods of recession and unemployment would be too severe, and periods of growth and prosperity would be too inflationary. Under Keynesianism the state's role was to maintain a balanced trade-off between unemployment and inflation. This idea was based on the famous Phillips curve, the taken-for-granted paradigmatic belief that there was an inverse causal relationship between unemployment and inflation. Furthermore, Keynesianism stipulated that during recession governments would temporarily have to incur budget deficits as they cut taxes and increased spending to stimulate the economy.[16]

During the late 1970s in both countries Keynesianism came under attack. Inflation, unemployment, and poor international competitiveness in an increasingly global economy were problems both countries faced. Their initial response was a set of neoliberal programs that included major tax reforms as well as reductions in the size of the public sector and welfare state. Central to the neoliberal program was the idea that by reducing taxes, particularly for business and wealthy taxpayers, capital would become available for investment. In turn, this would improve innovation, productivity, economic growth, international competitiveness, and employment without exacerbating inflation.

In the United States this approach was embodied in the Reagan administration's 1981 Economic Recovery Tax Act. The average effective corporate tax rate was cut from 33 percent to 16 percent by 1982, and personal income taxes were cut in ways that disproportionately benefited upper-income families (Moon and Sawhill 1984, 324–25; Quick 1984, 298). These supply-side tax cuts, so-called because they were supposed to increase the supply of investment capital, were motivated in part by concerns about U.S. international competitiveness, trade deficits, and capital flight (Roberts 1984; Steinmo 1993, 165). In particular, decision makers were worried that trade deficits and flagging international competitiveness were contributing to the stagflation that was gripping the country—the simultaneous increase in unemployment and inflation (Martin 1991, chap. 5). Similarly, the 1986 Tax Reform Act was initiated partly due to concerns over capital flight. But the 1986 act was also driven by worries over the increasing complexity of the tax code and the need to make it neutral with respect to the incentives it created for investing in different sectors of the economy. This was an effort to level the playing field for capital and reduce further the federal government's influence in the economy. The legislation cut corporate and individual income tax rates and simplified the tax code by paring back or eliminating a variety of tax expenditures (Martin 1991, chap. 7).

Several influential theorists and supporting organizations advanced the neoliberal program. During the 1970s, the concurrent rise in unemployment and inflation undermined the basic assumptions of the Phillips

[16] In chapter 2, I discussed Hall's (1992, 1993) analysis of what he called a paradigm shift from Keynesianism to monetarism. Hall borrowed the concept of paradigm from Thomas Kuhn (1962), who developed it in the philosophy of science to distinguish between evolutionary and revolutionary changes in scientific theory. As elaborated later, for me Keynesianism is a program, not a paradigm, that is based on a deeper set of paradigmatic principles. In addition to the Phillips curve assumptions, these include the basic principles of neoclassical economics.

curve. As a result, Keynesianism fell into disrepute, creating an environment of intellectual crisis among economists and decision makers, who began searching for an alternative program (Heilbroner and Milberg 1995). A variety of alternatives emerged in the ensuing debate, but neoliberalism won. It was advocated by a number of high-profile economists, particularly those who developed rational expectations theory, which suggested that the Keynesian program had failed because people anticipated the government's policy moves and adjusted their behavior in advance in ways that neutralized the impact of policy. Neoliberalism was also extolled publicly by editorialists writing in the *Wall Street Journal* and other popular publications. Of course, other academics and pundits tried to advance alternative programs. The most important was industrial policy, an approach that called for more, not less, government intervention into the economy. For instance, industrial policy called for the creation of corporatist economic decision-making institutions, new government agencies to channel investment capital to key industries and firms, and other expensive and complex forms of intervention. The neoliberal view, however, was backed by a much more sophisticated and well-funded organizational infrastructure than the alternatives. Conservative think tanks, such as the Heritage Foundation and the American Enterprise Institute, aggressively promoted neoliberalism in general and the supply-side position in particular. In contrast to the moderate and liberal think tanks that supported industrial policy and other views, conservative think tanks had developed great expertise in packaging and marketing the programs of academic economists to decision makers and viewed political advising more as an exercise in intellectual salesmanship than scholarship. Advocates of other programs were at a distinct disadvantage without comparable forms of organizational support (Allen 1994; Campbell 1998).

In Sweden the impetus for tax reform was also related to globalization. During the 1970s and 1980s, wage restraint, a mainstay of Sweden's famous corporatist wage bargain between the Swedish Employers Federation and the national industrial labor union (Shonfield 1965, 199–211), deteriorated as the public and service sectors grew, their employees joined other unions, and centralized wage bargaining collapsed (Pontusson and Swenson 1996). Compared to traditional industrial workers, these newly organized workers did not have as much incentive to restrain their wage demands because their jobs did not depend on their industries remaining competitive internationally. Increased wage demands from public employees as well as demands for public services led to higher taxes. In turn, higher taxes led to further wage demands and, therefore, inflation. In 1991, to break this vicious cycle, at the behest of the business community, the newly elected conservative government cut the top marginal tax rate on personal income from 80 percent to 50 percent and eliminated so many deductions that most people no longer had to file income tax returns after their employers withheld their taxes. The new government also reduced the tax rate on capital income to a flat 30 percent and rolled back deductions. Finally, it cut the marginal rate on corporate profits from 57 percent to 30 percent and, again, eliminated many generous tax expenditures (Steinmo 2002).

As in the United States, theorists and supporting organizations were responsible for convincing decision makers to adopt the neoliberal program. First, prominent economists began to abandon Keynesianism. Most notably, Assar Lindbeck, who had always been a staunch social democratic Keynesian, resigned from the Social Democratic Party in 1976 and by the early 1980s had begun to embrace elements of rational expectations, public choice, and monetarist theories. By the late 1970s a majority of Swedish economists had turned to foreign intellectual influences and had become highly critical of Swedish Keynesianism. In turn, the new neoliberal program soon rose to prominence within the Swedish economics profession (Blyth 2002, chap. 7; Pekkarinen 1989, 321). Second, the Swedish Employers Federation backed two conservative think tanks, the Center for Business and Policy Studies (SNS) and Timbro, which aggressively marketed the neoliberal program just as their counterparts were doing in the United States. Timbro in particular tried to influence the mainstream and financial press. These organizations were successful. Research suggests that as their campaign escalated, academic discourse shifted sharply in a neoliberal direction in important economics journals and official government reports. Their ability to shift discourse turned in part on the substantial financing made available to them by the Swedish Employers Federation—an organization whose financial resources dwarfed those of all the Swedish political parties combined and were more than twice as large as those of Sweden's major labor union (Blyth 2002, 210–19; Pestoff 1991, 77).

Both U.S. and Swedish decision makers set out to adopt very similar neoliberal tax reform programs in part because economists favored them and think tanks and other influential organizations successfully pushed them. Clearly, neoliberal programs carried weight because they were favored by influential, well-financed, interested organizational actors. But also important were the strategic actions of those actors who had to sell neoliberalism to the public and their fellow decision makers. Framing was important in this regard.

The Frames

Frames are normative ideas in the foreground of decision-making debates that elites use strategically to legitimate programs to the public and each other, and, therefore, to facilitate their adoption. One reason why the 1981 tax reform was passed in the United States is that it was deftly framed by conservative Republicans (Ackerman 1982, chap. 2). First, they combined the tax cut strategy with Jeffersonian images of a big, centralized, and expanding government whose consequences were devastating to the country and that could best be brought under control by limiting politicians' access to revenues. They argued, for example, that high taxes jeopardized individual freedom and public safety by encouraging tax evasion and threatened the traditional American family by reducing net family income, which forced wives into the labor market, threatened their husbands' manhood, and fueled higher divorce rates (e.g., Gilder 1981, chaps. 1–2). This frame was a bricolage combining cherished beliefs in family and freedom with suspicions of big government. The Reagan administration used similar frames to push the 1986 Tax Reform Act, arguing that this legislation would simultaneously be pro-family, pro-fairness, and pro-growth (Bennett and Asard 1995, 66).

Supply-siders also used historical examples to frame their arguments. Notably, Reagan and his advisors argued that their plan to cut business taxes was exactly what President Kennedy did in 1963 to combat recession. Democrats who advocated different approaches, including industrial policy, had great difficulty countering these frames. They were also often put on the defensive when conservatives attacked their frames. For instance, they had trouble rebutting the frequent conservative charge that industrial policy was really an incipient form of socialist state planning. Another important reason why the supply-siders won the framing battle was that they had substantially more financial resources with which to monitor public opinion to determine which frames might best resonate with the public (Allen 1994; Campbell 1998; Jamieson 1996, 397–89). In the end, observers agreed that an important reason why the supply side program carried the day was that its supporters were better at framing their arguments in ways that were appealing politically (Graham 1992, 158).

Framing was also important to passage of the 1991 tax reform in Sweden, and it brought to light two important points. First, the Swedish economic elite and conservative politicians defined the economic situation at the time as a "crisis" that had resulted from the breakdown of wage restraint, the need for a new approach to managing the country's economic problems, and exorbitant demands for welfare state services. Framing issues as constituting a crisis was also a strategy used by conservatives in other countries, such as Britain and the United States, who sought tax reductions and other neoliberal reforms (e.g., Campbell 1998; Hay 2001). Second, critics of the Swedish tax system charged that high tax rates had created a society of wranglers, cheaters, and tax evaders. They argued that even ordinary taxpayers were trying to avoid paying high taxes by working in the underground economy and engaging in a variety of other evasive activities. Hence, it was said that the tax system was creating new forms of injustice insofar as people were not paying their fair shares. Similarly, neoliberal critics of the Swedish welfare state charged that its generous provisions had created opportunities for abuse and waste. This frame was apparently so effective that when the Social Democratic Party returned to power in 1994 they trimmed several welfare programs. This was not a wholesale slashing of programs, but rather a more modest effort to remove some of the more egregious opportunities for abuse that had existed previously and that the conservatives had emphasized. As discussed later, it was also intended to help balance the budget (Steinmo 2002).

All of these framing strategies were couched within a much broader frame that conservatives had been crafting since the late 1970s, in which the traditional Swedish *solutions* for managing economic troubles (i.e., centralized wage bargaining, full employment policy, high taxes, large welfare state) were cast as *problems* causing inflation, labor unrest, and other difficulties. Since the 1930s, to win the support of business, the Social Democratic Party had framed their lavish redistributive programs as being desirable on efficiency grounds in the sense that full employment, broad-based wage bargaining, and a tax cap on profits would ensure the full utilization of human and other economic resources. Now, to attract the support of the public, the conservatives framed the market, not traditional social democratic programs, as the most efficient form of social organization and warned that the government must refrain from meddling with the economy if it wanted to avoid jeopardizing the economy's efficient operation and long-term health (Blyth 1999). Once again, the Swedish Employers Federation dedicated increasingly large amounts of money to ensure that this message got out in ways that would curry favor with the public and influence the political agenda (Pestoff 1991).

The Paradigm

Regardless of their strategic capabilities, decision makers are often constrained in how much change they can achieve. One constraint involves the institutionalized intellectual paradigms within which they operate. Paradigms are cognitive assumptions that typically reside in the background of debates about change and that constrain action by limiting the range of alternatives that decision makers are likely to perceive as useful and worth considering. Their effects are substantial because they define the terrain of programmatic debate (Block 1990; Schön and Rein 1994). Neoclassical economics was the dominant paradigm within the economics profession in both the United States and Sweden.

In the United States during the 1970s and 1980s the major economics departments (such as Harvard, Stanford, and the University of Chicago), the top economics journals like the *American Economic Review*, and virtually all the liberal and conservative think tanks subscribed to the paradigmatic principles of neoclassical economics. At its core, the neoclassical paradigm was premised on a belief in the sanctity of private property and free markets, and the notion that governments should leave market forces alone whenever possible. Among other things, this paradigm implied reducing taxes because it treated high taxes as a form of government intervention that undermined the initiative of corporations, workers, and thus market efficiency. It also implied that tax deductions, loopholes, and other tax incentives that might undermine the efficient allocation of capital and labor should be minimized. Finally, the neoclassical approach meant balancing government budgets (Heilbroner and Milberg 1995).

Although based on the neoclassical paradigm, Keynesianism was a program that allowed for considerable government intervention under certain circumstances, notably during recessions when governments were supposed to intervene forcefully to stimulate aggregate demand. But when Keynesianism fell into disrepute, it created a situation that was ripe for new programs emphasizing a more laissez-faire approach like neoliberal supply-side economics, which fit most closely with the prevailing theoretical pessimism of the economics profession and the core assumptions of the neoclassical paradigm. Indeed, the discrediting of Keynesianism had thrown the economics profession into disarray. Because economists lacked a well-articulated alternative to Keynesianism, they tended to fall back on their neoclassical principles (Heilbroner and Milberg 1995). Alternative programs that were discussed at the time did not resonate as well with the neoclassical paradigm and were disadvantaged in decision-making circles as a result. For instance, industrial policy was much farther from the core neoclassical principles than was the neoliberal approach, because it called for all sorts of government intervention and institution building.

The role of paradigms in tax reform was complex. Remember that Keynesianism's fall from grace turned in part on recognition that one of its most important underlying paradigmatic assumptions no longer held. Keynesianism was based on the taken-for-granted assumption of the Phillips curve that there was a trade-off between inflation and unemployment. When that paradigmatic assumption was discredited, so was the Keynesian program that rested upon it. So although the basic tenets of the neoclassical paradigm remained rock solid and, therefore, constrained the range of program options that decision makers took seriously after Keynesianism was discredited, a shift in one of the paradigmatic assumptions underlying Keynesianism triggered the quest for a program change in the first place.[17]

The story was similar in Sweden. The neoclassical paradigm dominated economic thinking even when the Social Democratic Party was in power. Although the Swedes had committed themselves to the creation of one of the world's largest and most generous welfare states, since the 1930s macroeconomic programs had rested on a neoclassical foundation insofar as the government believed in the sanctity of private ownership and markets. According to Peter Gourevitch (1986, 204), unlike its counterparts in some other European countries, the Swedish Social Democratic Party accepted the necessity of the market and, as a result, sought "to infuse a neoclassical framework with socialist values." Swedish programs did not involve direct state intervention in production, and state-owned enterprises did not play a significant role in the economy. Even the government's quest for full employment through elaborate Keynesian macroeconomic interventions, active labor market policies, and corporatist bargaining was guided by the paradigmatic belief that government could most effectively improve market performance and stimulate economic growth by encouraging private investment and the success of leading private corporations. To that end, state intervention was designed to remove obstacles to the free flow of labor and capital in the market place (Blyth 2002, 113–23; Pekkarinen 1989).

As in the United States, Swedish economists and decision makers fell back on core neoclassical principles as questions emerged about the validity of Keynesianism. Indeed, the power of these paradigmatic assumptions was great and perhaps best illustrated by Lindbeck's defection from the Social Democratic Party. He left in response to the party's call in 1975 for the creation of a program of wage-earner funds—a program through which unions would gradually buy stock, gain controlling interest in corporations, and, therefore, usher in the transition to collective employee ownership and power sharing with management. The wage-earner funds represented a sharp albeit temporary break from the neoclassical model and Lindbeck refused to accept such a break, as did many others.[18] More

---

[17] This underscores the point made briefly in chapter 4 (note 4) that paradigms, and for that matter public sentiments, vary in the degree to which their various elements are taken for granted or not. In this case, Keynesianism was a program that rested on a set of assumptions, including those associated with the Phillips curve, which, in turn, rested on an even deeper set of assumptions, the basic neoclassical paradigm.

[18] The experiment with wage-earner funds reflected a conflict within the Social Democratic Party over the degree to which it was committed to the neoclassical model. Certainly a move toward collective ownership by labor was intended as a step toward socialism. But even proponents of the plan recognized that firms would still function in the marketplace, meet their payroll obligations, and have to generate profits just like regular capitalist firms. In any case, as noted later, the party's flirtation with this alternative was short-lived.

important, however, was the effect that the return to neoclassical principles had for the broader public debate over new programs. According to Mark Blyth (2002, 215–16), Keynesianism's fall from grace and the shift in ideas among Swedish economists and opinion makers dramatically enhanced the ability of SNS and Timbro, the conservative think tanks, to push their neoliberal program. In turn, support increased sharply in both the liberal and conservative press for neoliberal ideas. And when conservative politicians called for cuts in tax rates, it resonated with the basic neoclassical view that had come forward in much professional and public discourse. Indeed, the economics profession was so unified around neoclassical principles by the late 1980s that it would have been very difficult for any government to pursue economic programs that deviated much from these basic ideas (Blyth 2002, 230). As a result, although talk about industrial policy and even nationalization occurred, it went nowhere because it did not resonate with the neoclassical view and because the Social Democratic Party had almost always agreed to keep industrial planning in the hands of private managers. The party even curtailed the wage-earner funds plan in 1982 after it cost them control of the government in 1976 (Gourevitch 1986, 203–4).

Before continuing, let me review briefly. A partial shift in paradigm, that is, suspicion about the Phillips curve's validity, helped precipitate a search for a new macroeconomic program in both countries. But once that search had begun, the institutionalized paradigm of neoclassical economics, which remained stable, constrained the range of options that decision makers were likely to consider seriously. In this regard, although other alternatives emerged, neoliberalism resonated most clearly with the neoclassical paradigm and, therefore, enjoyed an advantage over its competitors. The neoliberal program gained further advantage thanks to clever and effective framing by its backers. So far, then, the combined force of programs, frames, and paradigms were propelling and channeling both countries toward dramatic tax reform.

However, the move toward neoliberal tax cuts also involved another type of idea. Public sentiments constrained the degree to which globalization led to a race to the bottom in taxation.

Public Sentiments

Public sentiments consist of broad-based values, attitudes, and normative assumptions about what is appropriate. They are held by large segments of the population and are perceived by decision makers through public opinion polls and other forms of feedback from their constituents. Public sentiments are often well institutionalized, reside in the background of decision-making debates, and constrain the normative range of solutions that decision makers view as acceptable. This was both good and bad news for neoliberalism.

To begin with, another reason why neoliberalism received so much political support in the United States was that it resonated with public sentiments about the wasteful and corrupt ways of big government in general and high taxes and budget deficits in particular. As I mentioned earlier, Jeffersonian values eschewing big government and high taxes had long been held dear by many Americans. By the late 1970s, over 70 percent of Americans felt that their federal taxes were too high. A vast majority had also become increasingly concerned about budget deficits, and associated deficits with government profligacy, and favored a balanced budget. Alternative programmatic proposals from Democrats, such as industrial policy, often entailed expensive government intervention and, therefore, either higher taxes or budget deficits. As a result, these alternatives were hobbled politically because they were contrary to these prevailing public sentiments (Campbell 1998). The effect of public sentiments regarding big government, taxes, and deficits reached still further. The unprecedented depth of the 1981 tax cuts was exacerbated by a bidding war that broke out between Republicans and Democrats. Each side repeatedly sought to increase the size of the cuts to score political points with its constituents. Here politicians were pursuing their electoral interests by playing directly to public sentiments. In these ways, public sentiments added to the momentum for neoliberal reform.

Initial momentum for neoliberal tax cuts, however, soon began to stall. A year later Congress passed the 1982 Tax Equity and Fiscal Responsibility Act, which *reduced* many of the tax cuts from the 1981 legislation. This was done to counteract a skyrocketing budget deficit that the 1981 tax cuts helped trigger (Martin 1991, chap. 6). Neoliberalism called for both lower taxes and balanced budgets, but budget balancing was supposed to be achieved by matching tax cuts with cuts in government spending. Congress was unwilling to cut spending (particularly for Medicare, social security, and the military) enough to compensate for the 1981 tax cuts. This was because these very large and expensive programs had developed formidable constituents with enough clout to defend them (Pierson 1994; Roberts 1984). Despite the public's aversion to big government and some welfare programs, particularly for the poor, it had long valued both a strong military and the sort of middle-class social programs that Medicare and social security represented—social programs that people felt they were entitled to by virtue of having contributed to them from their wages during their working years (Skocpol 2000). In this way, public sentiments undermined the momentum for neoliberal reform.

Congress moved to cut taxes again through the 1986 act in order to stimulate investment, but it also reduced or eliminated a variety of tax expenditures, such as those regarding accelerated depreciation and investment tax credits. Reducing these loopholes was done for two reasons. First, it was supposed to make the tax code more neutral with respect to business investment by ridding it of incentives that would cause capital to flow to one industry or another for reasons having to do with government policy, not market signals. Second, decision makers closed loopholes to compensate for revenue lost through tax cuts and to avoid further budget deficits. By now they had become extremely sensitive to the deficit issue. Again, programs were being made in ways that were influenced by public sentiment. However, by closing loopholes the bill actually resulted in a $120 billion *increase* in corporate taxes paid to the federal government over the next five years. Again, this was not consistent with the intent of the neoliberal program (Martin 1991, chap. 7; Steinmo 1993, 165).

So, the role of public sentiments was especially complex. This was due to the fact that public sentiments are often inconsistent bundles of values, attitudes, and assumptions that do not always mix well when it comes to specific programs. On the one hand, the public valued low taxes, which facilitated neoliberal change and which balanced budgets. On the other hand, the public valued some of the government's most expensive programs, which made it hard for decision makers to cut them and, therefore, inhibited neoliberal change. In this case, then, different public sentiments conspired to create a difficult and contradictory situation for decision makers. Given their inability to cut spending more, tax reductions necessarily exacerbated budget deficits, but reducing deficits required tax increases. The politics involved were complex and have been reviewed elsewhere (Roberts 1984). But the important point is that decision makers were hemmed in during the 1980s by these different aspects of public sentiment. As a result, they vacillated between lower taxes to resolve stagflation and higher taxes to control budget deficits. In the end, the impetus to sustain deep neoliberal tax cuts was lost.

Public sentiments played a similar role in Sweden. When the Social Democratic Party returned to power in 1994 it encountered two problems. In the first place, it discovered that the 1991 reforms had shifted the tax burden from wealthy individuals and corporations to the middle and lower classes. In the second place, recession had hit in the early 1990s and so the conservative government had been forced to increase spending for unemployment and other social programs, which raised the budget deficit to 13 percent. This was especially serious because by then Sweden was poised to join the European Union in 1995 and was preparing for European monetary integration, which compelled member countries to hold deficits to 3 percent of GDP. As a result, the new Social Democratic government moved to control the deficit by trimming social programs, as noted earlier, and with a progressive tax increase. The progressive nature of the tax increase was designed to shift the tax burden back toward wealthy individuals and corporations. The social democrats had long used tax increases to balance budgets (Gourevitch 1986, 200). They raised the top marginal rate on very-high-income earners by 5 percent. Taxes on capital income were also increased.

This was quite consistent with prevailing public sentiment because most Swedes had long held progressively redistributive programs in high regard, including the progressive structure of the tax code. Furthermore, public opinion polls showed that while most Swedes believed that taxes were too high, very few were willing to support tax cuts if it meant whole-sale reductions in public spending. Public support for welfare spending had been strong for decades, even when bourgeois coalitions controlled the government, because Swedes believed deeply in and took for granted the value of a strong welfare state (Gourevitch 1986, 201). By the early 1990s at least two thirds of Swedes received some sort of direct public subsidy. In contrast to the United States, most Swedes believed that they got a lot for their taxes and so there was relatively less public pressure to cut taxes in the first place and very little opposition, other than from business, to raising them later (Steinmo 2002). Public sentiments limited how far neoliberal reforms could be pushed (Blyth 2002, 246).

In sum, governments in both countries cut taxes in response to global-ization and other pressures. They were able to do so thanks to the inter-play of programmatic ideas and frames, which operated generally as forces for change. Paradigms contributed to change too. Shifts in underly-ing Keynesian assumptions (the Phillips curve's demise) triggered a search for new programs, but the stability of even deeper neoclassical assump-tions constrained the range of options considered seriously during that search in ways that channeled change toward neoliberal tax cuts. How-ever, the ability of governments to make these cuts stick permanently was hampered by deep-seated public sentiments reflected in concerns with budget deficits, fiscal stability, hefty government programs, and, in the Swedish case, fairness and the progressivity of the tax code. In the United States, tax cuts in 1981, which were supported by the public, were re-versed when budget deficits, which were anathema to the public, emerged a year later. And for similar reasons the 1986 tax cuts were more than offset by a reduction in tax loopholes and deductions. In Sweden, tax cuts were also balanced in this way. And although the Swedish tax burden was high by international standards, these cuts were later partly reversed with little opposition from a public that grumbled about high taxes but ac-cepted them as a quid pro quo for deeply valued welfare state programs. As a result, in both countries government revenues remained fairly stable and little tax shifting occurred (see tables 5.1 and 5.2).

Of course, ideational factors were not the whole story. The regulative mechanisms previously discussed as well as complex political battles were at work in both countries and helped prevent a more substantial neoliberal overhaul of tax institutions. Groups with vested interests played key roles too. Similar stories unfolded in many other advanced capitalist countries. Decision makers almost everywhere faced political limits on the size of deficits and debt they could run up, the amount of welfare state retrenchment they could achieve, and, as a result, the degree of neoliberal tax reform they could realize (Schmidt 2001; Swank 1998, 608). In the end, decision makers in most countries chose to maintain a stable revenue base despite globalization pressures to cut taxes. This helped mitigate the race to the bottom that globalization theory predicts (Swank and Steinmo 2002).

DIFFUSION, TRANSLATION, AND PATH-DEPENDENCE MECHANISMS

So far I have shown that the regulative, normative, and cognitive institutions within which decision makers were embedded both enabled and constrained their capacities to reform tax institutions in response to globalization pressures. These reforms were limited. Indeed, the result was a path-dependent process where tax codes were changed a bit but still largely resembled those of the past.

I argued in chapter 3 that one important way in which path-dependent change occurs is through diffusion and translation. Translation is a process in which new ideas that arrive from elsewhere through diffusion are combined with, rather than replace, already existing local institutions. Translation was evident as nation-states moved to adopt the neoliberal program in response to the pressures of globalization during the late twentieth century. Many observers agree that the neoliberal program of tax reform, welfare reform, and deregulation diffused primarily from the United States to the rest of the world, often with strong assistance from international agencies like the International Monetary Fund, World Bank, and OECD as well as the U.S. economics profession (e.g., Bennett and Asard 1995, 16; Fligstein 2001a, 220–21; Helleiner 1996; Sassen 1996, 19; Palan and Abbott 1999, chap. 6; Wade and Veneroso 1998a, 1998b).

In the area of taxation, one example of translation is the blending of neoliberal tax cuts with other policies, notably efforts to broaden the tax base by closing tax loopholes, that were designed to preserve the revenue base upon which various long-standing social programs rested. Another example is the translation of the idea of the Earned Income Tax Credit (EITC) into practice in Europe. As developed in the United States, the EITC provides a cash transfer to working families with dependent children who fall below a certain income threshold. It works by reducing the income tax burdens of the working poor and near-poor. If the family's income is low enough, it can generate a tax refund (Howard 1997, 15). The idea has inspired policy initiatives in Europe designed to contain the rise of the working poor and encourage the creation of better low-wage service jobs. In countries like Belgium, France, the Netherlands, and Germany, the idea has been to reduce the social security taxes employers pay for their workers if employers create better low-wage jobs—sort of an EITC for employers insofar as the policy is designed to offset the disemployment effects of high payroll taxes associated with corporatist welfare regimes (Zeitlin 2003). The process of diffusion and translation, however, was even more evident in the area of economic deregulation.

Steven Vogel (1996) showed that the ideology of deregulation emerged first in the United States. This initiative produced a competitive dynamic whereby other countries feared that they would lose business to the more permissive U.S. market and so followed suit with regulatory reforms of their own. However, as discussed briefly in chapter 4, this culminated less in deregulation than *reregulation*, a process whereby neoliberal ideas were translated into local practice in nationally specific ways. Reforms were implemented by decision makers and bureaucrats who struggled over the specifics of reform and shaped them according to their institutionally defined interests. These interests were defined by their positions within the formal regulatory apparatus, their normative perceptions about the appropriate role of government in the economy, and their cognitive assumptions regarding the sorts of reform that could be considered seriously in the first place. According to Vogel (1996, 38), "U.S. experience provided a stimulus, but . . . domestic interest groups often interpreted the U.S. experience in a way to buttress their own cases." Translation of the neoliberal model into local institutional practice resulted in much diversity across countries in the character of regulatory reform.

The Japanese telecommunications industry is a good example. The Japanese had long believed in a strong managerial role for government in the economy and, as a result, political elites had developed formal institutional capacities, such as the powerful Ministry of International Trade and Industry (MITI), to restructure markets and guide industrial development (Samuels 1987). But in 1980, motivated in part by the example of U.S. deregulation during the 1970s, the legislature started to talk about liberalizing the use of telephone lines and in 1984 privatized the national telecommunications carrier, the Nippon Telegraph and Telephone Public Corporation (NTT). Neoliberal deregulation had arrived. However, the Ministry of Posts and Telecommunications used this as an opportunity to enhance its role as protector and promoter of the industry and thus to reassert the state's control over the industry albeit in a new form. Previously, the ministry enjoyed only limited supervisory control over NTT. But as privatization proceeded, the ministry played a key role, helping to craft legislation that afforded it extensive capacities to regulate prices and the introduction of new services—a maneuver that elevated it to a position of power and prominence among Japan's elite ministries, including the MITI. Reform ended up conforming more than anyone had expected to the institutional traditions (cognitive, normative, and regulative) of strong, centralized, state bureaucracies holding sway over industrial development and operation. Because regulatory reform in other countries in telecommunications, finance, and other industries was also combined with long-standing national institutional traditions, Vogel argued that there was not a convergence toward neoliberal deregulation or a regulatory race to the bottom, but rather the development of new styles of regulation, often with more, not fewer, rules, and with new regulatory capacities that varied substantially across countries (1996).

To be sure, privatization was a major change in property rights regarding *ownership* of the Japanese telecommunications infrastructure. It was an important move in the neoliberal direction. However, the ascendence of the ministry's control over pricing, the introduction of new services, and the like, involved changes in property rights regarding the *use* of that infrastructure that flew directly in the face of neoliberalism. It also represented institutional change that still conformed in important ways to the general principles of past Japanese practice. In this regard, according to Vogel, institutional change was translated into local practice in ways that constrained what would otherwise have been a much more revolutionary institutional change.

The process of translation also occurred in other areas of economic regulation. For instance, in Denmark pressures of international competition led decision makers to search for ways to incorporate neoliberal principles into traditional Danish institutions, where industrial policy had long been the norm and a product of elaborate negotiations between the state and private actors at the national level. These formal bargaining institutions were reinforced by the pervasive Danish belief that the only appropriate way to conduct policy-making was through inclusive, corporatist negotiations. Indeed, it was difficult for Danes to imagine doing things differently (Nielsen and Pedersen 1991; Pedersen 1993). Nonetheless, they were attracted to neoliberalism insofar as it emphasized the decentralization of political control over the economy. So rather than abandoning industrial policy and absolving the state of its responsibilities for industrial development, Danish leaders reorganized their institutions by establishing a more decentralized set of institutional links between the government, local authorities, business, labor, and other private organizations. The result was a new, decentralized, but still negotiated and corporatist form of decision making that encouraged firms to adopt new technologies and production practices (Kjaer and Pedersen 2001). Neoliberalism was translated into traditional Danish practices rather than replacing them. Similarly, the Danish state reformed labor market policy by decentralizing it, rather than abandoning it. Labor market policy became coordinated through negotiations between employers and state authorities at the regional rather than the national level (Swank and Martin 2001).

The phenomena of international diffusion and translation are widespread and help account for the persistence, rather than the disappearance, of unique, nationally specific institutional arrangements during the period of late-twentieth-century globalization. When organizations like the European Union and Mercosur, South America's open market project, issue directives that are intended specifically to harmonize the regulation of trade and other economic practices among states, national governments often translate them into their own law in unique ways, thereby leaving more heterogeneity than might otherwise be expected. Moreover, even when directives are translated into formal law as intended, their eventual implementation often varies across countries in ways that are consistent with local institutions (Duina 1999, 2003). Scholars have also noted that the same sort of institutionally mediated translation process occurs with the global diffusion of new models and ideas in institutional areas less directly linked to neoliberalism, such as citizenship (Soysal 1994) and human rights (Keck and Sikkink 1998).

It is worth mentioning briefly that translation also occurs in the private sector as firms engage in more global economic activity (Whitley 1997, 255). Certainly when firms move across borders they tend to operate in ways that are similar to how they operate at home because they have institutionalized certain ways of doing business that are buttressed by deep-seated cognitive and normative views of how to operate (Doremus et al. 1998). But they also adapt to some local practices. For example, when U.S. and Japanese automobile manufacturing firms set up subsidiaries in Mexico, they imported many aspects of their human resource management systems, such as employee training practices, which continued to mirror practices back home in the headquarters country. Labor relations in both subsidiaries, however, bore a distinct Mexican imprint. Notably, labor relations are typically more flexible in Mexico than in the United States, but less so than in Japan. Both firms had to adjust for this and conform to some local labor practices (Hibino 1997). Presumably, they made similar concessions to local practices at subsidiary sites elsewhere around the world. This certainly contradicts the argument that economic institutions are inexorably converging on the neoliberal or any other model (see also Davis and Marquis 2001; Hall and Soskice 2001a; Whitley and Kristensen 1997).

I am not arguing that the evidence offered here on regulatory reform is definitive. But it does raise further questions about the adequacy of the globalization thesis by showing how bits and pieces of the neoliberal model are often translated into local contexts in ways that result in a bricolage of the new and the old—a process of path-dependent change best understood from the perspective of institutional analysis.

Let me bring into sharper focus all of my arguments about institutional mechanisms and their effects on globalization and neoliberal reform. First, across the OECD countries the regulative mechanisms associated with the organization of labor, capital, and their integration into national decision making constrained the sort of race to the bottom in taxation that globalization theory predicts. The same is true for the regulative mechanisms associated with different types of electoral institutions. Scholars have made similar arguments about neoliberal welfare reform. Second, in at least two very different countries, the United States and Sweden, the normative and cognitive mechanisms associated with different types of ideas facilitated an initial impetus toward neoliberal tax reform, but in significant ways eventually helped constrain the degree to which this program was sustained on a more permanent basis. Third, there is at least anecdotal evidence to suggest that globalization has not precipitated the sort of wholesale institutional change in other areas, notably economic deregulation, that globalization theory anticipates. The reason is that when decision makers adopt neoliberal programs they still have to translate them into practice in ways that are consistent with local institutional legacies. Thus, it appears that the predictions of globalization theory have substantially missed the mark; the more radical institutional changes it forecast have turned out to be much more modest and evolutionary. I have explained why this is so by utilizing institutional analysis in the ways elaborated earlier in this book.[19]

TIME FRAMES REDUX: WHAT IF WE WAIT A LITTLE LONGER?

At the beginning of this chapter I argued that selecting the appropriate time frame was important for determining whether the globalization thesis is correct. I showed that by extending our time frame back to the beginning of the twentieth century, we could gain important insights

---

[19] I am not arguing that the factors identified above are the only reasons why globalization has failed to result in more convergence on the neoliberal model. For further discussion of some of the additional factors involved, see, for example, Campbell (2003), Hollingsworth and Streeck (1994), Mann (2001), Mittelman (2000), Palan and Abbott (1999), and Whitley and Kristensen (1997).

about globalization that threw the globalization thesis into question. Am I not vulnerable to the same sort of criticism? That is, might not skeptics of my arguments ask, what if we wait a little longer? After all, according to globalization theory it has only been about thirty years since the forces of globalization have been unleashed. If countries are punished for resisting neoliberalism through higher interest rates, more capital flight, reduced economic growth, and higher levels of unemployment, as globalization theory suggests, then perhaps they will eventually succumb. We may yet see neoliberal convergence and a race to the bottom. Again, there are good reasons to doubt that this will happen.

First, there is only scant evidence to support the claim by globalization theorists that countries are punished for not towing the neoliberal line. It is true that budget deficits in most OECD countries increased somewhat during the early 1990s, and where they did, countries tended to incur slightly higher real long-term interest rates, as globalization theorists predict (Garrett 1998a, chap 6). However, several facts should trouble globalization theorists. To begin with, higher levels of spending, taxation, or budget deficits did not cause capital to flee to other countries (Garrett 1998b). Moreover, higher levels of taxation and spending, typical for social democratic and Christian democratic governments, did not undermine economic growth (Hicks and Kenworthy 1998). Furthermore, the literature is not at all clear that social democratic and Christian democratic governments were more prone to unemployment than neoliberal ones (Hicks and Kenworthy 1998), although it does appear that disinvestment caused unemployment to increase (Western and Beckett 1999; Western 2001). Again, the evidence is far from overwhelming in its support for the globalization thesis. At most, governments may have been punished by the financial markets through higher interest rates for running budget deficits, but higher interest rates did not seem to deter governments from running deficits. Indeed, in the aggregate, governments seemed to be quite willing to incur slightly higher interest rates if the deficits that caused them helped these governments remain in power and maintain political stability (Garrett 1998a, 1998b).

Second, for institutional reasons, the behavior of firms and investors is not necessarily defined solely, or even primarily, by an interest in seeking geographical locations with the lowest production costs, including the lowest costs of taxation and social wages (Doremus et al. 1998). Indeed, since 1970 the vast majority of FDI flowed among the OECD countries rather than from the OECD to developing countries, which have much lower labor costs. Moreover, research suggests that the main factor affecting FDI outflows was the unionization and strike levels of labor, not wages. That is, FDI was a labor control strategy, not a cost reduction strategy (Alderson 2002). Of course, some firms do compete by minimizing costs, but others compete by being fast innovators, producing high-quality goods, and pursuing other factors that depend less on cost reduction than other factors. The ability to innovate and compete on the basis of quality rather than price and cost is affected by the institutional environment in which firms and investors operate.

For instance, the liberal market economies, such as the Anglo-Saxon countries, are good for firms that want to compete by keeping costs low and moving capital quickly from sector to sector and region to region. This is because they have an institutional infrastructure that includes weak unions and business associations, deregulated labor markets, and firm-level industrial bargaining between labor and management. Their institutions also encourage short-term corporate investment and profit horizons and have strong competition requirements that limit possible cooperation among firms. They also have educational systems that emphasize general rather than vocational training. In contrast, coordinated market economies, such as Germany and the Northern European countries, are good for firms that want to compete on the basis of high quality or the capacity for flexible specialization. The reason is that these economies have institutions that support strong labor unions and business associations as well as cooperative industrial relations between unions and managers both within and across firms. Their institutions encourage long-term corporate investment and profit horizons and interfirm cooperation in areas like research and development. They also have extensive vocational training systems (Hall 1998; Soskice 1999). Furthermore, in comparison to liberal market economies, states in coordinated market economies tend to pursue developmental and distributive goals more vigorously and directly, such as by providing financial support to firms or sectors for economic development projects, active labor market policies, and hefty welfare state programs to maintain a comparatively high social wage (Albert 1993; Best 1990; Hicks and Kenworthy 1998; Weiss 1998).

In other words, firms compete on the basis of comparative *institutional* advantage as well as comparative *cost* advantage (Hall and Soskice 2001b). Firms, investors, and states often understand this strategy in advanced capitalist countries (Hall 1998; Hollingsworth and Streeck 1994; Soskice 1999). They also understand it in developing countries (Guillén 2001a, 13). Certainly in the area of technology development, perhaps one of the most important insofar as global competition is concerned, differences in national institutional arrangements offer policymakers and businesses comparative advantages upon which they can capitalize if they recognize them (e.g., Ziegler 1997). Understanding their comparative institutional advantage is why large German employers continue to support corporatist wage bargaining—a way of keeping wage conflict out of cooperative shop-floor relations, which they believe is crucial for maintaining the flexibility in production that is necessary to compete internationally (Thelen 2000c). And, as noted earlier, in many advanced capitalist countries employers associations defend social spending programs because they see these programs contributing to human capital development, cultivating trust with workers and the general public, and facilitating a well-functioning economy in other ways (Swank and Martin 2001). The recognition of nationally specific comparative institutional advantage is another important reason why there is not likely to be more convergence toward neoliberalism. It is also why the threat of capital flight itself may be less pronounced than globalization theory assumes. That is, firms may not be as eager to flee to low-cost areas if they realize that they already enjoy comparative institutional advantages where they are currently located (Garrett 1998b). If so, then globalization theory's assumption about the essential mechanism driving the race to the bottom is wrong and there is no reason to expect convergence in the future, no matter how long we wait.

CONCLUSION

One final question remains. If the evidence contradicting the globalization thesis is so substantial, why does it continue to attract so much attention and be taken for granted by so many as the truth? This is a complicated question but a few thoughts are in order. The idea of globalization has been used by conservatives to create an ideological climate that suggests that government intervention is futile and could hurt national economic competitiveness (Block 1996; Bourdieu 1998; Gilpin 2000, 313; Piven 1995). Some leftists have also accepted the globalization thesis and used it to legitimize various socialist projects (Gordon 1988). In other words, arguments about globalization afford policymakers as well as business leaders some justification for making decisions that may be unpopular with the general public. Indeed, in 1993 the Clinton administration in the United States invoked the pressures of globalization to legitimize painful spending cuts that it claimed were necessary to reduce federal budget deficits (Krugman 1994). Of course, the globalization thesis also provides scholars with trendy subject matter for their articles and books!

The point is that the globalization thesis is politically and perhaps intellectually expedient. Not only does it constitute a cognitive paradigm that constrains how people view the world, but it also can be used as a frame for legitimizing a variety of activities and interests. Until we think more carefully from an institutional perspective about the relationships between international economic activity and national-level institutions, the power of the globalization thesis will remain unchecked. My intent is that the arguments developed throughout this book will fortify institutional analysis and increase its power not only to understand globalization better but also many other important phenomena in the world.

Chapter 6

WHERE DO WE GO FROM HERE?

I HAVE MADE several arguments in this book. First, I have shown that to recognize institutional change more accurately for what it is, rather than mistaking revolutionary for more evolutionary shifts, or vice versa, we need carefully to consider two things: the important dimensions of an institution that we track over time and the time frame itself. Second, I have explained that we need to specify more carefully the mechanisms underlying the causal concepts, such as path dependence and diffusion, which we use to account for institutional change. And I have argued that the mechanisms of bricolage and translation are particularly helpful in this regard. Third, I have discussed how different types of cognitive and normative ideas facilitate and constrain institutional change in important ways that are often neglected in studies that focus only on the impact of regulative institutions and the pursuit of self-interests. Finally, I have suggested that all of these issues have been serious problems for institutionalists, regardless of their specific approaches to institutional analysis, and that by strengthening institutional analysis in the ways suggested in this book we can better understand important social phenomena in the world around us. To illustrate the point, I applied the conceptual, methodological, and theoretical insights developed in chapters 2, 3, and 4 to the phenomenon of globalization. Contrary to much conventional wisdom, I established that the extent of globalization has been misunderstood, the causal mechanisms by which globalization is said to influence national institutions have been oversimplified, the effects of globalization have been exaggerated, and the national-level institutional changes that have been attributed to globalization have been far more evolutionary than revolutionary.

As I stipulated at the beginning of this book, my hunch is that institutional change tends to be more evolutionary than we often realize. Yet whether it is, or not, in a particular case is ultimately a question that can be answered only on empirical grounds. By developing institutional analysis along the lines suggested in this book, we can do a better job of identifying and explaining institutional change when it happens. We can also begin to resolve some of the analytic problems that rational choice, organizational, and historical institutionalists share. In turn, we may also be able to craft better theories of institutional change and perhaps a more unified paradigm of institutional analysis. So where do we go from here?

This chapter addresses that question. I begin by offering a theory of institutional change that integrates several insights from previous chapters and provides the basis for further theorizing and for empirical work in the future. Second, I explain that this theory also demonstrates the importance and payoffs of drawing upon the lessons of all three of the institutionalist paradigms with which this book is concerned. As a result, it also contributes to the second movement in institutional analysis, mentioned briefly in chapter 1. Recall that the second movement in institutional analysis is an emergent intellectual trend whose proponents seek to move beyond the traditional acrimonious debates in which rational choice, organizational, and historical institutionalists attacked each other's work. Instead, the second movement seeks to establish a more constructive dialogue among these paradigms that may result in building bridges and reconciling some of the intellectual disagreements among them (Campbell and Pedersen 2001b). Finally, I discuss the implications and opportunities of all these insights for future research.

Toward a Theory of Institutional Change

I noted in chapter 1 that institutional analysis has been criticized for having an inadequate understanding of institutional change. I think that we are now in a position to improve the situation if we take the lessons of previous chapters seriously. What follows is an effort to articulate a rudimentary theory of institutional change. It consists of a set of theoretical propositions based directly on the literatures and arguments discussed in preceding chapters.[1] These propositions are first approximations in that they are likely to be modified by further research. They are certainly not the last word on the subject, but should help us better focus our thinking and research in the future. Moreover, these propositions should provide the basis for the development of more precise hypotheses that can be tailored to research on specific instances of institutional change. In this sense, I hope that they will stimulate more theorizing and empirical research by providing a theoretical tool kit from which scholars can draw as they study institutions. Together they constitute a middle-range theory—one that is sensitive to the fact that historically specific institutional contexts constrain institutional change (e.g., Merton 1967).

The theory can best be described as one of *constrained innovation*. It provides, on the one hand, an account of creative institutional innovation, particularly by institutional entrepreneurs, and, on the other hand,

---

[1] Because the discussion that follows is based on arguments presented previously in considerable detail, I will be brief and will dispense with most citations to the relevant literature.

an account of structural constraints, which include the institutional processes, cultural frames, and cognitive beliefs that tend to limit the range of options available to these entrepreneurs. As a result, the theory offers insights about micro- and macro-level effects and how both agency and structure influence institutional change. More specifically, it explains how objective conditions give rise to problems that trigger episodes of institutional change; how institutional entrepreneurs and others play key roles in defining and framing these problems as well as proposing remedies for them; how the actions of entrepreneurs are constrained by the institutional and other contexts within which they operate; and how all of these phenomena affect the probabilities that institutional change will result.

Remember from chapter 1 that institutions are sets of formal and informal rules, monitoring and enforcement mechanisms, and systems of meaning that define the context within which people and organizations interact. They result in durable practices that are legitimated by widely held beliefs. Moreover, remember that institutional change is defined as the extent of variation that occurs, or not, over a given period of time in the important dimensions that constitute an institution. As discussed in chapter 2, these are critical issues that researchers must consider carefully if they want to determine how much change has actually occurred in any given episode of change. Revolutionary change involves simultaneous change across most, if not all, dimensions of an institution over a given period of time; evolutionary change consists of change in only a few of these dimensions; and stability consists of the absence of change in most, if not all, of these dimensions. So, for any episode of change, change may be located on a continuum, which ranges from stability on one end, through increasing degrees of evolutionary change in the middle, and through increasing degrees of revolutionary change on the other end.

But what causes institutional change? To begin with, institutional change can be triggered by either exogenous or endogenous factors. Exogenous factors typically receive most of the attention among institutionalists. They include war, economic catastrophe, and other calamities as well as abrupt shifts in prices and transaction costs, changes in state policy, dramatic technological innovations, and the like. They are generally alluded to by those of us who favor punctuated equilibrium or punctuated evolutionary models of change. However, if we accept the notion, suggested in chapter 2, that institutions are multidimensional entities that are composed of different institutional logics guiding action, then we should expect that there may be much inconsistency among these dimensions and logics. That is, institutions may create potentially contradictory incentives and opportunities for action. Such inconsistency may generate enough tension, friction, and other problems to cause actors to seek new institutional arrangements. In other words, constellations of institutions may themselves generate endogenous pressures for change (Friedland and Alford 1991; Lieberman 2002; Schneiberg 1999). Indeed, some have argued that for this reason institutions are far less stable than we tend to assume (e.g., Orren and Skowronek 1994). To wit,

> **Proposition 1**: *Institutional change can be triggered by problems that are either exogenous or endogenous to the institution in question.*

Of course, arguing simply that problems (sometimes we call them crises) cause change is not very useful. First, it implies a mindless knee-jerk reaction, which assumes that actors know a problem when they see one and then respond automatically to it by altering their institutions. The process involved is far more complex than this, as I will soon elaborate. Indeed, the process is so complex that there are no guarantees that problems will always precipitate institutional change. Actors may fail to recognize problems as such for a long time. They may also disagree about how serious a problem is, how to solve it, or whether anything can or should be done about it in the first place. In this sense, problems are socially constructed. Furthermore, struggles to change institutions may result in stalemates, inertia may set in, and problems may fester for a long time without much being done to resolve them.[2] And, of course, actors may try to address problems without resorting to institutional change per se. To wit,

> **Proposition 2**: *Problems are necessary, but not sufficient, conditions for institutional change.*

Second, to argue simply that problems cause change begs an important question: How, as analysts, do we recognize such problems a priori? Can we determine in advance when problems are likely to reach a point at which actors begin to suspect that they need to make institutional adjustments to cope with them?

I propose that such problems manifest themselves when exogenous or endogenous factors create situations that actors perceive as a threat to the fundamental distribution of resources or power that they need to pursue whatever self-interested, altruistic, or other goals they may have. For instance, during the 1970s and 1980s, the advent of new production technologies among European steel manufacturers threatened the domestic market share for U.S. steel producers, who then successfully urged Con-

---

[2] There is a substantial literature that explores why actors do not recognize problems when they emerge and why, even if they recognize them, they fail to take action to resolve them. For example, see Crenson (1971), Gaventa (1980), and Lukes (1974).

gress to pass protectionist trade legislation (Scherrer 1991). Engagement in the First World War caused the U.S. War Department to experience supply shortages, which led to the creation of temporary corporatist-style planning boards that were designed to improve industrial governance and increase production for the war effort (Cuff 1973). And, as discussed in chapter 4, the U.S. Atomic Energy Commission's contradictory institutional mandate to promote and regulate the development of commercial nuclear power triggered conflict between government bureaucrats and scientists over each other's jurisdiction regarding nuclear reactor safety policy—a conflict that sparked a legitimation crisis for the agency and an overhaul of regulatory institutions. In each case, situations developed that actors believed threatened their access to resources or power (markets, customers, profits; military supplies; regulatory authority) and then precipitated institutional change (new rules regarding international trade; industrial governance; regulatory policy). If institutions are settlements over the distribution of resources or power that are reached through struggle and bargaining, as I suggested in the opening paragraph of this book, then anything that threatens to upset this distribution is a problem that could trigger new struggles and bargains and eventually institutional change. To wit,

> **Proposition 3:** *Problems trigger a struggle over institutional change when actors perceive that these problems jeopardize the current distribution of resources or power.*

Furthermore, if actors perceive that a situation has emerged that provides them with an opportunity to change institutions in ways that will increase their resources or power, then they will likely seek change in these institutions. For example, as noted in chapter 2, after international attention began to focus intensely on civil rights abuses in the United States during the 1950s, U.S. civil rights activists perceived that their opportunities for achieving institutional change had increased. In turn, the movement's activities escalated and activists pressed harder for constitutional changes, notably voting rights legislation, that would have increased the political power of African Americans. Conversely, if actors perceive that a situation has emerged that threatens to reduce their resources or power, then they will likely resist change to the institutions that provide these things, as many Southern politicians did in response to the civil rights movement's constitutional initiatives. To wit,

> **Proposition 4:** *Actors are more likely to pursue / resist change in the institutions affecting the distribution of resources or power if they perceive that it will increase / decrease their resources or power.*

One caveat is in order regarding the last proposition. To preserve the institutional status quo in one place, and thus the current distribution of resources or power, actors may seek to change institutions in another place. For instance, to curb the civil rights movement's quest for equal voting rights, local politicians often changed ancillary institutions to check the movement's advance. In particular, they resorted to increasingly oppressive law enforcement policies for dealing with demonstrators, and turned an increasingly blind eye to vigilante groups, like the Ku Klux Klan, who terrorized civil rights organizers. In both cases, defensive institutional reforms were designed in one place (local law enforcement policy) to maintain the institutional status quo in another place (the U.S. Constitution). Similarly, when the threat of hostile corporate takeovers became prevalent in the United States during the 1980s, firms often adopted defensive institutional reforms, such as staggered terms for directors, golden parachutes for executives, super-majority rules for boards, poison pill strategies, and the like (Useem 1996, 28). These changes in corporate rules did not directly affect the distribution of resources or power between corporate raiders and their targets—that is, raiders could still launch a hostile takeover bid if they wanted—but modifications in ancillary corporate institutions made such a move less appealing.

I have suggested repeatedly that the perceptions of actors are important. But how do actors develop their perceptions about problems and solutions that involve institutional change in the first place? We still need to know much more about how these perceptions are formulated, but we have made some headway. For example, following the arguments in chapters 3 and 4, ideas and the actors associated with them are central to this process. Of particular importance are institutional entrepreneurs and others who frame situations as problems. After all, one thing that institutional entrepreneurs do is deliberately articulate a vision of the problem in ways that can be understood by the relevant decision makers and constituents. This means that they must frame and communicate the situation in clear and simple enough terms for these groups to understand.[3] Of course, what constitutes "clear and simple" depends on the prevailing normative and cognitive beliefs that are already in place. Things will more likely appear to be clear and simple if institutional entrepreneurs frame them in ways that resonate with these prevailing beliefs. To wit,

Proposition 5: *Problems are more likely to be perceived as requiring institutional changes if there are institutional entrepreneurs*

---

[3] Institutional entrepreneurs are not always elites, such as high-level political or corporate advisors. They may also be people less centrally located to decision-making processes, such as labor leaders, social movement activists, academics, and the like, who try to change institutions.

on hand who can articulate and frame them as such in clear and simple terms.

Recognition of a problem by itself, however, is not enough for decision makers to initiate change. For that to happen entrepreneurs must formulate alternative institutional programs and convince decision makers to adopt them. But where do these alternatives come from? How do entrepreneurs generate ideas about new institutional arrangements in the first place? Here we return to the arguments in chapter 3 about path dependence, bricolage, diffusion, and translation. Institutional innovations usually consist of a creative recombination—a bricolage—of institutional principles and practices that entrepreneurs have inherited from the past and that are available as part of their repertoire. Entrepreneurs with more diverse social, organizational, and institutional connections tend to have more expansive repertoires with which to work and tend to be exposed to more ideas about how to recombine elements creatively in their repertoires. As a result, they are more likely to propose relatively more revolutionary than evolutionary institutional changes. Similarly, entrepreneurs who are positioned socially, organizationally, and institutionally in ways that expose them to the diffusion of *new* ideas, which then become part of their repertoire, are more likely to create relatively more revolutionary than evolutionary ideas for change. Particularly as new ideas are incorporated into the mix, change tends to be less path dependent. To wit,

> **Proposition 6**: *Institutional change is likely to be relatively more revolutionary than evolutionary to the extent that entrepreneurs are located at the interstices of several social networks, organizations, and institutions, especially if their location exposes them to new ideas.*

It is important to remember that entrepreneurs do not enjoy complete autonomy. They cannot do entirely as they please. No matter how brilliant they may be, or how wonderful their ideas for change might appear, their efforts will have little impact unless they mobilize supporters and garner the financial, political, organizational, or other resources that are necessary to gain access to key decision-making arenas and convince decision makers to adopt their innovations.[4] Access to these resources is especially critical when, as is often the case, the process of institutional change involves several entrepreneurs jockeying for position and competing to

---

[4] Of course, existing institutions themselves affect the likelihood that various entrepreneurs can gain access to these decision makers. For instance, porous political institutions afford access to a wider range of entrepreneurs than more insulated institutions. For a fascinating discussion of how different types of political institutions affect both the likelihood and substance of institutional change, see Sheingate (forthcoming).

win the favor of these decision makers. For instance, as detailed in chapter 5, this was one reason why neoliberal proposals for change, which were backed by well funded think tanks, more readily captured the imagination of Swedish decision makers for a time than proposals from less well funded groups when Sweden grappled with the problem of stagflation in the 1980s and early 1990s. Indeed, institutional change is a process of struggle and bargaining to which resources are central. To wit,

> **Proposition 7:** *One program for institutional innovation is more likely to precipitate institutional change than another if the entrepreneurs who advocate it command more resources with which to sway key decision makers than their competitors.*

Once entrepreneurs have formulated an alternative institutional program and gained access to decision makers, they need to convince them that their program will provide an effective solution to the problem at hand as they have defined it. Their ability to do so depends on several things. First, as discussed in chapter 4, they must establish the credibility of their program. Credibility depends in part on whether there is available evidence that the proposed innovation will resolve the problem. Why? Because, as organizational institutionalists are fond of arguing, unless decision makers are forced to adopt certain institutional practices, they tend to copy things that seem to have worked for others in similar predicaments (e.g., Strang and Macy 2001). To wit,

> **Proposition 8:** *One program for institutional innovation is more likely to precipitate institutional change than another if entrepreneurs present evidence to decision makers indicating that it has worked effectively elsewhere.*

Second, entrepreneurs must convince decision makers that the innovations they propose resonate favorably with the local institutional context. The better they do this, the more likely it is that decision makers will adopt their programs and sustain them over time. Generally speaking, these programs must appear to fit reasonably well with the given regulative environment by, for example, not threatening to raise legal questions and, therefore, the ire of local authorities. Entrepreneurs must also convince decision makers that their programs fit the decision makers' dominant cognitive paradigm. If decision makers cannot be convinced of this, then they will likely be suspicious of the program or have difficulty understanding it because it is not familiar to them. Finally, entrepreneurs must convince decision makers that the new program is legitimate in the sense that it resonates with the prevailing normative sentiments and sensibilities of decision makers themselves as well as their constituents (e.g., voters, customers, stockholders, etc.) and their peers, to whom decision makers look for acceptance and support. Otherwise concerns may arise that the innovation will trigger opposition regarding its appropriateness. If this happens, then it will be difficult to sustain the institutional innovation. In sum, decision makers must be convinced that the proposed innovations can be translated into practice with relative ease. Making this case to decision makers requires institutional entrepreneurs to frame their proposals for change in convincing terms. To wit,

> **Proposition 9:** *Institutional change is more likely to be initiated by decision makers if entrepreneurs can present programs for innovation that appear to translate well into the prevailing regulative environment, the cognitive paradigm of decision makers, and the normative sentiments of decision makers, their constituents, and their peers.*

Once decision makers have been convinced to adopt an innovation, they need actually to translate it into the local institutional context. Decision makers and others work hard to translate innovations into practice. Some innovations translate more easily than others. This is because existing institutional arrangements provide greater incentives and opportunities for some innovations than for others. The need to translate and fit innovations into the local context is one of the most important ways in which currently existing institutional arrangements mediate the process of institutional change. It stands to reason that those innovations that fit best are not only more likely to be adopted in the first place, but are also more likely to last than those that do not fit as well. After all, those that do not fit well are more likely to trigger resistance, opposition, and other difficulties after they have been implemented. These difficulties may then lead to modifications later where actors try to bring their initial innovations into closer conformity with the existing institutional context. For instance, in postcommunist Poland during the early 1990s quite radical changes in policies regarding social expenditures, enterprise subsidies, and privatization sparked so much opposition and protest that the new government dramatically scaled back and modified these reforms (Campbell 2001). In the extreme, innovations may be abandoned entirely if the fit is particularly poor. To wit,

> **Proposition 10:** *Innovations that best fit the prevailing institutional context will be more likely to persist over time once they are implemented than those that do not fit as well.*

It also stands to reason that the more actors try to fit their innovations to the existing institutional context, the less likely these innovations are to be relatively revolutionary. This is because better fit implies greater compatibility and less change in the status quo. Thus, because sustained implementation often depends on how well actors translate and fit innovations into existing institutional practice, institutional change tends to be relatively more evolutionary than revolutionary. As a result, change also tends to be more path dependent insofar as new institutional arrangements continue to resemble those of the immediate past. To wit,

Proposition 11: *Innovations that best fit the prevailing institutional context will be more likely to result in evolutionary rather than revolutionary change than those that do not fit as well.*

Finally, I suggested briefly in chapter 3 that even when decision makers agree to try an innovation, they are more likely to implement it substantively, rather than in just a symbolic or half-hearted way, if they are sympathetic and ideologically committed to the innovation and if they have the financial, administrative, and other implementation capacities necessary to support it. Again, resources are important. These practical considerations are real, and decision makers often take them seriously. It follows, then, that even if they are enamored with a relatively more revolutionary innovation, they will pursue a less revolutionary one if they do not believe that they have the capacities to implement and sustain the more radical one. To wit,

Proposition 12: *Institutional change is likely to be relatively more revolutionary than evolutionary not only if decision makers take the idea seriously, but also if they believe that they have the necessary resources to implement and sustain it effectively.*

Let me make several clarifications. First, the process of institutional change is often not as neat, clean, and linear as the sequencing I have used to present these twelve propositions. Although actors may try to be logical, systematic, and strategic, sometimes things happen in more chaotic and unpredictable ways (e.g., Cohen et al. 1972; Kingdon 1995). For instance, problems may be redefined after actors begin to craft institutional solutions for them. Hence, institutional change is a process that can be full of stops, starts, reversals, and redirections.

Second, none of what I have argued here implies a functionalist theory of institutional change. Just because an innovation is adopted and implemented on a sustained basis does not necessarily mean that it is successful (i.e., functional) in resolving the problem that triggered it. Why? Beside the possibility that people simply make mistakes, change involves much struggle, bargaining, and compromise. People also try to respond to problems in ways that they deem to be culturally appropriate. All of this means that the changes that people actually make may not be entirely effective for solving the problem at hand. And even though their innovations may be suboptimal in this regard, they may still be relatively permanent and locked in due to the support they have from various quarters, including those who managed to dominate the innovation process.

Third, the theory I am proposing probably sheds the most light on the process by which planned institutional innovation and change occurs, particularly insofar as it emphasizes the role of institutional entrepreneurs. Not all instances of institutional innovation are entirely planned, deliberate, and intentional. For example, judge-made law is often said to evolve in ways that result eventually in important shifts in legal institutions through the unintended cumulative effects of many small judicial decisions, but without much planning or deliberate design (Rutherford 1994, chap. 5). In other words, while actors may be purposive in their actions, the institutional changes that follow from these actions are not always entirely intended.

Fourth, my emphasis on actors, especially institutional entrepreneurs, in this theory does not imply that we should rely exclusively on rational choice theory to inform our understanding of institutional change. For instance, although rational choice institutionalism may help us understand how actors strategically pursue their interests within certain constraints, other paradigms have much to offer in helping us understand how actors perceive and interpret their interests and constraints in the first place. As I will elaborate momentarily, an understanding of institutional change, as I have outlined it, requires insights from all three institutionalist paradigms. I have paid close attention to actors simply because it helps to infuse our thinking about institutional change with a sense of agency. Even scholars who are favorably disposed to institutional analysis have argued that institutionalists from all three paradigms—rational choice, organizational, and historical—tend to invoke excessively structural explanations (Hirsch 1997; Lieberman 2002). The propositions I have outlined acknowledge the importance and interplay of both structure and agency. As such they blend a theory of constraint with a theory of action. On the one hand, institutional structure generates the tensions, frictions, and problems that endogenously spark attempts at change. It also affects the likelihood that institutional entrepreneurs will gain access to resources, innovative ideas, and decision makers. After all, access of this kind is determined largely by the location of entrepreneurs within a constellation of social networks, organizations, and institutions. Finally, structure matters insofar as existing regulative, cognitive, and normative institutions make up the context into which innovations must be translated and fit. On the other hand, entrepreneurs enjoy a modicum of agency, autonomy, and choice as they concoct innovations through bricolage, frame their innovations in ways that affect the likelihood of adoption, and work to translate and fit them into practice. These are all creative albeit constrained processes. Moreover, they all involve considerable struggle and bargaining. In sum, structure constrains the range of *possibilities* for institutional change that are generally available to creative actors and from which these actors may choose. Structure does not completely determine choices and outcomes, but it influences the *probabilities* that one innovation will be created, selected, implemented, and sustained rather than another. Of course, occasionally, very creative, well-positioned, and even lucky actors may defy the probabilities and beat the odds. But this is rare. In general, then, as I mentioned earlier, this is a process of constrained innovation.

The Second Movement in Institutional Analysis

The theoretical approach that I have outlined provides a more integrated view of the process of institutional change than any of the three institutionalist paradigms does alone. In this regard, it advances the second movement in institutional analysis—a movement that seeks to build bridges and reconcile some of the intellectual differences among these paradigms (Campbell and Pedersen 2001b). Let me explain.

First, the theory builds on some of the most important insights offered by rational choice institutionalists regarding institutional change. It accepts that exogenous shocks, which might include things like changes in prices (North 1990), transaction costs (Williamson 1985), threats of war (Levi 1997), and the like, may provide the initial spark for institutional change. It also recognizes that institutional change is driven by actors that are strategic and goal oriented (North 1990, 1998); that their goals are not necessarily restricted to self-interested ones, but may also include altruism, the pursuit of the collective good, or anything else that they believe to be appropriate (Elster 1989, pp. 23–24); that their pursuit of these goals is institutionally constrained (Ingram and Clay 2000); and that the outcome of any episode of institutional change depends on conflict, struggle, and bargaining as configured by the distribution of resources among the actors involved (Knight 2001, 1992). Indeed, rational choice theory's major contribution here may be the light it can shed on the processes of strategic bargaining and negotiation that are often central to institutional change. The theory I have proposed, however, modifies and expands upon these insights. For instance, it suggests that the problems that precipitate institutional change may be endogenous as well as exogenous in origin. It also stresses how the perception of these problems as well as opportunities for change play heavily in any episode of institutional change and that there are key actors (e.g., institutional entrepreneurs) who play central roles in socially constructing these perceptions in the first place. And, in an effort to heed Douglass North's (1998, p. 20) call for a more cognitively oriented approach to the study of institutional change, it acknowledges that the cognitive dimensions of institutional contexts, especially the paradigmatic assumptions of decision makers, constrain the choices that actors are likely to make.

Second, the theory draws upon some of the core ideas of historical institutionalism. Specifically, it recognizes that the endogenous triggers for much institutional change emerge from the tensions, frictions, inconsistencies, and contradictions within institutions themselves (Orren and Skowronek 1994); that most institutional change tends to be path dependent and evolutionary (Pierson 2000b); and that for institutional innovations to stick and succeed they need to fit the local economic, political, and administrative context (Hall 1989b; Lieberman 2002). It also accepts that for decision makers to be convinced that an institutional innovation ought to be attempted, they need to be convinced by substantial evidence that current institutions cannot resolve the problem at hand and that new ones will (Hall 1993, 1992; McNamara 1998). It improves on these ideas, however, by suggesting how the process of defining problems, elaborating possible solutions, and fitting these solutions to local conditions involves much entrepreneurial activity and agency, such as the ability of actors to frame problems and solutions in convincing ways. It also shows that the process of path-dependent change stems not only from institutional and other constraints but also from the creative process whereby actors draw upon the pre-given principles and practices around them and engage in bricolage. In this sense, institutions are enabling as well as constraining.

Finally, the theory benefits from the insights of organizational institutionalism. It accepts that institutional change occurs when actors try to resolve problems that generate uncertainty—particularly uncertainty over the distribution of resources or power (Fligstein 1990); that relatively more revolutionary changes are typically associated with the diffusion of new ideas for innovation into a field of organizations and other actors (DiMaggio and Powell 1983; Meyer et al. 1997a, 1997b); that change often involves a process of bricolage by which actors recombine already available institutional principles and practices that exist in their repertoires (Clemens 1993; Swidler 1986); and that institutional entrepreneurs are central to much of this activity (Fligstein 2001b, 1997). It also relies on the important argument that institutions consist of cognitive and normative elements as well as the regulative elements most often discussed by rational choice and historical institutionalists (Dobbin 1994; Scott 2001, chap. 3). Yet it expands and modifies some of these notions. Notably, it contends that the capacity of entrepreneurs to innovate in evolutionary or revolutionary ways depends on their social, organizational, and institutional locations, which determine the degree to which they are exposed to the diffusion of new ideas for innovation. Furthermore, it holds that the process of diffusion includes a critical translation step whereby innovative ideas are fit to local institutional contexts in ways that yield significant differences across locations. Lastly, this theory suggests that the distribution of resources and power play an important role in determining what entrepreneurs can do. It addresses the concern of critics who have lamented the tendency, when it comes to explaining change, of organizational institutionalists to privilege the determinative effects of normative and cognitive constructs at the expense of an analysis of power, conflict, and struggle (Hirsch 1997; Stinchcombe 1997).

My point is straightforward. Viewing institutional change as I have outlined it here requires that we recognize the relative strengths and weaknesses of all three institutionalist paradigms. More important, a complete understanding of institutional change demands that we blend insights from all three paradigms. In this sense, in order to improve our understanding of the process of institutional change a second movement in institutional analysis is imperative.

IMPLICATIONS FOR FUTURE RESEARCH

The preceding discussion as well as previous chapters raise several issues that require considerably more attention in the future. What follows is a brief discussion of some of those that are especially important and that point toward exciting opportunities for research and theorizing. They include the endogenous origins of institutional change; the role of institutional entrepreneurs; the process of bricolage; the importance of perception and framing; and the translation and fitting of innovations to local contexts.

To begin with, although we are beginning to shift our attention from exogenous to endogenous sources of institutional change, our understanding of the latter is far from adequate. Notably, although scholars have argued recently that institutional friction, such as mismatches among competing institutional logics, often spark change, identifying and measuring friction remains a serious problem for institutionalists, particularly for those of us who are interested in predicting institutional change or specifying the conditions under which it is more or less likely to happen (Lieberman 2002, 703). In short, we need to pay much more attention to the origins of endogenous problems.

One way to proceed would be to examine carefully the professional backgrounds of actors who are systematically responsible for decision making and their institutional locations. Following much early work in the sociology of organizations and professions (Friedson 1994, chap. 8; Waters 1989), we should expect, for instance, that the more decision-making authority is shared by actors with substantially different kinds of training and experience, such as professionals, scientists, and other experts, on the one hand, and bureaucrats or managers, on the other hand, the more likely it is that friction will arise over how to define and handle problems when they emerge. Another way to proceed would be to pay close attention to the organizing logics of institutions (e.g., Scott et al. 2000). As some scholars have argued, institutions are probably more prone to friction and change when they consist of contradictory logics that create conflicting and perhaps irreconcilable incentives and motivations (Lieberman 2002; Schneiberg 1999). In any case, several questions can guide our work in the future. Do endogenous problems stem from differences in the normative orientations or identities among different types of institutional actors; from conflicts of material self-interest; from discrepant cognitive paradigms; or from some combination of them all? Which of these possibilities is likely to spark the most serious problems— that is, the problems that are most likely to precipitate the most extreme, revolutionary forms of institutional change? Assuming that all institutions generally have inconsistencies and contradictions like these, under what conditions are they most likely to manifest to the point where actors become concerned enough to begin thinking about changing institutions to resolve these problems?

We also need to know more about institutional entrepreneurs. These people play critical roles in changing institutions. As I mentioned briefly in chapter 3, there is a substantial literature on entrepreneurialism that has come from economics, organizational studies, and economic sociology (e.g., Swedberg 2000). Much of it is concerned with the establishment and survival of business enterprises and other types of organizations rather than with institutional change per se. Howard Aldrich's (1999, chap. 4) work is a good example insofar as he is concerned with how entrepreneurs affect organizational, not institutional, change. Nevertheless, his work is particularly useful insofar as he situates entrepreneurs in a broader social structural context and raises a variety of questions that could easily be applied to the study of institutional change. In particular, how do entrepreneurs' positions in broader social networks affect their capacities for changing institutions? How do different types of network ties affect entrepreneurial activity, such as the kind of bricolage that entrepreneurs are likely to devise? Are heterogenous ties more or less beneficial than homogenous ties in changing institutions? Are stronger ties with close friends or familiar organizations more important for changing institutions than weaker ties with distant acquaintances or less familiar organizations? Can entrepreneurs strategically manage and change their network locations? If so, how do they do it, and what effect does this have with respect to their ability to garner resources, gather new ideas, and devise innovations that result in institutional changes that are relatively more revolutionary than evolutionary?

Recently, a few institutionalists have begun to think seriously about how entrepreneurs affect institutional change. Notably, Neil Fligstein (2001b, 1997) has developed an interactionist theory of entrepreneurs, which stipulates that the most successful entrepreneurs are those that are skilled at inducing cooperation among contending groups of actors. Despite its many merits, especially its focus on interaction, Fligstein's theory largely neglects the important point that the skills with which entrepreneurs do this and, presumably, the patterns of interaction in which they engage, are determined in part by their social, organizational, and institutional locations. Insofar as this blind spot is shared by other institutionalists, we would all do well to pay closer attention to the vast literature on social networks upon which Aldrich relies—literature that shows, for instance, that an individual's network location has a big influence on his or her ability to access information and other resources (Granovetter 1974), gain competitive advantage (Burt 1992), and, ultimately, achieve entrepreneurial success (Uzzi 1996). Indeed, access to information and resources, gaining competitive advantage vis-à-vis other institutional entrepreneurs, and successfully persuading decision makers to adopt their institutional innovations are all central to the process of institutional change that I have theorized. There is also some potentially helpful research in the social movements literature, which recognizes that successful social movement mobilization depends on the social networks within which movement leaders are embedded and that connect rank-and-file members (Ganz 2000; Gould 1993). Both of these literatures offer us important insights into entrepreneurialism and leadership that may shed light on the nature of institutional change. Importantly, they both remind us that institutional change does not exist in a vacuum. The people that populate institutions and are responsible for changing them are situated in a broader set of social structures that institutionalists have often neglected, but that should be incorporated into our theories of institutional change.

This bears directly on the process of bricolage. Although some interesting work has been done to document that institutional bricolage occurs (e.g., Haveman and Rao 1997; Stark 1996), we actually know very little about how this process unfolds. I have suggested that it depends heavily on the social, organizational, and institutional location of entrepreneurs, but we still need to know more about why entrepreneurs make one bricolage rather than another. To my knowledge, very few people have studied this intriguing question. It would be fascinating, for instance, to interview people whose job it is to devise institutional innovations and find out more about why they concocted the innovations they did, and not other ones, and how they blended ideas from different places and why they did so. It would also be very helpful to understand more about how astute entrepreneurs, who understand that their location matters, seek to shift locations and strategically create connections, if possible, with new actors when they feel that it is necessary to expand their repertoires and possibilities for bricolage (e.g., Piore 1995).

Much of what I have argued here about institutional change turns on how actors—particularly entrepreneurs—perceive their problems, possible solutions, opportunities for change, and eventual courses of action. Most institutionalists have paid remarkably little attention to the issue of perception other than to note that perceptions matter and are influenced by the institutional contexts that they have inherited from the past and within which they operate. Recall, for instance, that Frank Dobbin (1994) argued that national political institutions influenced how policymakers in France, Britain, and the United States perceived their options when they set out to build national railway systems, but that he focused much more on how these perceptions affected policy outcomes than on how these perceptions were formulated in the first place. Similarly, Victoria Hattam (1993) showed how a shift in the perceptions of the U.S. labor movement affected its strategies for institutional change, but she said little about how these perceptions shifted. And rational choice institutionalists have long been criticized for relegating perceptual issues to the distant background, ignoring, for instance, how actors perceive the interests that are pivotal to rational choice explanations. This generic blind spot among institutionalists is attributable to the excessively structural quality of most institutional analysis.

To eliminate this blind spot, we can benefit enormously by borrowing from two literatures. First, again, is the literature on social movements, which offers several insights about how people come to recognize opportunities for mobilization—that is, change—when they come to pass. The initial work was done by David Snow and his colleagues (Snow and Benford 1992; Snow et al. 1986), who theorized how leaders mobilize support by framing opportunities as well as possible solutions, strategies, and tactics. This work pays close attention to how movement leaders draw upon various types of ideas, culture, systems of meaning, and identities to create shared understandings of the world; how frames are constructed to diagnose problems and propose solutions; why some frames are more successful than others in mobilizing people for action; and how framing itself is a contested process involving movement and countermovement leaders as well as external actors, such as political authorities. Recently, more traditional social movement theorists who have explained movement success in terms of the ability of leaders to mobilize resources or exploit political opportunities have incorporated an analysis of framing into their work with great benefit (McAdam et al. 1996; McCarthy et al. 1996; Tarrow 1994, 1996). The affinities between social movements theory and some versions of institutional analysis in this regard have become increasingly apparent (Campbell forthcoming) and are already being exploited by some researchers (Davis et al. forthcoming).

Discourse analysis is a second literature that promises to shed light on these sorts of perceptual issues. Discourse analysis is often based on close readings of print media, documents, and other texts seeking to determine how language and rhetoric that lead—successfully or not—to change in organizations and political institutions are constructed (e.g., Creed et al. 2002a, 2002b; de Goede 1996; Pedersen 1991; Phillips 1996; Schmidt 2002, 2001). Some of this work is highly technical, particularly to the extent that it tries to detect common rhetorical patterns in large numbers of texts (e.g., Lewis 2003). This too can be a useful place for us to look for insights about how institutional entrepreneurs interpret and define interests, problems, solutions, and the like for themselves, decision makers, and others.

Researchers who work in these two areas have raised and grappled with several interesting questions that relate to the process of institutional change as I have described it. First, how do institutional entrepreneurs construct frames and seek to alter perceptions? What are the conditions under which institutional entrepreneurs are more or less likely to copy the rhetoric and ideas of those around them (e.g., Lewis 2003)? Second, do these entrepreneurs use the same frames and discourse for diagnosing problems as they do for articulating solutions? Do their frames depend on their access to different kinds of resources or different arenas in which institutional problems are discussed? How do entrepreneurs shape their framing and rhetoric in different ways depending on whom they are addressing? In other words, do they offer different frames to decision makers, on the one hand, and to decision makers' constituents, on the other (e.g., Schmidt 2002)? Third, why are some frames more influential than others in either fostering or blocking institutional change? Can we specify different types of frames and discourse? Are arguments that are cloaked in scientific rhetoric and the trappings of quantification more likely to persuade than those that are not (McCloskey 1985)? Certainly an exciting possibility for research is to determine the conditions under which a particular type of frame is more or less successful in altering perceptions and precipitating institutional change. Another possibility is to examine why one frame among several competing frames is more likely to have contributed to institutional change than the rest (e.g., McCammon et al. 2001). Attending to these sorts of questions would help us infuse our theories with a bit more agency.

Finally, I have said a great deal about the necessity for translating and fitting innovative programs into local institutional contexts. We need to learn much more about this process too. What does it take for an innovation to fit, or not? Is fit really a function of the amount of political or organizational support an innovation has such that greater levels of support mean that people will simply try harder to make it work and be more forgiving when the innovation creates problems? Or is fit a function of something else? Researchers have begun to generate careful studies of the translation process, particularly in the area of comparative political economy (Djelic 1998; Duina 1999; Marjoribanks 2000), but we need more of this sort of work. Again, it would be extremely useful to know more about how people who devise and implement innovations take the issue of fit into account. Do they try to anticipate problems, take steps to avoid them preemptively, garner support in advance from constituents for translation, and perhaps make adjustments in already existing local institutions to prepare for translation of an innovation? If so, how do they do these things? Until we know more about translation and fit, our arguments about institutional change will remain poorly specified.

FINAL THOUGHT

Throughout this book I have tried to provide insights into some of the most important problems that rational choice, organizational, and historical institutionalists share. I have also made a number of suggestions about how we ought to begin to solve them. Along the way I have raised a number of questions that still require answers. In the end, as one colleague remarked after reading an earlier draft of this book, I have probably raised more questions than answers. But at this stage of the game, I think this is necessary, particularly insofar as these questions can orient future work across the three institutionalist paradigms and push the entire enterprise of institutional analysis forward. If we can answer these questions, then the future for institutional analysis is very bright.

ANALYSIS OF TAX LEVELS AND STRUCTURES

FOR COUNTRY SUBGROUPS

THIS APPENDIX examines whether there is support for globalization theory's prediction of a race to the bottom in tax institutions if we examine different types of OECD countries. Some scholars have argued that we should expect this sort of homogenization to occur within country subgroups (e.g., Kitschelt et al. 1999). The following analysis examines whether the level of taxation and the structure of taxation are affected by globalization in either different types of welfare states or in countries whose economies are coordinated by different types of institutional arrangements.

LEVEL OF TAXATION

One useful way to differentiate among countries is to distinguish among types of welfare states. The *social democratic* welfare states of Northern Europe have traditionally been the most generous to their citizens and, thus, ought to be associated with the highest tax burdens insofar as these states utilize tax revenue to finance welfare spending. In contrast, *residual* welfare states, like those in the Anglo-Saxon countries, have been stingier historically, and so should be associated with lower tax burdens. Finally, because *Christian democratic* welfare states fall between these extremes, so should their tax burdens (Esping-Andersen 1999; Stephens et al. 1999). Following globalization theory, we would expect countries with the highest tax burdens, the social democratic welfare states, to cut their taxes the most, followed by the Christian democratic welfare states, and then the residual welfare states.

Table A.1 shows changes in total tax revenues as a percentage of gross domestic product (GDP) in eighteen OECD countries from 1970 to 1998 for these three types of welfare states. Countries were classified as having residual, Christian democratic, or social democratic welfare states according to the index developed by Herbert Kitschelt and his colleagues (1999, 436). Table A.1 confirms that since 1970 average tax burdens were

TABLE A.1.
Total Tax Revenues in Residual, Christian Democratic,
and Social Democratic Welfare States (as a percentage of GDP)

	1970	1980	1990	1998
Residual				
Australia	22.9	27.4	29.3	29.9
Canada	31.2	32.0	36.1	37.4
Ireland	29.9	31.5	33.6	32.2
Japan	19.7	25.4	30.9	28.4
New Zealand	27.4	33.0	38.1	35.2
United Kingdom	37.0	35.3	36.0	37.2
United States	27.7	27.0	26.7	28.9
Mean	27.97	30.23	32.96	32.74
Median	27.70	31.50	33.60	32.20
Standard deviation	5.63	3.65	4.14	3.86
Interquartile range	5.40	5.30	5.95	6.80
Christian Democratic				
Austria	34.9	39.5	40.2	44.4
Belgium	35.7	43.1	43.1	45.9
France	35.1	40.6	43.0	45.2
Germany	32.9	33.1	32.6	37.0
Italy	26.1	30.3	38.9	42.7
Netherlands	37.1	43.4	42.8	41.0
Switzerland	22.5	28.9	30.9	35.1
Mean	32.04	36.99	38.79	41.61
Median	34.90	39.50	40.20	42.70
Standard deviation	5.53	6.10	5.08	4.17
Interquartile range	5.90	10.15	7.15	5.80

Source: OECD (2000a, table 3, pp. 67–68).

TABLE A.1. (*cont'd*)

	1970	1980	1990	1998
Social Democratic				
Denmark	40.4	43.9	47.1	49.8
Finland	32.5	36.2	44.7	46.2
Norway	34.9	42.7	41.8	43.6
Sweden	39.8	47.1	53.7	52.0
Mean	36.90	42.48	46.83	47.90
Median	37.35	43.30	45.90	48.00
Standard deviation	3.83	4.58	5.07	3.73
Interquartile range	5.65	3.63	4.78	4.80

Source: OECD (2000a, table 3, pp. 67–68).

lowest in residual welfare states, followed by Christian democratic welfare states, and then social democratic welfare states, which had the highest tax burdens. Within each group of countries, however, tax burdens *increased* over time. In residual welfare states, the means and medians rose from 28 to 33 percent of GDP and from 28 to 32 percent of GDP, respectively. In Christian democratic welfare states, the means and medians rose from 32 to 42 percent of GDP and from 35 to 43 percent of GDP, respectively. In social democratic welfare states, the means and medians both rose from about 37 to 48 percent of GDP. These upward trends contradict globalization theory. In all three sets of countries the standard deviations declined albeit in varying degree. The interquartile range barely declined from 5.9 to 5.8 in the Christian democratic welfare states, but dropped from 5.7 to 4.8 in the social democratic welfare states. It rose from 5.4 to 6.8 in the residual welfare states. Overall, this suggests a modest tendency for all three types of welfare states to converge in varying degree on *higher* tax burdens, not lower ones as globalization theory predicts.

Another useful distinction that we can draw between types of countries is that made between coordinated and liberal market economies (Soskice 1999). *Coordinated market economies,* such as Germany and the Northern European countries, are those whose institutions facilitate strong labor unions and business associations, cooperative industrial relations between unions and managers both within and across firms, long-term corporate investment and profit horizons, interfirm cooperation in areas like research and development, and extensive vocational training systems.

In contrast, *liberal market economies*, such as the Anglo-Saxon countries, have weaker unions and business associations, deregulated labor markets and firm-level, rather than sectoral or industrial, bargaining between labor and management, short-term corporate investment and profit horizons, strong competition requirements that limit possible cooperation among firms, and educational systems that emphasize general rather than vocational training. Furthermore, in comparison to liberal market economies, states in coordinated market economies tend to pursue developmental and distributive goals much more vigorously and directly than their counterparts in liberal market economies, such as by providing financial support to firms or sectors for economic development projects, active labor market policies, and hefty welfare state programs to maintain a comparatively high social wage (Albert 1993; Best 1990; Hicks and Kenworthy 1998; Weiss 1998). Of course, these are policies that are expensive and require relatively high levels of taxation.

Table A.2 compares the tax burdens in coordinated and liberal market economies from 1970 to 1998. Countries were classified as either coordinated or liberal market economies according to the index developed by Bruce Western (2001, 78). An analysis of the means and medians reveals, as expected, that tax burdens are consistently lower in the liberal market economies. An inspection of the means shows that in the liberal market economies the average tax burden increased from 30 to 36 percent of GDP, and in the coordinated market economies it increased from 33 to 42 percent of GDP. The medians show similar trends rising from 29 to 36 percent of GDP in the liberal market economies, and from 35 to 44 percent in the coordinated market economies. Furthermore, in the liberal market economies the standard deviation increased from 4.7 to 5.8, and in the coordinated market economies it increased from 6.8 to 7.1. The interquartile range also rose from 5.1 to 7.1 in the liberal economies, and from 4.2 to 8.1 in the coordinated economies. So average tax burdens in both types of societies *increased* during this period, and measures of dispersion showed no tendency toward convergence. There is little support within these country types for globalization theory.

STRUCTURE OF TAXATION

To determine whether globalization affects the structure of taxation in country subgroups, table A.3 examines tax shifting in different types of welfare states in seventeen OECD countries between 1990 and 1998.[1]

---

[1] Although included in previous tables, Japan is omitted in tables A.3 and A.4 due to missing data.

TABLE A.2.
Total Tax Revenues in Liberal and Coordinated Market Economies
(as a percentage of GDP)

	1970	1980	1990	1998
Liberal Economies				
Australia	22.9	27.4	29.3	29.9
Canada	31.2	32.0	36.1	37.4
France	35.1	40.6	43.0	45.2
Ireland	29.9	31.5	33.6	32.2
Italy	26.1	30.3	38.9	42.7
New Zealand	27.4	33.0	38.1	35.2
United Kingdom	37.0	35.3	36.0	37.2
United States	27.7	27.0	26.7	28.9
Mean	29.66	32.14	35.21	36.09
Median	28.80	31.75	36.05	36.20
Standard deviation	4.68	4.39	5.26	5.80
Interquartile range	5.10	4.00	5.78	7.10
Coordinated Economies				
Austria	34.9	39.5	40.2	44.4
Belgium	35.7	43.1	43.1	45.9
Denmark	40.4	43.9	47.1	49.8
Finland	32.5	36.2	44.7	46.2
Germany	32.9	33.1	32.6	37.0
Japan	19.7	25.4	30.9	28.4
Netherlands	37.1	43.4	42.8	41.0
Norway	34.9	42.7	41.8	43.6
Sweden	39.8	47.1	53.7	52.0
Switzerland	22.5	28.9	30.9	35.1
Mean	33.04	38.33	40.78	42.34
Median	34.90	41.10	42.30	44.00
Standard deviation	6.83	7.19	7.42	7.14
Interquartile range	4.15	9.45	9.80	8.13

Source: OECD (2000a, table 3, pp. 67–68).

TABLE A.3.
Central Government Revenues by Tax Type in Residual, Christian Democratic,
and Social Democratic Welfare States
(as a percentage of total government revenues)

	Income & Profit Taxes		Social Security Taxes		Taxes on Goods & Services	
	1990	1998	1990	1998	1990	1998
Residual						
Australia	65.0	68.0	0.0	0.0	21.0	21.0
Canada	51.0	54.0	16.0	19.0	17.0	17.0
Ireland	37.0	42.0	15.0	13.0	38.0	37.0
New Zealand	53.0	62.0	0.0	0.0	27.0	28.0
United Kingdom	39.0	39.0	17.0	17.0	28.0	31.0
United States	52.0	57.0	35.0	32.0	3.0	3.0
Mean	49.50	53.67	13.84	13.50	22.33	22.83
Median	51.50	55.50	15.50	15.00	24.00	24.50
Standard deviation	10.27	11.29	13.01	12.24	11.86	12.04
Interquartile range	10.75	15.75	12.99	15.24	9.75	12.25
Christian Democratic						
Austria	19.0	26.0	37.0	40.0	25.0	25.0
Belgium	35.0	37.0	35.0	33.0	24.0	25.0
France	17.0	20.0	44.0	42.0	28.0	29.0
Germany	16.0	15.0	53.0	48.0	24.0	20.0
Italy	37.0	33.0	29.0	31.0	29.0	26.0
Netherlands	31.0	25.0	35.0	41.0	22.0	23.0
Switzerland	15.0	15.0	51.0	51.0	23.0	23.0
Mean	24.29	24.43	40.57	40.86	25.00	24.43
Median	19.00	25.00	37.00	41.00	24.00	25.00
Standard deviation	9.64	8.48	8.98	7.24	2.58	2.82
Interquartile range	16.50	12.00	12.50	8.50	3.00	2.50

Source: World Bank (2001, table 4.13, pp. 242–44).

TABLE A.3. (cont'd)

	Income & Profit Taxes		Social Security Taxes		Taxes on Goods & Services	
	1990	1998	1990	1998	1990	1998
Social Democratic						
Denmark	37.0	36.0	4.0	4.0	41.0	42.0
Finland	31.0	29.0	9.0	10.0	47.0	44.0
Norway	16.0	21.0	24.0	23.0	34.0	38.0
Sweden	18.0	14.0	31.0	34.0	29.0	28.0
Mean	25.50	25.00	17.00	17.75	37.75	38.00
Median	24.50	25.00	16.50	16.50	37.50	40.00
Standard deviation	10.15	9.56	12.62	13.43	7.89	7.12
Interquartile range	15.00	11.50	18.00	17.25	9.75	7.00

Source: World Bank (2001, table 4.13, pp. 242–44).

Residual welfare states experienced little tax shifting other than an *increase* in the amount of revenue generated through income and profit taxes. Contrary to the predictions of globalization theory, the corresponding means and medians climbed from about 50 to 54 percent of total revenue and from 52 to 56 percent of total revenue, respectively. Both measures of dispersion increased. The mean, median, and standard deviation for social security taxes declined very slightly, but the interquartile range increased from about 13 to 15. Mean and median taxes on goods and services increased marginally as did the measures of dispersion.

Christian democratic welfare states also encountered little tax shifting in line with globalization theory. For income and profit taxes the mean rose very slightly but the median rose from 19 to 25 percent of total revenues collected. The standard deviation declined from 9.6 to 8.5, and the interquartile range decreased from 16.5 to 12. For social security taxes the mean and median values also increased while the measures of dispersion decreased. So for both types of taxation to the extent that any trend is evident it is one of convergence toward a *greater* reliance on income and profit taxes and social security taxes, evidence that does not square well with globalization theory. The results for taxes on goods and services are inconclusive. The mean declined slightly and the standard deviation increased. Conversely, the median increased slightly and the interquartile range decreased.

The results for social democratic welfare states reveal little change. For income and profit taxes an examination of the means reveals a very slight decline from 25.5 to 25 percent in the amount of total revenue collected. But there was a very slight rise in the median from 24.5 to 25 percent of total revenue collected. Both measures of dispersion declined. For social security taxes the mean increased quite modestly from 17 to 17.8 and the median remained unchanged while the standard deviation increased and the interquartile range decreased. For taxes on goods and services the mean was basically stable and the median rose from 37.5 to 40 percent of total revenue collected. The standard deviation declined slightly from 7.9 to 7.1, and the interquartile range declined from 9.8 to 7. Thus, in the social democratic welfare states there is no consistent evidence to support globalization theory.

Table A.4 examines whether there might be different results for liberal and coordinated market economies. Contrary to globalization theory, table A.4 shows that within the liberal market economies there was a slight *increase* in the amount of revenue collected through income and profit taxes between 1990 and 1998. The mean and median rose from 44 to 47 percent of total revenues collected and from 45 to 48 percent of total revenues collected, respectively. The measures of dispersion increased as well. Indeed, the increase in income and profit taxation is surprising insofar as these are the countries that tend to favor lower income taxes, at least judging by the rhetoric of ruling politicians like Ronald Reagan, Margaret Thatcher, and other conservatives in power who called frequently since 1980 for lower taxes on individuals and corporations. The mean for social security taxes in liberal market economies was virtually stable, and the median increased from 16.5 to 18 percent of total revenues collected. The standard deviation declined slightly from 15.7 to 15.1, and the interquartile range rose from 19.3 to 21.5. For taxes on goods and services, the mean, median, and standard deviation remained quite stable, but the interquartile range increased slightly from 8.3 to 9.5. Insofar as the liberal market economies are concerned, these results provide no support for globalization theory.

For the coordinated market economies, table A.4 reveals that the percentage of revenues collected through income and profit taxes did not decline. The mean remained unchanged and the median rose from 19 to 25 percent of total revenues collected. Furthermore, the standard deviation and interquartile range declined very slightly from 9.1 to 8.8 and from 15 to 14, respectively. There was virtually no change in the proportion of revenues collected either through social security

TABLE A.4.

Central Government Revenues by Tax Type in Liberal and Coordinated Market Economies
(as a percentage of total government revenues)

	Income & Profit Taxes		Social Security Taxes		Taxes on Goods & Services	
	1990	1998	1990	1998	1990	1998
Liberal Economies						
Australia	65.0	68.0	0.0	0.0	21.0	21.0
Canada	51.0	54.0	16.0	19.0	17.0	17.0
France	17.0	20.0	44.0	42.0	28.0	29.0
Ireland	37.0	42.0	15.0	13.0	38.0	37.0
Italy	37.0	33.0	29.0	31.0	29.0	26.0
New Zealand	53.0	62.0	0.0	0.0	27.0	28.0
United Kingdom	39.0	39.0	17.0	17.0	28.0	31.0
United States	52.0	57.0	35.0	32.0	3.0	3.0
Mean	43.88	46.88	19.50	19.25	23.88	24.00
Median	45.00	48.00	16.50	18.00	27.50	27.00
Standard deviation	14.57	16.16	15.72	15.13	10.43	10.43
Interquartile range	15.25	20.75	19.25	21.50	8.25	9.50
Coordinated Economies						
Austria	19.0	26.0	37.0	40.0	25.0	25.0
Belgium	35.0	37.0	35.0	33.0	24.0	25.0
Denmark	37.0	36.0	4.0	4.0	41.0	42.0
Finland	31.0	29.0	9.0	10.0	47.0	44.0
Germany	16.0	15.0	53.0	48.0	24.0	20.0
Netherlands	31.0	25.0	35.0	41.0	22.0	23.0
Norway	16.0	21.0	24.0	23.0	34.0	38.0
Sweden	18.0	14.0	31.0	34.0	29.0	28.0
Switzerland	15.0	15.0	51.0	51.0	23.0	23.0
Mean	24.22	24.22	31.00	31.56	29.89	29.78
Median	19.00	25.00	35.00	34.00	25.00	25.00
Standard deviation	9.07	8.76	16.64	16.26	8.92	9.05
Interquartile range	15.00	14.00	13.00	18.00	10.00	15.00

Source: World Bank (2001, table 4.13, pp. 242–44).

TABLE A.5.
Corporate Income Taxes in Residual, Christian Democratic, and Social
Democratic Welfare States (as a percentage of total government revenues)

	1975	1985	1998
Residual			
Australia	15.5	11.5	19.4
Canada	20.9	13.9	15.9
Ireland	6.2	3.9	12.4
Japan	29.4	30.7	22.3
New Zealand	12.8	8.9	11.5
United Kingdom	8.8	18.2	14.3
United States	21.6	13.6	16.9
Mean	16.46	14.39	16.10
Median	15.50	13.60	15.90
Standard deviation	8.08	8.46	3.83
Interquartile range	10.45	5.85	4.80
Christian Democratic			
Austria	6.9	5.0	6.3
Belgium	10.5	7.9	21.0
France	10.1	9.4	13.8
Germany	5.2	7.6	5.6
Italy	11.3	14.4	12.0
Netherlands	13.1	13.4	19.0
Switzerland	6.3	5.7	8.4
Mean	9.06	9.06	12.30
Median	10.10	7.90	12.00
Standard deviation	2.93	3.62	6.04
Interquartile range	4.30	4.75	9.05

Source: OECD (2000a, table 131, p. 202).

TABLE A.5. (*cont'd*)

	1975	1985	1998
Social Democratic			
Denmark	3.9	6.0	7.8
Finland	3.4	2.9	9.7
Norway	3.1	26.7	14.1
Sweden	3.8	5.7	9.9
Mean	3.55	10.33	10.38
Median	3.60	5.85	9.80
Standard deviation	0.37	11.01	2.66
Interquartile range	0.50	6.18	1.73

Source: OECD (2000a, table 131, p. 202).

taxes or taxes on goods and services. Nor did the standard deviations change much. However, the interquartile range increased from 13 to 18 for social security taxes and from 10 to 15 for taxes on goods and services. Again, these results offer virtually no support for globalization theory.

Finally, let us examine whether governments in different types of countries shifted the tax burden off corporations. Table A.5 examines the percentage of total government revenues collected just from corporate income taxes between 1978 and 1998. In the residual welfare states, there is no clear evidence to support the globalization thesis. The mean barely declined from 16.5 to 16.1 percent of government revenues, and the median increased by a similarly small amount, rising from 15.5 to 15.9 percent. In Christian democratic welfare states, the mean rose from about 9.1 to 12.3 percent, and the median rose from 10.1 to 12.0 percent. In the social democratic welfare states, the mean and median rose sharply from 3.6 to 10.4 percent and 3.6 to 9.8 percent of government revenues, respectively. Again, the globalization thesis is not supported.

Table A.6 shows the results for liberal and coordinated market economies. In liberal market economies, the mean and median rose from 13.4 to 14.5 percent and from 12.1 to 14.1 percent of government revenues, respectively. In the coordinated market economies, the mean increased from 8.6 to 12.4 percent of government revenues, and the median rose from 5.8 to 9.8 percent. None of these results supports globalization theory.

Corporate Income Taxes in Liberal and Coordinated Market Economies
(as a percentage of total government revenues)

	1975	1985	1998
Liberal Economies			
Australia	15.5	11.5	19.4
Canada	20.9	13.9	15.9
France	10.1	9.4	13.8
Ireland	6.2	3.9	12.4
Italy	11.3	14.4	12.0
New Zealand	12.8	8.9	11.5
United Kingdom	8.8	18.2	14.3
United States	21.6	13.6	16.9
Mean	13.40	11.73	14.53
Median	12.05	12.55	14.05
Standard deviation	5.56	4.34	2.72
Interquartile range	7.08	4.75	3.85
Coordinated Economies			
Austria	6.9	5.0	6.3
Belgium	10.5	7.9	21.0
Denmark	3.9	6.0	7.8
Finland	3.4	2.9	9.7
Germany	5.2	7.6	5.6
Japan	29.4	30.7	22.3
Netherlands	13.1	13.4	19.0
Norway	3.1	26.7	14.1
Sweden	3.8	5.7	9.9
Switzerland	6.3	5.7	8.4
Mean	8.56	11.16	12.41
Median	5.75	6.80	9.80
Standard deviation	8.02	9.68	6.26
Interquartile range	5.78	6.33	9.83

Source: OECD (2000a, table 131, p. 202).

In sum, globalization appears to have had virtually none of the effects predicted by globalization theory on either the level or structure of taxation in either different types of welfare states or in liberal and coordinated market economies. Nor did it seem to influence the burden of taxation borne by corporations through the corporate income tax alone. Hence, these findings do not lend much support to those who have argued that globalization will produce homogenization within country subgroups.

REFERENCES

Abbott, Andrew. 2001. *Time Matters: On Theory and Method*. Chicago: University of Chicago Press.

———. 1997. "On the Concept of the Turning Point." *Comparative Social Research* 16:85–105.

———. 1992. "From Causes to Events: Notes on Narrative Positivism." *Sociological Methods and Research* 20(4): 428–55.

———. 1988. "Transcending General Linear Reality." *Sociological Theory* 6(Fall): 169–86.

Abrahamson, Eric, and Gregory Fairchild. 1999. "Management Fashion: Lifecycles, Triggers, and Collective Learning Processes." *Administrative Science Quarterly* 44:708–40.

Ackerman, Frank. 1982. *Reaganomics: Rhetoric vs. Reality*. Boston: South End.

Albert, Michel. 1993. *Capitalism vs. Capitalism*. New York: Four Walls Eight Windows.

Alderson, Arthur S. 2002. "Explaining the Upswing in Direct Investment from 18 OECD Nations: A Test of Mainstream and Heterodox Theories of Globalization." Paper presented at the annual meeting of the American Sociological Association, Chicago.

Aldrich, Howard E. 2000. "Entrepreneurial Strategies in New Organizational Populations." Pp. 211–28 in *Entrepreneurship: The Social Science View*, edited by Richard Swedberg. New York: Oxford University Press.

———. 1999. *Organizations Evolving*. Thousand Oaks, Calif.: Sage.

Allen, Michael Patrick. 1994. "Elite Social Movement Organizations and the State: The Rise of the Conservative Policy-Planning Network." *Research in Politics and Society* 4:87–109.

Allen, Michael Patrick, and John L. Campbell. 1994. "State Revenue Extraction from Different Income Groups: Variations in Tax Progressivity in the United States, 1916–1986." *American Sociological Review* 59(2): 169–86.

Alt, James E., and Kenneth A. Shepsle. 1990a. "Editor's Introduction." Pp. 1–8 in *Perspectives on Positive Political Economy*, edited by James E. Alt and Kenneth A. Shepsle. New York: Cambridge University Press.

———, eds. 1990b. *Perspectives on Positive Political Economy*. New York: Cambridge University Press.

Aminzade, Ronald. 1992. "Historical Sociology and Time." *Sociological Methods and Research* 20(4): 456–80.

Anthony, Denise, Douglas Heckathorn, and Steven Maser. 1994. "Rational Rhetoric in Politics: The Debate over Ratifying the U.S. Constitution." *Rationality and Society* 6(4): 489–518.

Arthur, W. Brian. 1994. *Increasing Returns and Path Dependence in the Economy*. Ann Arbor: University of Michigan Press.

Astley, W. Graham. 1985. "The Two Ecologies: Population and Community Perspectives on Organizational Evolution." *Administrative Science Quarterly* 30:224–41.

Austen-Smith, David. 1990. "Information Transmission in Debate." *American Journal of Political Science* 34(1): 124–52.

Austen-Smith, David, and William H. Riker. 1990. "Asymmetric Information and the Coherence of Legislation: A Correction." *American Political Science Review* 84(1): 243–45.

———. 1987. "Asymmetric Information and the Coherence of Legislation." *American Political Science Review* 81(3): 897–918.

Axelrod, Robert. 1984. *The Evolution of Cooperation*. New York: Basic.

Babb, Sarah. 1996. " 'A True American System of Finance': Frame Resonance in the U.S. Labor Movement, 1866 to 1886." *American Journal of Sociology* 61:1033–52.

Bailey, K. D. 1975. "Cluster Analysis." Pp. 59–128 in *Sociological Methodology 1975*, edited by David Heise. San Francisco: Jossey-Bass.

Barley, Stephen R., and Pamela S. Tolbert. 1997. "Institutionalization and Structuration: Studying the Links Between Action and Institution." *Organization Studies* 18(1): 93–117.

Bartley, Tim, and Marc Schneiberg. 2002. "Rationality and Institutional Contingency: The Varying Politics of Economic Regulation in the Fire Insurance Industry." *Sociological Perspectives* 45:47–80.

Barzel, Yoram. 1989. *Economic Analysis of Property Rights*. New York: Cambridge University Press.

Bates, Robert H., Avner Greif, Margaret Levi, Jean-Laurent Rosenthal, and Barry Weingast. 1998. *Analytic Narratives*. Princeton: Princeton University Press.

Bauman, Zygmunt. 1998. *Globalization: The Human Consequences*. New York: Cambridge University Press.

Baumgartner, Frank R., and Bryan D. Jones. 1993. *Agendas and Instability in American Politics*. Chicago: University of Chicago Press.

Bebchuk, Lucian Ayre, and Mark J. Roe. 1999. "A Theory of Path Dependence in Corporate Ownership and Governance." *Stanford Law Review* 52(1): 127–70.

Bendor, Jonathan, Terry M. Moe, and Kenneth W. Shotts. 2001. "Recycling the Garbage Can: An Assessment of the Research Program." *American Political Science Review* 95(1): 169–90.

Bendor, Jonathan, Serge Taylor, and Roland Van Gaalen. 1987. "Politicians, Bureaucrats, and Asymmetric Information." *American Journal of Political Science* 31:796–828.

Bennett, W. Lance, and Erik Asard. 1995. "The Marketplace of Ideas: The Rhetoric and Politics of Tax Reform in Sweden and the United States." *Polity* 28(1): 1–23.

Bensen, J. Kenneth. 1973. "The Analysis of Bureaucratic-Professional Conflict: Functional Versus Dialectical Approaches." *Sociological Quarterly* 14:376–94.

Berger, Peter, and Thomas Luckman. 1967. *The Social Construction of Reality*. New York: Doubleday Anchor.

Berger, Suzanne. 1996. "Introduction." Pp. 1–25 in *National Diversity and Global Capitalism*, edited by Suzanne Berger and Ronald Dore. Ithaca: Cornell University Press.

Berger, Suzanne, and Ronald Dore, eds. 1996. *National Diversity and Global Capitalism*. Ithaca: Cornell University Press.

Berman, Sheri. 2001. "Ideas, Norms, and Culture in Political Analysis." *Comparative Politics* 33(2): 231–50.

———. 1998. *The Social Democratic Movement: Ideas and Politics in the Making of Interwar Europe*. Cambridge: Harvard University Press.

Best, Michael. 1990. *The New Competition: Institutions of Industrial Restructuring*. Cambridge: Harvard University Press.

Blau, Peter, and W. Richard Scott. 1962. *Formal Organizations: A Comparative Perspective*. San Francisco: Chandler.

Block, Fred. 1996. *The Vampire State: And Other Myths and Fallacies about the U.S. Economy*. New York: New Press.

———. 1990. *Postindustrial Possibilities: A Critique of Economic Discourse*. Berkeley: University of California Press.

Blyth, Mark. 2002. *Great Transformations: Economic Ideas and Institutional Change in the Twentieth Century*. New York: Cambridge University Press.

———. 1999. "The Transformation of the Swedish Model: Economic Ideas, Distributional Conflict, and Institutional Change." Unpublished paper, Department of Political Science, Johns Hopkins University.

———. 1998. "From Ideas and Institutions to Ideas and Interests: Beyond the Usual Suspects?" Paper presented at the Eleventh Conference of Europeanists, Baltimore.

———. 1997. "Any More Bright Ideas? The Ideational Turn of Comparative Political Economy." *Comparative Politics* 29(2): 229–50.

Boli, John, and John W. Meyer. 1987. "The Ideology of Childhood and the State: Rules Distinguishing Children in National Constitutions." Pp. 217–41 in *Institutional Structure: Constituting State, Society, and the Individual*, edited by George M. Thomas, John W. Meyer, Francisco O. Ramirez, and John Boli. Beverly Hills, Calif.: Sage.

Boli, John, and George M. Thomas, eds. 1999a. *Constructing World Culture: International Nongovernmental Organizations since 1875*. Stanford: Stanford University Press.

———. 1999b. "Introduction." Pp. 1–12 in *Constructing World Culture: International Nongovernmental Organizations since 1875*, edited by John Boli and George M. Thomas. Stanford: Stanford University Press.

Boudon, Raymond. 1998. "Social Mechanisms Without Black Boxes." Pp. 172–203 in *Social Mechanisms: An Analytical Approach to Social Theory*, edited by Peter Hedström and Richard Swedberg. New York: Cambridge University Press.

Bourdieu, Pierre. 1998. *Acts of Resistance: Against the Tyranny of the Market*. New York: The New Press.

Braun, Rudolf. 1975. "Taxation, Sociopolitical Structure, and State-Building: Great Britain and Brandenburg-Prussia." Pp. 243–327 in *The Formation of National States in Western Europe*, edited by Charles Tilly. Princeton: Princeton University Press.

Braybrooke, David, and Charles Lindblom. 1963. *A Strategy of Decision*. New York: Free Press.

Brinton, Mary C., and Victor Nee, eds. 1998. *The New Institutionalism in Sociology*. New York: Russell Sage.

Bromley, Daniel. 1989. *Economic Interests and Institutions*. New York: Blackwell.

Brownlee, W. Elliot. 1996. *Federal Taxation in America*. New York: Cambridge University Press.

Brunner, Hans-Peter. 1994. "Technological Diversity, Random Selection in a Population of Firms and Technological Institutions in Government." Pp. 33–43 in *Evolutionary Economics and Chaos Theory*, edited by Loet Lydesdorff and Peter Van den Besselaar. New York: St. Martin's.

Burawoy, Michael. 1979. *Manufacturing Consent*. Chicago: University of Chicago Press.

Burawoy, Michael, and Pavel Krotov. 1993. "The Soviet Transition from Socialism to Capitalism: Worker Control and Economic Bargaining in the Wood Industry." Pp. 56–90 in *What About the Workers? Workers and the Transition to Capitalism in Russia*, edited by Simon Clarke, Peter Fairbrother, Michael Burawoy, and Pavel Krotov. London: Verso.

Burstein, Paul. 1998. "Bringing the Public Back In: Should Sociologists Consider the Impact of Public Opinion on Public Policy?" *Social Forces* 77(1): 27–62.

———. 1991. "Policy Domains: Organization, Culture, and Policy Outcomes." *Annual Review of Sociology* 17:327–50.

Burt, Ronald S. 1992. *Structural Holes: The Social Structure of Competition*. Cambridge: Harvard University Press.

Burton, M. Diane, Jesper B. Sørensen, and Christine M. Beckman. 2002. "Coming From Good Stock: Career Histories and New Venture Formation." *Research in the Sociology of Organizations* 19:229–62.

Calvert, Randall L. 1998. "Rational Actors, Equilibrium, and Social Institutions." Pp. 57–94 in *Explaining Social Institutions*, edited by Jack Knight and Itai Sened. Ann Arbor: University of Michigan Press.

———. 1985. "The Value of Biased Information: A Rational Choice Model of Political Advice." *Journal of Politics* 47:531–55.

Cameron, David. 1978. "The Expansion of the Public Economy: A Comparative Analysis." *American Political Science Review* 72:1243–61.

Campbell, John L. Forthcoming. "Where Do We Stand? Common Mechanisms in Organizations and Social Movements Research." In *Social Movements and Organization Theory*, edited by Gerald F. Davis, Doug McAdam, W. Richard Scott, and Mayer N. Zald. New York: Cambridge University Press.

———. 2003. "States, Politics, and Globalization: Why Institutions Still Matter." Pp. 234–59 in *The Nation-State in Question*, edited by T. V. Paul, G. John Ikenberry, and John A. Hall. Princeton: Princeton University Press.

———. 2002. "Ideas, Politics and Public Policy." *Annual Review of Sociology* 28:21–38.

———. 2001. "Convergence or Divergence? Globalization, Neoliberalism and Fiscal Policy in Postcommunist Europe." Pp. 107–39 in *Globalization and the*

European Political Economy, edited by Steven Weber. New York: Columbia University Press.

———. 1998. "Institutional Analysis and the Role of Ideas in Political Economy." *Theory and Society* 27:377–409.

———. 1997. "Recent Trends in Institutional Political Economy." *International Journal of Sociology and Social Policy* 17(7/8): 15–56.

———. 1993a. "The State and Fiscal Sociology." *Annual Review of Sociology* 19:163–85.

———. 1993b. "Property Rights and Governance Transformations in Eastern Europe and the United States." Pp. 151–70 in *Institutional Change: Theory and Empirical Findings*, edited by Sven-Erik Sjostrand. Armonk, N.Y.: M. E. Sharpe.

———. 1988. *Collapse of an Industry: Nuclear Power and the Contradictions of U.S. Policy*. Ithaca: Cornell University Press.

Campbell, John L., and Michael Patrick Allen. 2001. "Identifying Shifts in Policy Regimes: Cluster and Interrupted Time-Series Analyses of U.S. Income Taxes." *Social Science History* 25(2): 37–65.

———. 1994. "The Political Economy of Revenue Extraction in the Modern State: Time-Series Analysis of U.S. Income Taxes, 1916–1986." *Social Forces* 72(3): 643–69.

Campbell, John L., J. Rogers Hollingsworth, and Leon N. Lindberg, eds. 1991. *Governance of the American Economy*. New York: Cambridge University Press.

Campbell, John L., and Leon N. Lindberg. 1991. "The Evolution of Governance Regimes." Pp. 319–55 in *Governance of the American Economy*, edited by John L. Campbell, J. Rogers Hollingsworth, and Leon N. Lindberg. New York: Cambridge University Press.

———. 1990. "Property Rights and the Organization of Economic Activity by the State." *American Sociological Review* 55:634–47.

Campbell, John L., and Ove K. Pedersen. 2001a. "The Rise of Neoliberalism and Institutional Analysis." Pp. 1–24 in *The Rise of Neoliberalism and Institutional Analysis*, edited by John L. Campbell and Ove K. Pedersen. Princeton: Princeton University Press.

———. 2001b. "The Second Movement in Institutional Analysis." Pp. 249–83 in *The Rise of Neoliberalism and Institutional Analysis*, edited by John L. Campbell and Ove K. Pedersen. Princeton: Princeton University Press.

———, eds. 2001c. *The Rise of Neoliberalism and Institutional Analysis*. Princeton: Princeton University Press.

———. 1996. "The Evolutionary Nature of Revolutionary Change in Postcommunist Europe." Pp. 207–51 in *Legacies of Change: Transformations of Postcommunist European Economies*, edited by John L. Campbell and Ove K. Pedersen. New York: Aldine de Gruyter.

Carroll, Glenn R., and Michael T. Hannan. 1989. "Density Dependence in the Evolution of Populations of Newspaper Organizations." *American Sociological Review* 54:524–48.

Carroll, Glenn R., and Anand Swaminathan. 2000. "Why the Microbrewery Movement? Organizational Dynamics of Resource Partitioning." *American Journal of Sociology* 106:715–62.

Cerny, Philip G. 1997. "International Finance and the Erosion of Capitalist Diversity." Pp. 173–81 in *Political Economy of Modern Capitalism: Mapping Convergence and Diversity*, edited by Colin Crouch and Wolfgang Streeck. Thousand Oaks, Calif.: Sage.

Chandler, Alfred D., Jr. 1977. *The Visible Hand: The Managerial Revolution in American Business*. Cambridge: Harvard University Press.

Chase-Dunn, Christopher, Andrew Jorgenson, Rebecca Giem, Shoon Lio, Thomas E. Reifer, and John Rogers. 2002. "Waves of Structural Globalization since 1800: New Results on Investment Globalization." Paper presented at the annual meeting of the American Sociological Association, Chicago.

Chase-Dunn, Christopher, Yukio Kawano, and Benjamin Brewer. 2000. "Trade Globalization since 1795: Waves of Integration in the World System." *American Sociological Review* 65:77–96.

Christensen, Søren, Peter Karnøe, Jesper Strangaard Pedersen, and Frank Dobbin. 1997. "Actors and Institutions: Editors' Introduction." *American Behavioral Scientist* 40(4): 392–96.

Clemens, Elisabeth S. 1997. *The People's Lobby: Organizational Innovation and the Rise of Interest Group Politics in the United States, 1890–1925*. Chicago: University of Chicago Press.

———. 1993. "Organizational Repertoires and Institutional Change: Women's Groups and the Transformation of U.S. Politics." *American Journal of Sociology* 98:755–98.

Clemens, Elisabeth S., and James M. Cook. 1999. "Politics and Institutionalism: Explaining Durability and Change." *Annual Review of Sociology* 25:441–66.

Cohen, Michael D., James G. March, and Johan P. Olsen. 1972. "A Garbage Can Model of Organizational Choice." *Administrative Science Quarterly* 17(1): 1–25.

Coleman, James S. 1990. *Foundations of Social Theory*. Cambridge: Harvard University Press.

Coleman, James S., E. Katz, and H. Menzel. 1966. *Medical Innovation*. Indianapolis: Bobbs-Merrill.

Crafts, Nicholas. 2000. "Globalization and Growth in the Twentieth Century." Pp. 1–51 in *World Economic Outlook: Supporting Studies*. Washington, D.C.: International Monetary Fund.

Crawford, Beverly, and Arend Lijphart. 1995. "Explaining Political and Economic Change in Post-Communist Eastern Europe: Old Legacies, New Institutions, Hegemonic Norms, and International Pressures." *Comparative Political Studies* 28:171–99.

Creed, W. E. Douglas, Maureen Scully, and John R. Austin. 2002a. "Clothes Make the Person? The Tailoring of Legitimating Accounts and the Social Construction of Identity." *Organization Science* 13(5): 475–96.

———. 2002b. "A Picture of the Frame: Frame Analysis as Technique and as Politics." *Organizational Research Methods* 5(1): 34–55.

Crenson, Matthew A. 1971. *The Un-Politics of Air Pollution: A Study of Non-Decisionmaking in the Cities*. Baltimore: Johns Hopkins University Press.

Cuff, Robert D. 1973. *The War Industries Board: Business-Government Relations During World War I*. Baltimore: Johns Hopkins University Press.

Czarniawska, Barbara, and Bernward Joerges. 1996. "Travels of Ideas." Pp. 13–48 in *Translating Organizational Change*, edited by Barbara Czarniawska and Guje Sevon. New York: Aldine de Gruyter.

Czarniawska, Barbara, and Guje Sevon. 1996. "Introduction." Pp. 1–12 in *Translating Organizational Change*, edited by Barbara Czarniawska and Guje Sevon. New York: Aldine de Gruyter.

David, Paul A. 1985. "Clio and the Economics of QWERTY." *American Economic Review* 75(2): 332–37.

David, Paul A., and Dominique Foray. 1994. "Dynamics of Competitive Technology Diffusion Through Local Network Structures: The Case of EDI Document Standards." Pp. 63–78 in *Evolutionary Economics and Chaos Theory*, edited by Loet Lydesdorff and Peter Van den Besselaar. New York: St. Martin's.

Davis, Gerald F., Kristina A. Diekmann, and Catherine H. Tinsley. 1994. "The Decline and Fall of the Conglomerate Firm in the 1980s: The Deinstitutionalization of an Organizational Form." *American Sociological Review* 59:547–70.

Davis, Gerald F., and Christopher Marquis. 2001. "The Globalization of Stock Markets and Convergence in Corporate Governance." Presented at the conference on the Economic Sociology of Capitalism, Cornell University.

Davis, Gerald F., Doug McAdam, W. Richard Scott, and Mayer N. Zald, eds. Forthcoming. *Social Movements and Organization Theory*. New York: Cambridge University Press.

Davis, Gerald F., and Tracy A. Thompson. 1994. "A Social Movement Perspective on Corporate Control." *Administrative Science Quarterly* 39:141–73.

Davis, Gerald F., and Michael Useem. 2000. "Top Management, Company Directors, and Corporate Control." Pp. 233–59 in *Handbook of Strategy and Management*, edited by Andrew Pettigrew, Howard Thomas, and Richard Whittington. London: Sage.

De Goede, Marieke. 1996. "Ideology in the U.S. Welfare Debate: Neo-liberal Representations of Poverty." *Discourse and Society* 7:317–57.

Dehejia, Vivek H., and Philipp Genschel. 1999. "Tax Competition in Europe." *Politics and Society* 27(3): 403–30.

Derthick, Martha, and Paul J. Quirk. 1985. *The Politics of Deregulation*. Washington, D.C.: Brookings Institution.

DiMaggio, Paul J. 1997. "Culture and Cognition." *Annual Review of Sociology* 223:263–87.

———. 1991. "Constructing an Organizational Field as a Professional Project: U.S. Art Museums, 1920–1940." Pp. 267–92 in *The New Institutionalism in Organizational Analysis*, edited by Walter W. Powell and Paul J. DiMaggio. Chicago: University of Chicago Press.

———. 1988. "Interest and Agency in Institutional Theory." Pp. 3–21 in *Institutional Patterns and Organizations: Culture and Environment*, edited by Lynne G. Zucker. Cambridge: Ballinger.

DiMaggio, Paul J. 1986. "Cultural Entrepreneurship in Nineteenth-Century Boston: The Creation of an Organizational Base for High Culture in America." Pp. 194–211 in *Media, Culture and Society*, edited by Richard Collins. Beverly Hills, Calif.: Sage.

DiMaggio, Paul J., and Walter W. Powell. 1991. "Introduction." Pp. 1–40 in *The New Institutionalism in Organizational Analysis*, edited by Walter W. Powell and Paul J. DiMaggio. Chicago: University of Chicago Press.

———. 1983. "The Iron Cage Revisited: Institutional Isomorphism and Collective Rationality in Organizational Fields." *American Sociological Review* 48:147–60.

Djelic, Marie-Laure. 1998. *Exporting the American Model: The Postwar Transformation of European Business*. New York: Oxford University Press.

Dobbin, Frank. 1994. *Forging Industrial Policy: The United States, Britain, and France in the Railway Age*. New York: Cambridge University Press.

———. 1993. "The Social Construction of the Great Depression: Industrial Policy During the 1930s in the United States, Britain and France." *Theory and Society* 22:1–56.

———. 1992. "The Origins of Private Social Insurance: Public Policy and Fringe Benefits in America." *American Journal of Sociology* 97:1416–50.

Dobbin, Frank, John R. Sutton, John W. Meyer, and W. Richard Scott. 1993. "Equal Opportunity Law and the Construction of Internal Labor Markets." *American Journal of Sociology* 99:396–427.

Dolowitz, David P. 2000. "Introduction." *Governance: An International Journal of Policy and Administration* 13(1): 1–4.

Dolowitz, David P., and David Marsh. 2000. "Learning from Abroad: The Role of Policy Transfer in Contemporary Policy-Making." *Governance: An International Journal of Policy and Administration* 13(1): 5–24.

———. 1996. "Who Learns What from Whom? A Review of the Policy Transfer Literature." *Political Studies* 44:343–57.

Domhoff, G. William. 2002. *Who Rules America? Power and Politics*. New York: McGraw-Hill

Dore, Ronald. 1983. "Goodwill and the Spirit of Market Capitalism." *British Journal of Sociology* 34:459–82.

Dore, Ronald, William Lazonick, and Mary O'Sullivan. 1999. "Varieties of Capitalism in the Twentieth Century." *Oxford Review of Economic Policy* 15(4): 102–20.

Doremus, Paul N., William W. Keller, Louis W. Pauly, and Simon Reich. 1998. *The Myth of the Global Corporation*. Princeton: Princeton University Press.

Douglas, Mary. 1986. *How Institutions Think*. Syracuse: Syracuse University Press.

Dowell, Glen, Anand Swaminathan, and James Wade. 2002. "Pretty Pictures and Ugly Scenes: Political and Technological Maneuvers in High Definition Television." Paper presented at the conference on Organizations and Social Movements, University of Michigan.

Duina, Francesco. 2003. "National Legislatures in Common Markets: Autonomy in the European Union and Mercosur." Pp. 183–212 in *The Nation-State in Question*, edited by T. V. Paul, G. John Ikenberry, and John A. Hall. Princeton: Princeton University Press.

————. 1999. *Harmonizing Europe: Nation States within the Common Market.* Albany: State University of New York Press.

Durkheim, Emile. 1938. *The Rules of Sociological Method.* New York: Free Press.

————. 1933. *The Division of Labor in Society.* New York: Free Press.

Edelman, Lauren B. 1992. "Legal Ambiguity and Symbolic Structures: Organizational Mediation of Civil Rights Law." *American Journal of Sociology* 97:1531–76.

————. 1990. "Legal Environments and Organizational Governance: The Expansion of Due Process in the American Workplace." *American Journal of Sociology* 95:1401–40.

Edsall, Thomas Byrne. 1984. *The New Politics of Inequality.* New York: Norton.

Eldredge, Niles. 1989. "Punctuated Equilibrium, Rates of Change and Large-Scale Entities in Evolutionary Systems." Pp. 103–20 in *The Dynamics of Evolution: The Punctuated Equilibrium Debate in the Natural and Social Sciences,* edited by A. Somit and S. A. Peterson. Ithaca: Cornell University Press.

Eldredge, Niles, and Stephen Jay Gould. 1972. "Punctuated Equilibria: An Alternative to Phyletic Gradualism." Pp. 82–115 in *Models in Paleobiology,* edited by Thomas Schopf. San Francisco: Freeman Cooper.

Elster, Jon. 2000. "Rational Choice History: A Case of Excessive Ambition." *American Political Science Review* 94(3): 685–95.

————. 1998a. "A Plea for Mechanisms." Pp. 47–73 in *Social Mechanisms: An Analytical Approach to Social Theory,* edited by Peter Hedström and Richard Swedberg. New York: Cambridge University Press.

————. 1998b. "Equal or Protection? Arguing and Bargaining over the Senate at the Federal Convention." Pp. 145–61 in *Explaining Social Institutions,* edited by Jack Knight and Itai Sened. Ann Arbor: University of Michigan Press.

————. 1989. *Nuts and Bolts for the Social Sciences.* New York: Cambridge University Press.

Elster, Jon, Claus Offe, and Ulrich K. Preuss. 1998. *Institutional Design in Post-Communist Societies: Rebuilding the Ship at Sea.* New York: Cambridge University Press.

Emirbayer, Mustafa, and Ann Mische. 1998. "What Is Agency?" *American Journal of Sociology* 103:962–1023.

Esping-Andersen, Gosta. 1999. *Social Foundations of Postindustrial Economies.* New York: Oxford University Press.

————. 1990. *The Three Worlds of Welfare Capitalism.* Princeton: Princeton University Press.

Evans, Peter. 1995. *Embedded Autonomy: States and Industrial Transformation.* Princeton: Princeton University Press.

Eyestone, Robert. 1977. "Confusion, Diffusion, and Innovation." *American Political Science Review* 71:441–47.

Eyre, Dana P., and Mark C. Suchman. 1996. "Status, Norms and the Proliferation of Conventional Weapons: An Institutional Theory Approach." Pp. 79–113 in *The Culture of National Security,* edited by Peter J. Katzenstein. New York: Columbia University Press.

Finnemore, Martha. 1996. "Norms, Culture, and World Politics: Insights from Sociology's Institutionalism." *International Organization* 50(2): 325–47.

Fligstein, Neil. 2001a. *The Architecture of Markets: An Economic Sociology of Twenty-First-Century Capitalist Societies*. Princeton: Princeton University Press.

———. 2001b. "Social Skills and the Theory of Fields." *Sociological Theory* 19:105–25.

———. 1997. "Social Skill and Institutional Theory." *American Behavioral Scientist* 40(4): 397–405.

———. 1996. "Markets as Politics: A Political-Cultural Approach to Market Institutions." *American Sociological Review* 61:656–73.

———. 1990. *The Transformation of Corporate Control*. Cambridge: Harvard University Press.

Fligstein, Neil, and Iona Mara-Drita. 1996. "How to Make a Market: Reflections on the Attempt to Create a Single Market in the European Union." *American Journal of Sociology* 102:1–32.

Forbes, Linda C., and John M. Jermier. 2002. "The Institutionalization of Voluntary Organizational Greening and the Ideals of Environmentalism: Lessons about Official Culture from Symbolic Organization Theory." Pp. 194–213 in *Organizations, Policy, and the Natural Environment: Institutional and Strategic Perspectives*, edited by Andrew J. Hoffman and Marc J. Ventresca. Stanford: Stanford University Press.

Friedland, Roger, and Robert A. Alford. 1991. "Bringing Society Back In: Symbols, Practices and Institutional Contradictions." Pp. 232–64 in *The New Institutionalism in Organizational Analysis*, edited by Walter W. Powell and Paul J. DiMaggio. Chicago: University of Chicago Press.

Friedman, David. 1988. *The Misunderstood Miracle: Industrial Development and Political Change in Japan*. Ithaca: Cornell University Press.

Friedson, Eliot. 1994. *Professionalism Reborn: Theory, Prophecy and Policy*. Chicago: University of Chicago Press.

Furniss, Norman, and Timothy Tilton. 1977. *The Case for the Welfare State*. Bloomington: Indiana University Press.

Galambos, Louis, and Joseph Pratt. 1988. *The Rise of the Corporate Commonwealth: United States Business and Public Policy in the 20th Century*. New York: Basic.

Ganz, Marshall. 2000. "Resources and Resourcefulness: Strategic Capacity in the Unionization of California Agriculture, 1959–1966." *American Journal of Sociology* 105:1003–62.

Garrett, Geoffrey. 1998a. *Partisan Politics in the Global Economy*. New York: Cambridge University Press.

———. 1998b. "Global Markets and National Politics: Collision Course or Virtuous Circle?" *International Organization* 52(4): 787–824.

Garrett, Geoffrey, and Peter Lange. 1996. "Internationalization, Institutions and Political Change." Pp. 48–75 in *International and Domestic Politics*, edited by Robert O. Keohane and Helen V. Milner. New York: Cambridge University Press.

Garrett, Geoffrey, and Barry R. Weingast 1993. "Ideas, Interests, and Institutions: Constructing the European Community's Internal Market." Pp. 173–206 in *Ideas and Foreign Policy: Beliefs, Institutions, and Political Change*, edited by Judith Goldstein and Robert O. Keohane. Ithaca: Cornell University Press.

Gaventa, John. 1980. *Power and Powerlessness: Quiescence and Rebellion in an Appalachian Valley.* Urbana: University of Illinois Press.

Genschel, Philipp. 2002. "Globalization, Tax Competition, and the Welfare State." *Politics and Society* 30(2): 245–77.

Gereffi, Gary. 1994. "The International Economy and Economic Development." Pp. 206–33 in *The Handbook of Economic Sociology*, edited by Neil Smelser and Richard Swedberg. Princeton: Princeton University Press.

Gerschenkron, Alexander. 1962. *Economic Backwardness in Historical Perspective.* Cambridge: Harvard University Press.

Giddens, Anthony. 2000. *Runaway World: How Globalization Is Reshaping our Lives.* New York: Routledge.

Gilder, George. 1981. *Wealth and Poverty.* New York: Bantam.

Gilpin, Robert. 2000. *The Challenge of Global Capitalism.* Princeton: Princeton University Press.

Glatzer, Miguel, and Dietrich Rueschemeyer. 2002. "Globalization and Social Welfare Policy." Unpublished manuscript, Watson Institute for International Relations, Brown University.

Goldstein, Judith. 1993. *Ideas, Interests, and American Trade Policy.* Ithaca: Cornell University Press.

Goldstein, Judith, and Robert O. Keohane, editors. 1993a. *Ideas and Foreign Policy.* Ithaca: Cornell University Press.

———. 1993b. "Ideas and Foreign Policy: An Analytic Framework." Pp. 3–30 in *Ideas and Foreign Policy*, edited by Judith Goldstein and Robert O. Keohane. Ithaca: Cornell University Press.

Gordon, David M. 1988. "The Global Economy: New Edifice or Crumbling Foundations?" *New Left Review* 168:24–65.

Gould, Roger. 1993. "Trade Cohesion, Class Unity, and Urban Insurrection: Artisanal Activism in the Paris Commune." *American Journal of Sociology* 98:721–54.

Gould, Stephen Jay. 1989. "Punctuated Equilibrium in Fact and Theory." Pp. 54–84 in *The Dynamics of Evolution: The Punctuated Equilibrium Debate in the Natural and Social Sciences*, edited by A. Somit and S. A. Peterson. Ithaca: Cornell University Press.

———. 1982. "Darwinism and the Expansion of Evolutionary Theory." *Science* 216(April 23):380–87.

Gould, Stephen Jay, and Niles Eldredge. 1977. "Punctuated Equilibrium: The Tempo and Mode of Evolution Reconsidered." *Paleobiology* 3:115–51.

Gouldner, Alvin. 1954. *Patterns of Industrial Bureaucracy.* New York: Free Press.

Gourevitch, Peter. 1986. *Politics in Hard Times: Comparative Responses to International Economic Crises.* Ithaca: Cornell University Press.

Graham, Otis L., Jr. 1992. *Losing Time: The Industrial Policy Debate.* Cambridge: Harvard University Press.

Granovetter, Mark. 1974. *Getting a Job: A Study of Contacts and Careers.* Chicago: University of Chicago Press.

Greenwood, Royston, and C. R. Hinings. 1996. "Understanding Radical Organizational Change: Bringing Together the Old and the New Institutionalism." *Academy of Management Review* 21:1022–54.

Greenwood, Royston, and C. R. Hinings. 1993. "Understanding Strategic Change: The Contribution of Archetypes." *Academy of Management Journal* 36: 1052–81.

Greider, William. 1997. *One World Ready or Not: The Manic Logic of Global Capitalism.* New York: Simon and Schuster.

Greve, Henrich. 1995. "Jumping Ship: The Diffusion of Strategy Abandonment." *Administrative Science Quarterly* 40:444–73.

Griffin, Larry J. 1992. "Temporality, Events, and Explanation in Historical Sociology." *Sociological Methods and Research* 20(4): 403–27.

Griffin, Larry J., and Larry W. Isaac. 1992. "Recursive Regression and the Historical Use of 'Time' in Time-Series Analysis of Historical Process." *Historical Methods* 25(4): 166–79.

Guéhenno, Jean-Marie. 1995. *The End of the Nation-State.* Minneapolis: University of Minnesota Press.

Guillén, Mauro. 2001a. *The Limits of Convergence: Globalization and Organizational Change in Argentina, South Korea, and Spain.* Princeton: Princeton University Press.

———. 2001b. "Is Globalization Civilizing, Destructive, or Feeble? A Critique of Five Key Debates in the Social Science Literature." *Annual Review of Sociology* 27:235–60.

———. 1994a. *Models of Management: Work, Authority and Organization in Comparative Perspective.* Chicago: University of Chicago Press.

———. 1994b. "The Age of Eclecticism: Current Organizational Trends and the Evolution of Managerial Models." *Sloan Management Review* 36(1): 75–86.

Gulati, Ranjay, and Martin Gargiulo. 1999. "Where Do Interorganizational Networks Come From?" *American Journal of Sociology* 104:1439–93.

Guthrie, Doug. 1999. *Dragon in a Three-Piece Suit: The Emergence of Capitalism in China.* Princeton: Princeton University Press.

Haas, Peter M. 1992. "Introduction: Epistemic Communities and International Policy Coordination." *International Organization* 46(1): 1–36.

Hall, John A. 2000. "Globalization and Nationalism." Unpublished manuscript, Department of Sociology, McGill University.

Hall, Peter A. 1998. "Organized Market Economies and Unemployment in Europe: Is It Finally Time to Accept Liberal Orthodoxy?" Paper presented at the Eleventh International Conference of Europeanists, Baltimore.

———. 1993. "Policy Paradigms, Social Learning and the State." *Comparative Politics* 25:275–96.

———. 1992. "The Movement from Keynesianism to Monetarism: Institutional Analysis and British Economic Policy in the 1970s." Pp. 90–113 in *Structuring Politics*, edited by Sven Steinmo, Kathleen Thelen, and Frank Longstreth. New York: Cambridge University Press.

———, ed. 1989a. *The Political Power of Economic Ideas: Keynesianism across Nations.* Princeton: Princeton University Press.

———. 1989b. "Conclusion: The Politics of Keynesian Ideas." Pp. 361–92 in *The Political Power of Economic Ideas: Keynesianism across Nations*, edited by Peter A. Hall. Princeton: Princeton University Press.

———. 1986. *Governing the Economy: The Politics of State Intervention in Britain and France*. New York: Oxford University Press.

Hall, Peter A., and David Soskice, eds. 2001a. *Varieties of Capitalism: The Institutional Foundations of Comparative Advantage*. New York: Oxford University Press.

Hall, Peter A., and David Soskice. 2001b. "An Introduction to Varieties of Capitalism." Pp. 1–70 in *Varieties of Capitalism: The Institutional Foundations of Comparative Advantage*, edited by Peter A. Hall and David Soskice. New York: Oxford University Press.

Hall, Peter A., and Rosemary C. R. Taylor. 1998. "The Potential of Historical Institutionalism: A Response to Hay and Wincott." *Political Studies* 46: 958–62.

———. 1996. "Political Science and the Three New Institutionalisms." *Political Studies* 44:936–57.

Hallerberg, Mark. 1996. "Tax Competition in Wilhelmine Germany and Its Implications for the European Union." *World Politics* 48(3): 324–57.

Hamilton, Gary, and Nicole Biggart. 1988. "Market, Culture, and Authority: A Comparative Analysis of Management and Organization in the Far East." *American Journal of Sociology* 94:S52–S94.

Hanley, Eric, Lawrence King, and Istvan Janos Tóth. 2002. "The State, International Agencies, and Property Transformations in Post-Communist Hungary." *American Journal of Sociology* 108:129–67.

Hannah, Leslie. 1980. "Visible and Invisible Hands in Great Britain." Pp. 41–76 in *Managerial Hierarchies*, edited by Alfred D. Chandler, Jr., and Herman Daems. Cambridge: Harvard University Press.

Hannan, Michael T., and John Freeman. 1989. *Organizational Ecology*. Cambridge: Harvard University Press.

Hansen, John Mark. 1991. *Gaining Access: Congress and the Farm Lobby, 1919–1981*. Chicago: University of Chicago Press.

Harrison, Bennett. 1994. *Lean and Mean: The Changing Landscape of Corporate Power in the Age of Flexibility*. New York: Basic.

Hartigan, J. A. 1975. *Clustering Algorithms*. New York: John Wiley.

Harvey, David. 1989. *The Condition of Postmodernity*. Oxford: Blackwell.

Hattam, Victoria C. 1993. *Labor Visions and State Power: The Origins of Business Unionism in the United States*. Princeton: Princeton University Press.

Haveman, Heather A. 2000. "The Future of Organizational Sociology: Forging Ties among Paradigms." *Contemporary Sociology* 29:476–86.

———. 1993. "Follow the Leader: Mimetic Isomorphism and Entry into New Markets." *Administrative Science Quarterly* 38:593–627.

Haveman, Heather A., and Hayagreeva Rao. 1997. "Structuring a Theory of Moral Sentiments: Institutional and Organizational Coevolution in the Early Thrift Industry." *American Journal of Sociology* 102:1606–51.

Hay, Colin. 2001. "The 'Crisis' in Keynesianism and the Rise of Neoliberalism in Britain: An Ideational Institutionalist Approach." Pp. 193–218 in *The Rise of Neoliberalism and Institutional Analysis*, edited by John L. Campbell and Ove K. Pedersen. Princeton: Princeton University Press.

Hay, Colin, and Daniel Wincott. 1998. "Structure, Agency, and Historical Institutionalism." *Political Studies* 46:951–57.

Haydu, Jeffrey. 1998. "Making Use of the Past: Time Periods as Cases to Compare and as Sequences of Problem Solving." *American Journal of Sociology* 104:339–71.

Hechter, Michael. 1987. *Principles of Group Solidarity.* Berkeley: University of California Press.

Hechter, Michael, and Satoshi Kanazawa. 1997. "Sociological Rational Choice Theory." *Annual Review of Sociology* 23:191–214.

Heclo, Hugh. 1974. *Modern Social Politics in Britain and Sweden.* New Haven: Yale University Press.

Hedström, Peter. 1998. "Rational Imitation." Pp. 306–27 in *Social Mechanisms: An Analytical Approach to Social Theory,* edited by Peter Hedström and Richard Swedberg. New York: Cambridge University Press.

Hedström, Peter, and Richard Swedberg, eds. 1998a. *Social Mechanisms: An Analytical Approach to Social Theory.* New York: Cambridge University Press.

———. 1998b. "Social Mechanisms: An Introductory Essay." Pp. 1–31 in *Social Mechanisms: An Analytical Approach to Social Theory,* edited by Peter Hedström and Richard Swedberg. New York: Cambridge University Press.

Heilbroner, Robert, and William Milberg. 1995. *The Crisis of Vision in Modern Economic Thought.* New York: Cambridge University Press.

Held, David, Anthony McGrew, David Goldblatt, and Jonathan Perraton. 1999. *Global Transformations: Politics, Economics and Culture.* Stanford: Stanford University Press.

Helleiner, Eric. 1996. "Post-Globalization: Is the Financial Liberalization Trend Likely to Be Reversed?" Pp. 193–210 in *States Against Markets: The Limits of Globalization,* edited by Robert Boyer and Daniel Drache. London: Routledge.

Hemerijck, Anton, and Jonathan Zeitlin. 2002. "Policy Innovation and Hybridization in European Welfare States." Unpublished manuscript, Department of Sociology, University of Wisconsin-Madison.

Hibbs, Douglas. 1977. "On Analyzing the Effects of Policy Interventions: Box-Jenkins and Box-Tiao vs. Structural Equation Models." Pp. 137–79 in *Sociological Methodology 1977,* edited by David Heise. San Francisco: Jossey-Bass.

Hibino, Barbara. 1997. "The Transmission of Work Systems: A Comparison of U.S. and Japan Auto's Human Resource Management Practices in Mexico." Pp. 158–70 in *Governance at Work: The Social Regulation of Economic Relations,* edited by Richard Whitley and Peer Hull Kristensen. New York: Oxford University Press.

Hicks, Alexander, and Lane Kenworthy. 1998. "Cooperation and Political Economic Performance in Affluent Democratic Capitalism." *American Journal of Sociology* 103:1631–72.

Hironaka, Ann, and Evan Schofer. 2002. "Decoupling in the Environmental Arena: The Case of Environmental Impact Statements." Pp. 214–34 in *Organizations, Policy, and the Natural Environment: Institutional and Strategic Perspectives,* edited by Andrew J. Hoffman and Marc J. Ventresca. Stanford: Stanford University Press.

Hirsch, Paul M. 1997. "Sociology Without Social Structure: Neoinstitutional Theory Meets Brave New World." *American Journal of Sociology* 102:1702–23.

———. 1972. "Processing Fads and Fashions: An Organization-Set Analysis of Cultural Industry Systems." *American Journal of Sociology* 77:639–59.

Hirsch, Paul M., and Michael Lounsbury. 1997. "Ending the Family Quarrel: Toward a Reconciliation of 'Old' and 'New' Institutionalisms." *American Behavioral Scientist* 40(4): 406–18.

Hirschman, Albert O. 1977. *The Passions and the Interests*. Princeton: Princeton University Press.

Hirst, Paul, and Grahame Thompson. 1996. *Globalization in Question*. Cambridge: Polity.

Hodgson, Geoffrey M. 1994. "The Return of Institutional Economics." Pp. 58–76 in *The Handbook of Economic Sociology*, edited by Neil J. Smelser and Richard Swedberg. Princeton: Princeton University Press.

———. 1988. *Economics and Institutions: A Manifesto for a Modern Institutional Economics*. Philadelphia: University of Pennsylvania Press.

Hoefer, Richard. 1996. "Swedish Corporatism in Social Welfare Policy, 1986–1994: An Empirical Examination." *Scandinavian Political Studies* 19(1): 67–80.

Hoffman, Andrew W. 1997. *From Heresy to Dogma: An Institutional History of Corporate Environmentalism*. San Francisco: New Lexington.

Hollingsworth, J. Rogers, and Robert Boyer, eds. 1997. *Contemporary Capitalism: The Embeddedness of Institutions*. New York: Cambridge University Press.

Hollingsworth, J. Rogers, Philippe C. Schmitter, and Wolfgang Streeck, eds. 1994. *Governing Capitalist Economies: Performance and Control of Economic Sectors*. New York: Oxford University Press.

Hollingsworth, J. Rogers, and Wolfgang Streeck. 1994. "Concluding Remarks on Performance, Convergence and Competitiveness." Pp. 270–300 in *Governing Capitalist Economies: Performance and Control of Economic Sectors*, edited by J. Rogers Hollingsworth, Philippe C. Schmitter, and Wolfgang Streeck. New York: Oxford University Press.

Holm, Petter. 1995. "The Dynamics of Institutionalization: Transformation Processes in Norwegian Fisheries." *Administrative Science Quarterly* 40(3): 398–422.

Hooks, Gregory. 1991. *Forging the Military-Industrial Complex: World War II's Battle of the Potomac*. Urbana: University of Illinois Press.

Howard, Christopher. 1997. *The Hidden Welfare State: Tax Expenditures and Social Policy in the United States*. Princeton: Princeton University Press.

Ikenberry, G. John. 1988. "Conclusion: An Institutional Approach to American Foreign Economic Policy." Pp. 219–43 in *The State and American Foreign Economic Policy*, edited by G. John Ikenberry, David A. Lake, and Michael Mastanduno. Ithaca: Cornell University Press.

Immergut, Ellen M. 1998. "The Theoretical Core of the New Institutionalism." *Politics and Society* 26(1): 5–34.

———. 1992. *Health Care Politics: Ideas and Institutions in Western Europe*. Cambridge: Cambridge University Press.

Ingram, Paul, and Karen Clay. 2000. "The Choice-Within-Constraints New Institutionalism and Implications for Sociology." *Annual Review of Sociology* 26:525–46.

Isaac, Larry W. 1997. "Transforming Localities: Reflections on Time, Causality, and Narrative in Contemporary Historical Sociology." *Historical Methods* 30(1): 4–12.

Isaac, Larry W., Susan M. Carlson, and Mary P. Mathis. 1994. "Quality of Quantity in Comparative / Historical Analysis: Temporally Changing Wage Labor Regimes in the United States and Sweden." Pp. 54–92 in *The Comparative Political Economy of the Welfare State*, edited by Thomas Janoski and Alexander M. Hicks. New York: Cambridge University Press.

Isaac, Larry W., and Larry J. Griffin. 1989. "Ahistoricism in Time-Series Analyses of Historical Process: Critique, Redirection and Illustrations from U.S. Labor History." *American Sociological Review* 54:873–90.

Jacobsen, John Kurt. 1995. "Much Ado about Ideas: The Cognitive Factor in Economic Policy." *World Politics* 47:283–310.

Jacoby, Sanford M. 1995. "Social Dimensions of Global Economic Integration." Pp. 3–30 in *The Workers of Nations: Industrial Relations in a Global Economy*, edited by Sanford M. Jacoby. New York: Oxford University Press.

Jamieson, Kathleen Hall. 1996. *Packaging the Presidency*. New York: Oxford University Press.

Janelli, Roger L. 1993. *Making Capitalism: The Social and Cultural Construction of a South Korean Conglomerate*. Stanford: Stanford University Press.

Jepperson, Ronald L. 1991. "Institutions, Institutional Effects, and Institutionalism." Pp. 143–63 in *The New Institutionalism in Organizational Analysis*, edited by Walter W. Powell and Paul J. DiMaggio. Chicago: University of Chicago Press.

Jepperson, Ronald L., Alexander Wendt, and Peter J. Katzenstein. 1996. "Norms, Identity and Culture in National Security." Pp. 33–75 in *The Culture of National Security*, edited by Peter J. Katzenstein. New York: Columbia University Press.

Jessop, Bob. 1997. "The Future of the National State: Erosion or Reorganization? General Reflections on the West European Case." Paper presented at the conference on Globalization: Critical Perspectives, University of Birmingham, United Kingdom.

Jones, Bryan D. 1999. "Bounded Rationality." *Annual Review of Political Science* 2:297–321.

Kapstein, Ethan B. 1994. *Governing the Global Economy: International Finance and the State*. Cambridge: Harvard University Press.

Katzenstein, Peter J. 1996a. "Introduction: Alternative Perspectives on National Security." Pp. 1–32 in *The Culture of National Security*, edited by Peter J. Katzenstein. New York: Columbia University Press.

———, ed. 1996b. *The Culture of National Security*. New York: Columbia University Press.

———. 1993. "Coping with Terrorism: Norms and Internal Security in Germany and Japan." Pp. 265–95 in *Ideas and Foreign Policy: Beliefs, Institutions, and Political Change*. Ithaca: Cornell University Press.

———. 1985. *Small States in World Markets*. Ithaca: Cornell University Press.

———, ed. 1978. *Between Power and Plenty: Foreign Economic Policies of Advanced Industrial States*. Madison: University of Wisconsin Press.

Katznelson, Ira. 1985. "Working-Class Formation and the State." Pp. 257–84 in *Bringing the State Back In*, edited by Peter Evans, Dietrich Rueschemeyer, and Theda Skocpol. New York: Cambridge University Press.

Kaufman, Jason. 1998. "Politics as Social Learning: Policy Experts, Political Mobilization, and AIDS Preventive Policy." *Journal of Policy History* 10(3): 289–329.

Keck, Margaret, and Kathryn Sikkink. 1998. *Activists Beyond Borders: Advocacy Networks in International Politics*. Ithaca: Cornell University Press.

Keller, Morton. 1981. "The Pluralist State: American Economic Regulation in Comparative Perspective, 1900–1930." Pp. 56–94 in *Regulation in Perspective*, edited by Thomas K. McCraw. Cambridge: Harvard University Press.

Kelman, Steven. 1988. "Why Public Ideas Matter." Pp. 31–53 in *The Power of Public Ideas*, edited by Robert Reich. Cambridge: Harvard University Press.

Kenworthy, Lane. 1997. "Globalization and Economic Convergence." *Competition and Change* 2:1–64.

Keohane, Robert O., and Helen V. Milner, eds. 1996. *Internationalization and Domestic Politics*. New York: Cambridge University Press.

King, Desmond, and Stewart Wood. 1999. "The Political Economy of Neoliberalism: Britain and the United States in the 1980s." Pp. 371–97 in *Continuity and Change in Contemporary Capitalism*, edited by Herbert P. Kitschelt, Peter Lange, Gary Marks, and John D. Stephens. New York: Cambridge University Press.

Kingdon, John. 1995. *Agendas, Alternatives, and Public Policies*, 2nd ed. New York: Harper Collins.

Kiser, Edgar, and Mike Abel. 2002. "State-Making by Imitation: A Case Study of the Administrative Reforms of Peter The Great." Unpublished manuscript, Department of Sociology, University of Washington, Seattle.

Kiser, Edgar, and Michael Hechter. 1998. "The Debate on Historical Sociology: Rational Choice and Its Critics." *American Journal of Sociology* 104:785–816.

———. 1991. "The Role of General Theory in Comparative-Historical Sociology." *American Journal of Sociology* 97:1–30.

Kiser, Edgar, and Joshua Kane. 2001. "Revolution and State Structure: The Bureaucratization of Tax Administration in Early Modern England and France." *American Journal of Sociology* 107:183–223.

Kiser, Edgar, and Aaron Laing. 2001. "Have We Overestimated the Effects of Neoliberalism and Globalization? Some Speculations on the Anomalous Stability of Taxes on Business." Pp. 51–68 in *The Rise of Neoliberalism and Institutional Analysis*, edited by John L. Campbell and Ove K. Pedersen. Princeton: Princeton University Press.

Kiser, Edgar, and April Linton. 2002. "The Hinges of History: State-Making and Revolt in Early Modern France." *American Sociological Review* 67:889–910.

Kitschelt, Herbert P. 1986. "Political Opportunity Structures and Political Protest: Anti-Nuclear Movements in Four Democracies." *British Journal of Political Science* 16:57–85.

Kitschelt, Herbert P., Peter Lange, Gary Marks, and John D. Stephens. 1999. "Convergence and Divergence in Advanced Capitalist Democracies." Pp. 427–60 in *Continuity and Change in Contemporary Capitalism*, edited by Herbert P. Kitschelt, Peter Lange, Gary Marks, and John D. Stephens. New York: Cambridge University Press.

Kjaer, Peter, and Ove K. Pedersen. 2001. "Translating Liberalization: Neoliberalism in the Danish Negotiated Economy." Pp. 219–48 in *The Rise of Neoliberalism and Institutional Analysis*, edited by John L. Campbell and Ove K. Pedersen. Princeton: Princeton University Press.

Knight, Jack. 2001. "Explaining the Rise of Neoliberalism: The Mechanisms of Institutional Change." Pp. 27–50 in *The Rise of Neoliberalism and Institutional Analysis*, edited by John L. Campbell and Ove K. Pedersen. Princeton: Princeton University Press.

———. 1998. "Models, Interpretations, and Theories: Constructing Explanations of Institutional Emergence and Change." Pp. 95–120 in *Explaining Social Institutions*, edited by Jack Knight and Itai Sened. Ann Arbor: University of Michigan Press.

———. 1992. *Institutions and Social Conflict*. New York: Cambridge University Press.

Knight, Jack, and Jean Ensminger. 1998. "Conflict Over Changing Norms: Bargaining, Ideology, and Enforcement." Pp. 105–26 in *The New Institutionalism in Sociology*, edited by Mary C. Brinton and Victor Nee. New York: Russell Sage.

Knight, Jack, and Douglass North. 1997. "Explaining Economic Change: The Interplay Between Cognition and Institutions." *Legal Theory* 3:211–26.

Knight, Jack, and Itai Sened, eds. 1998a. *Explaining Social Institutions*. Ann Arbor: University of Michigan Press.

———. 1998b. "Introduction." Pp. 1–14 in *Explaining Social Institutions*, edited by Jack Knight and Itai Sened. Ann Arbor: University of Michigan Press.

Kocka, Jürgen. 1980. "The Rise of the Modern Industrial Enterprise in Germany." Pp. 77–116 in *Managerial Hierarchies*, edited by Alfred D. Chandler, Jr., and Herman Daems. Cambridge: Harvard University Press.

Kolko, Gabriel. 1963. *The Triumph of Conservatism*. Chicago: Quadrangle.

Kornai, Janos. 1992. *The Socialist System: The Political Economy of Communism*. Princeton: Princeton University Press.

Kornhauser, William. 1962. *Scientists in Industry: Conflict and Accommodation*. Berkeley: University of California Press.

Korpi, Walter. 2001. "Contentious Institutions: An Augmented Rational-Action Analysis of the Origins and Path Dependency of Welfare State Institutions in Western Countries." *Rationality and Society* 13(2): 235–83.

Kowert, Paul A., and Jeff Legro. 1996. "Norms, Identity and Their Limits: A Theoretical Reprise." Pp. 351–97 in *The Culture of National Security*, edited by Peter J. Katzenstein. New York: Columbia University Press.

Krasner, Stephen D. 1984. "Approaches to the State: Alternative Conceptions and Historical Dynamics." *Comparative Politics* 16(2): 223–46.

Krugman, Paul. 1994. "Competitiveness: A Dangerous Obsession." *Foreign Affairs* 74(2): 28–44.

Kuhn, Thomas S. 1962. *The Structure of Scientific Revolutions*. Chicago: University of Chicago Press.

Kuran, Timor. 1995. *Private Truths, Public Lies*. Cambridge: Harvard University Press.

Laitin, David. 1998. *Identity in Formation: The Russian-Speaking Populations in the Near Abroad*. Ithaca: Cornell University Press.

Langlois, Richard N. 1986. "Rationality, Institutions, and Explanation." Pp. 225–55 in *Economics as a Process: Essays in the New Institutional Economics*, edited by Richard N. Langlois. New York: Cambridge University Press.

Lash, Scott, and John Urry. 1987. *The End of Organized Capitalism*. Madison: University of Wisconsin Press.

Lazonick, William. 1991. *Business Organization and the Myth of the Market Economy*. New York: Cambridge University Press.

Levi, Margaret. 1997. *Consent, Dissent, and Patriotism*. New York: Cambridge University Press.

———. 1988. *Of Rule and Revenue*. Berkeley: University of California Press.

Levine, Ross, and Sara Zervos. 1998. "Stock Markets, Banks, and Economic Growth." *American Economic Review* 88:537–54.

Levi-Strauss, Claude. 1966. *The Savage Mind*. Chicago: University of Chicago Press.

Levy-Leboyer, Maurice. 1980. "The Large Corporation in Modern France." Pp. 117–60 in *Managerial Hierarchies*, edited by Alfred D. Chandler, Jr., and Herman Daems. Cambridge: Harvard University Press.

Lewis, Eleanor T. 2003. *Influences on Isomorphism in the Rhetoric of Organizational Language*. Ph.D. diss., Department of Social and Decision Sciences, Carnegie Mellon University.

Lieberman, Robert C. 2002. "Ideas, Institutions, and Political Order: Explaining Political Change." *American Political Science Review* 96:697–712.

Lieberson, Stanley, and Freda B. Lynn. 2002. "Barking up the Wrong Branch: Scientific Alternatives to the Current Model of Sociological Science." *Annual Review of Sociology* 28:1–19.

Lillrank, P. 1995. "The Transfer of Management Innovations from Japan." *Organization Studies* 16:971–89.

Lin, Anchi. 1995. *The Social and Cultural Bases of Private Corporate Expansion in Taiwan*. Ph.D. diss., Department of Sociology, Harvard University.

Lindberg, Leon N., and John L. Campbell. 1991. "The State and the Organization of Economic Activity." Pp. 356–95 in *Governance of the American Economy*, edited by John L. Campbell, J. Rogers Hollingsworth, and Leon N. Lindberg. New York: Cambridge University Press.

Lindberg, Leon N., and Charles S. Maier, eds. 1985. *The Politics of Inflation and Economic Stagnation*. Washington, D.C.: Brookings Institution.

Lindblom, Charles. 1959. "The Science of Muddling Through." *Public Administration Review* 19:79–88.

Locke, Richard M., and Kathleen Thelen. 1995. "Apples and Oranges Revisited: Contextualized Comparisons and the Study of Comparative Labor Politics." *Politics and Society* 23(3): 337–67.

Lounsbury, Michael. 2001. Institutional Sources of Practice Variation: Staffing College and University Recycling Programs." *Administrative Science Quarterly* 46:29–56.

Lukes, Steven. 1974. *Power: A Radical View*. London: MacMillan.

Lupia, Arthur. 1992. "Busy Voters, Agenda Control, and the Power of Information." *American Political Science Review* 86(2): 390–403.

Maddison, Angus. 1982. *Phases of Capitalist Development*. New York: Oxford University Press.

Mahoney, James. 2000a. "Path Dependence in Historical Sociology." *Theory and Society* 29:507–48.

———. 2000b. "Raising the Standard: New Guidelines for Designing Social Inquiry." Unpublished paper, Department of Sociology, Brown University.

Mann, Michael. 2001. "Globalization and September 11." *New Left Review* 12:51–72.

———. 1988. "State and Society, 1130–1815: An Analysis of English State Finances." Pp. 73–123 in *States, War, and Capitalism*, edited by Michael Mann. New York: Basil Blackwell.

Mann, Michael, and Dylan Riley. 2002. "Globalization and Inequality: The Enduring Impact of Macro-Regional Ideologies and Nation-States." Unpublished manuscript, Department of Sociology, University of California, Los Angeles.

Mansbridge, Jane J. 1986. *Why We Lost the ERA*. Chicago: University of Chicago Press.

March, James G. 1996. "Continuity and Change in Theories of Organizational Action." *Administrative Science Quarterly* 41(2): 278–87.

March, James G., and Johan P. Olsen. 1993. "Institutional Perspectives on Governance." Unpublished manuscript, Norwegian Research Center in Organization and Management, Bergen.

———. 1989. *Rediscovering Institutions: The Organizational Basis of Politics*. New York: Free Press.

———. 1984. "The New Institutionalism: Organizational Factors in Political Life." *American Political Science Review* 78:734–49.

March, James G., and Herbert Simon. 1958. *Organizations*. New York: Wiley.

Marcussen, Martin. 2000. *Ideas and Elites: The Social Construction of Economic and Monetary Union*. Aalborg: Aalborg University Press.

Marjoribanks, Timothy. 2000. *News Corporation, Technology and the Workplace: Global Strategies, Local Change*. New York: Cambridge University Press.

Martin, Cathie Jo. 2000. *Stuck in Neutral: Business and the Politics of Human Capital Investment Policy*. Princeton: Princeton University Press.

———. 1991. *Shifting the Burden: The Struggle Over Growth and Corporate Taxation*. Chicago: University of Chicago Press.

Marx, Karl. [1887] 1973. *Capital: A Critique of Political Economy*, vol. 1. New York: International Publishers.

McAdam, Doug, and W. Richard Scott. Forthcoming. "Organizations and Movements." In *Social Movements and Organization Theory*, edited by Gerald F. Davis, Doug McAdam, W. Richard Scott, and Mayer N. Zald. New York: Cambridge University Press.

McAdam, Doug, and William H. Sewell, Jr. 2001. "It's About Time: Temporality in the Study of Social Movements and Revolutions." Pp. 89–125 in *Silence and Voice in the Study of Contentious Politics*, edited by Ronald Aminzade. New York: Cambridge University Press.

McAdam, Doug, John D. McCarthy, and Mayer N. Zald. 1996. "Introduction: Opportunities, Mobilizing Structures, and Framing Processes—Toward a Synthetic, Comparative Perspective on Social Movements." Pp. 1–20 in *Comparative Perspectives on Social Movements*, edited by Doug McAdam, John D. McCarthy, and Mayer N. Zald. New York: Cambridge University Press.

McAdam, Doug, Sidney Tarrow, and Charles Tilly. 2001. *Dynamics of Contention*. New York: Cambridge University Press.

McCammon, Holly J., Karen E. Campbell, Ellen M. Granberg, and Christine Mowery. 2001. "How Movements Win: Gendered Opportunity Structures and U.S. Women's Suffrage Movements, 1866–1919." *American Sociological Review* 66:49–70.

McCarthy, John D., Jackie Smith, and Mayer N. Zald. 1996. "Accessing Public, Media, Electoral, and Governmental Agendas." Pp. 291–311 in *Comparative Perspectives on Social Movements*, edited by Doug McAdam, John D. McCarthy and Mayer N. Zald. New York: Cambridge University Press.

McCloskey, Donald N. 1985. *The Rhetoric of Economics*. Madison: University of Wisconsin Press.

McDonough, John E. 1997. *Interests, Ideas, and Deregulation*. Ann Arbor: University of Michigan Press.

McDowall, D., R. McCleary, E. E. Meidinger, and R. A. Hay. 1980. *Interrupted Time Series Analysis*. Beverley Hills, Calif.: Sage.

McGuire, Patrick, Mark Granovetter, and Michael Schwartz. 1993. "Thomas Edison and the Social Construction of the Early Electricity Industry in America." Pp. 213–46 in *Explorations in Economic Sociology*, edited by Richard Swedberg. New York: Russell Sage.

McKenzie, Richard B., and Dwight R. Lee. 1991. *Quicksilver Capital*. New York: Free Press.

McNamara, Kathleen R. 1998. *The Currency of Ideas: Monetary Politics in the European Union*. Ithaca: Cornell University Press.

Merton, Robert K. 1967. "On Sociological Theories of the Middle Range." Pp. 39–72 in *On Theoretical Sociology*. New York: Free Press.

Meyer, Alan D., Geoffrey R. Brooks, and James B. Goes. 1990. "Environmental Jolts and Industry Revolutions: Organizational Responses to Discontinuous Change." *Strategic Management Journal* 11:93–110.

Meyer, John W., John Boli, and George M. Thomas. 1987. "Ontology and Rationalization in the Western Cultural Account." Pp. 12–37 in *Institutional Structure: Constituting State, Society and the Individual*, edited by George M. Thomas, John W. Meyer, Francisco O. Ramirez, and John Boli. Beverly Hills, Calif.: Sage.

Meyer, John W., John Boli, George M. Thomas, and Francisco O. Ramirez. 1997a. "World Society and the Nation State." *American Journal of Sociology* 103(1): 144–81.

Meyer, John W., David Frank, Ann Hironaka, Evan Schofer, and Nancy B. Tuma. 1997b. "The Structuring of a World Environmental Regime, 1870–1990." *International Organization* 51:623–51.

Meyer, John W., and Brian Rowan. 1977. "Institutionalized Organizations: Formal Structure as Myth and Ceremony." *American Journal of Sociology* 83:340–63.

Milner, Helen V., and Robert O. Keohane. 1996. "Internationalization and Domestic Politics: An Introduction." Pp. 3–24 in *Internationalization and Domestic Politics*, edited by Robert O. Keohane and Helen V. Milner. New York: Cambridge University Press.

Mittelman, James H. 2000. *The Globalization Syndrome: Transformation and Resistance*. Princeton: Princeton University Press.

Mizruchi, Mark S., and Lisa C. Fein. 1999. "The Social Construction of Organizational Knowledge: A Study of the Uses of Coercive, Mimetic, and Normative Isomorphism." *Administrative Science Quarterly* 44:653–83.

Moe, Terry. 1987. "Interests, Institutions, and Positive Theory: The Politics of the NLRB." *Studies in American Political Development* 2:236–99.

Moon, Marilyn, and Isabel V. Sawhill. 1984. "Family Incomes: Gainers and Losers." Pp. 317–46 in *The Reagan Record*, edited by John L. Palmer and Isabel V. Sawhill. Cambridge: Ballinger.

Moore, David W. 1995. *The Superpollsters*. New York: Four Walls Eight Windows Press.

Moore, Mark H. 1988. "What Sort of Ideas Become Public Ideas?" Pp. 55–83 in *The Power of Public Ideas*, edited by Robert Reich. Cambridge: Harvard University Press.

Morrill, Calvin. Forthcoming. "Institutional Change Through Interstitial Emergence: The Growth of Alternative Dispute Resolution in American Law, 1965–1995." In *How Institutions Change*, edited by Walter W. Powell and Daniel L. Jones. Chicago: University of Chicago Press.

Morris, Aldon. 2000. "Reflections on Social Movement Theory: Criticisms and Proposals." *Contemporary Sociology* 29:445–54.

Nee, Victor. 2001. "North's Theory of Institutional Change and State Capitalism in China." Paper presented at the conference on the Economic Sociology of Capitalism, Center for the Study of Economy and Society, Cornell University.

———. 1998. "Sources of the New Institutionalism." Pp. 1–16 in *The New Institutionalism in Sociology*, edited by Mary C. Brinton and Victor Nee. New York: Russell Sage.

Nelson, Richard R. 1994a. "Evolutionary Theorizing about Economic Change." Pp. 108–36 in *The Handbook of Economic Sociology*, edited by Neil J. Smelser and Richard Swedberg. Princeton: Princeton University Press.

———. 1994b. "Economic Growth via the Coevolution of Technology and Institutions." Pp. 21–32 in *Evolutionary Economics and Chaos Theory*, edited by Loet Lydesdorff and Peter Van den Besselaar. New York: St. Martin's.

Nelson, Richard R., and Sidney G. Winter. 1982. *An Evolutionary Theory of Economic Change*. Cambridge: Harvard University Press.

Nielsen, Klaus, and Ove K. Pedersen. 1991. "From the Mixed Economy to the Negotiated Economy: The Scandinavian Countries." Pp. 145–67 in *Morality,*

Rationality, and Efficiency: New Perspectives on Socio-Economics, edited by Richard M. Coughlin. Armonk, N.Y.: M. E. Sharpe.

North, Douglass C. 2001. "The Need for a Cognitive Social Science." Keynote address at the Conference on the Economic Sociology of Capitalism, Center for the Study of Economy and Society, Cornell University.

———. 1998. "Five Propositions about Institutional Change." Pp. 15–26 in *Explaining Social Institutions*, edited by Jack Knight and Itai Sened. Ann Arbor: University of Michigan Press.

———. 1990. *Institutions, Institutional Change and Economic Performance*. New York: Cambridge University Press.

———. 1981. *Structure and Change in Economic History*. New York: Norton.

Oakes, Leslie S., Barbara Townley, and David J. Cooper. 1998. "Business Planning as Pedagogy: Language and Control in a Changing Institutional Field." *Administrative Science Quarterly* 43:257–92.

Ó Riain, Seán. 2000. "States and Markets in an Era of Globalization." *Annual Review of Sociology* 26:187–213.

OECD. 2000a. *Revenue Statistics, 1965–1999*. Paris: Organization for Economic Cooperation and Development.

———. 2000b. *Toward Global Tax Cooperation: Report to the 2000 Ministerial Council Meeting and Recommendations by the Committee on Fiscal Affairs*. Paris: Organization for Economic Cooperation and Development.

Ohmae, Kenichi. 1995. *The End of the Nation State*. New York: Free Press.

———. 1990. *The Borderless World: Power and Strategy in the Interlinked Economy*. New York: Harper Collins.

Orren, Karen. 1991. *Belated Feudalism: Labor, the Law, and Liberal Development in the United States*. New York: Cambridge University Press.

Orren, Karen, and Stephen Skowronek. 1994. "Beyond the Iconography of Order: Notes for a 'New Institutionalism.'" Pp. 311–30 in *The Dynamics of American Politics*, edited by Lawrence D. Dodd and Calvin Jillson. Boulder: Westview.

Ostrom, Elinor. 1991. "Rational Choice Theory and Institutional Analysis: Toward Complementarity." *American Political Science Review* 85(1): 237–43.

———. 1990. *Governing the Commons: The Evolution of Institutions for Collective Action*. New York: Cambridge University Press.

Ouchi, William G. 1981. *Theory Z: How American Business Can Meet the Japanese Challenge*. New York: Avon.

Padgett, John F. 1998. "Organizational Genesis, Identity and Control: The Transformation of Banking in Renaissance Florence." Paper presented at the seminar on Social and Institutional Change at the Robert Wood Johnson Foundation, organized through the Princeton University Center for the Study of Social Organization and Change.

Pagano, Marcello, and Kimberlee Gauvreau. 1993. *Principles of Biostatistics*. Belmont, Mass.: Duxbury.

Palan, Ronen, and Jason Abbott. 1999. *State Strategies in the Global Political Economy*. London: Pinter.

Parsons, Talcott. 1963. "Social Change and Medical Organization in the United States: A Sociological Perspective." *The Annals of the American Academy of Political and Social Science* 356:21–33.

———. 1951. *The Social System*. New York: Free Press.

Pedersen, Ove K. 1993. "The Institutional History of the Danish Polity: From a Market and Mixed Economy to a Negotiated Economy." Pp. 277–300 in *Institutional Change: Theory and Empirical Findings*, edited by Sven-Erik Sjöstrand. Armonk, N.Y.: M. E. Sharpe.

———. 1991. "Nine Questions to a Neo-Institutional Theory in Political Science." *Scandinavian Political Studies* 14(2): 125–18.

Pekkarinen, Jukka. 1989. "Keynesianism and the Scandinavian Models of Economic Policy." Pp. 311–46 in *The Political Power of Economic Ideas*, edited by Peter A. Hall. Princeton: Princeton University Press.

Perrow, Charles. 2002. *Organizing America: Wealth, Power, and the Origins of Corporate Capitalism*. Princeton: Princeton University Press.

———. 1986. *Complex Organizations: A Critical Essay*, 3rd. ed. New York: Random House.

Pestoff, Victor. 1991. "The Politics of Private Business, Cooperatives and Public Enterprise in a Corporate Democracy: The Case of Sweden." Department of Business Administration, University of Stockholm.

Peters, B. Guy. 1999. *Institutional Theory in Political Science: The "New Institutionalism."* London: Pinter.

Phillips, Louise. 1996. "Rhetoric and the Spread of the Discourse of Thatcherism." *Discourse and Society* 7:209–41.

Pierson, Paul. 2000a. "Not Just What, but When: Timing and Sequence in Political Processes." *Studies in American Political Development* 14(Spring): 72–92.

———. 2000b. "Increasing Returns, Path Dependence, and the Study of Politics." *American Political Science Review* 94(2): 251–67.

———. 2000c. "Big, Slow-Moving, and . . . Invisible: Macro-Social Processes in the Study of Comparative Politics." Unpublished manuscript, Department of Government, Harvard University.

———. 1994. *Dismantling the Welfare State?* New York: Cambridge University Press.

———. 1993. "When Effect Becomes Cause: Policy Feedback and Political Change." *World Politics* 45:595–628.

Pierson, Paul, and Theda Skocpol. 2000. "Historical Institutionalism in Contemporary Political Science." Presented at the annual meeting of the American Political Science Association, Washington, D.C.

Piore, Michael J. 1995. *Beyond Individualism: How Social Demands of the New Identity Groups Challenge American Political and Economic Life*. Cambridge: Harvard University Press.

Piore, Michael J., and Charles F. Sabel. 1984. *The Second Industrial Divide*. New York: Basic.

Piven, Frances Fox. 1995. "Is it Global Economics or Neo-Laissez-Faire?" *New Left Review* 123:107–14.

Polanyi, Karl. 1944. *The Great Transformation: The Political and Economic Origins of Our Time*. Boston: Beacon.

Pontusson, Jonas, and Peter Swenson. 1996. "Labor Markets, Production Strategies, and Wage Bargaining Institutions: The Swedish Employer Offensive in Comparative Perspective." *Comparative Political Studies* 29(2): 223–50.

Powell, Walter W. 1991. "Expanding the Scope of Institutional Analysis." Pp. 183–203 in *The New Institutionalism in Organizational Analysis*, edited by Walter W. Powell and Paul J. DiMaggio. Chicago: University of Chicago Press.

———. 1987. "Hybrid Organizational Arrangements." *California Management Review* 30(1): 67–87.

———. 1985. *Getting into Print*. Chicago: University of Chicago Press.

Powell, Walter W., and Paul J. DiMaggio, eds. 1991. *The New Institutionalism in Organizational Analysis*. Chicago: University of Chicago Press.

Pressman, Jeffrey, and Aaron Wildavsky. 1979. *Implementation*. Berkeley: University of California Press.

Price, Richard, and Nina Tannenwald. 1996. "Norms and Deterrence: The Nuclear and Chemical Weapons Taboos." Pp. 114–52 in *The Culture of National Security: Norms and Identity in World Politics*, edited by Peter J. Katzenstein. New York: Columbia University Press.

Quadagno, Jill, and Stan J. Knapp. 1992. "Have Historical Sociologists Forsaken Theory? Thoughts on the History/Theory Relationship." *Sociological Methods and Research* 20(4): 481–507.

Quick, Perry D. 1984. "Businesses: Reagan's Industrial Policy." Pp. 287–16 in *The Reagan Record*, edited by John L. Palmer and Isabel V. Sawhill. Cambridge: Ballinger.

Rao, Hayagreeva, Phillipe Monin, and Rodolphe Durand. 2003. "Institutional Change in Toque Ville: Nouvelle Cuisine as an Identity Movement in French Gastronomy." *American Journal of Sociology* 108:795–843.

Rao, Hayagreeva, Calvin Morrill, and Mayer N. Zald. 2000. "Power Plays: How Social Movements and Collective Action Create New Organizational Forms." *Research in Organization Behavior* 22:239–82.

Rao, Hayagreeva, and Kumar Sivakumar. 1999. "Institutional Sources of Boundary-Spanning Structures: The Establishment of Investor Relations Departments in the *Fortune 500* Industrials." *Organization Science* 10(1): 27–42.

Reich, Robert. 1991. *The Work of Nations*. New York: Vintage.

Reskin, Barbara F. 2003. "Including Mechanisms in Our Models of Ascriptive Inequality." *American Sociological Review* 68:1–21.

Ricci, David M. 1993. *The Transformation of American Politics: The New Washington and the Rise of Think Tanks*. New Haven: Yale University Press.

Riker, William H. 1998. "The Experience of Creating Institutions: The Framing of the United States Constitution." Pp. 121–44 in *Explaining Social Institutions*, edited by Jack Knight and Itai Sened. Ann Arbor: University of Michigan Press.

Risse, Thomas, Stephen C. Ropp, and Kathryn Sikkink, eds. 1999. *The Power of Human Rights: International Norms and Domestic Change*. New York: Cambridge University Press.

Risse, Thomas, and Kathryn Sikkink. 1999. "The Socialization of International Human Rights Norms into Domestic Practices: Introduction." Pp. 1–38 in *The Power of Human Rights: International Norms and Domestic Change*, edited by

Thomas Risse, Stephen C. Ropp, and Kathryn Sikkink. New York: Cambridge University Press.

Risse-Kappen, Thomas. 1994. "Ideas Do Not Float Freely: Transnational Coalitions, Domestic Structures, and the End of the Cold War." *International Organization* 48(2): 185–214.

Roberts, Paul Craig. 1984. *The Supply-Side Revolution*. Cambridge: Harvard University Press.

Rodrik, Dani. 1997. *Has Globalization Gone Too Far?* Washington, D.C.: Institute for International Economics.

———. 1996. "Why Do More Open Economies Have Bigger Governments?" Working paper no. 5537, National Bureau of Economic Research. Cambridge: National Bureau of Economic Research.

Roe, Mark J. 1999. "Lifetime Employment: Labor Peace and the Evolution of Japanese Corporate Governance." *Columbia Law Review* 99(2): 508–40.

———. 1996. "Chaos and Evolution in Law and Economics." *Harvard Law Review* 109(3): 641–68.

———. 1994. *Strong Managers, Weak Owners*. Princeton: Princeton University Press.

Rogers, Joel, and Wolfgang Streeck. 1994. "Workplace Representation Overseas: The Works Councils Story." Pp. 97–156 in *Working Under Different Rules*, edited by Richard Freeman. New York: Russell Sage.

Rohrlich, Paul Egon. 1987. "Economic Culture and Foreign Policy: The Cognitive Analysis of Economic Policy Making." *International Organization* 41(1): 61–92.

Rosenberg, Justin. 2000. *The Follies of Globalization Theory*. New York: Verso.

Roy, William G. 1997. *Socializing Capital: The Rise of the Large Industrial Corporation in America*. Princeton: Princeton University Press.

Rueschemeyer, Dietrich, and Theda Skocpol, editors. 1996a. *States, Social Knowledge, and the Origins of Modern Social Policies*. Princeton: Princeton University Press.

———. 1996b. "Conclusion." Pp. 296–312 in *States, Social Knowledge, and the Origins of Modern Social Policies*, edited by Dietrich Rueschemeyer and Theda Skocpol. Princeton: Princeton University Press.

Rutherford, Malcolm. 1994. *Institutions in Economics: The Old and the New Institutionalism*. New York: Cambridge University Press.

Sabel, Charles. 1993. "Studied Trust: Building New Forms of Cooperation in a Volatile Economy." Pp. 104–44 in *Explorations in Economic Sociology*, edited by Richard Swedberg. New York: Russell Sage.

Sacks, Michael Alan. 2002. "The Social Structure of New Venture Funding: Stratification and the Differential Liability of Newness." *Research in the Sociology of Organizations* 19:263–94.

Samuels, Richard J. 1987. *The Business of the Japanese State*. Ithaca: Cornell University Press.

Sassen, Saskia. 1998. *Globalization and Its Discontents*. New York: New Press.

———. 1996. *Losing Control: Sovereignty in an Age of Globalization*. New York: Columbia University Press.

Saxenian, Annalee. 1994. *Regional Advantage: Culture and Competition in Silicon Valley and Route 128*. Cambridge: Harvard University Press.

Scharpf, Fritz W. 1997. *Games Real Actors Play: Actor-Centered Institutionalism in Policy Research*. Boulder: Westview.

Scherrer, Christoph. 1991. "Governance of the Steel Industry: What Caused the Disintegration of the Oligopoly?" Pp. 182–208 in *Governance of the American Economy*, edited by John L. Campbell, J. Rogers Hollingsworth, and Leon N. Lindberg. New York: Cambridge University Press.

Schmidt, Vivien A. 2002. *The Futures of European Capitalism*. New York: Oxford University Press.

———. 2001. "Discourse and the Legitimation of Economic and Social Policy Change in Europe." Pp. 229–72 in *Globalization and the European Political Economy*, edited by Steven Weber. New York: Columbia University Press.

———. 2000. "Democracy and Discourse in an Integrating Europe and a Globalizing World." *European Law Journal* 6:277–300.

Schneiberg, Marc. 2002. "Organizational Heterogeneity and the Production of New Forms: Politics, Social Movements and Mutual Companies in American Fire Insurance, 1900–1930." *Research in the Sociology of Organizations* 19:39–89.

———. 1999. "Political and Institutional Conditions for Governance by Association: Private Order and Price Controls in American Fire Insurance." *Politics and Society* 27(1): 67–103.

Schneiberg, Marc, and Tim Bartley. 2001. "Regulating American Industries: Markets, Politics, and the Institutional Determinants of Fire Insurance Regulation." *American Journal of Sociology* 107:101–46.

Schneiberg, Marc, and Elisabeth S. Clemens. Forthcoming. "The Typical Tools for the Job: Research Strategies in Institutional Analysis." In *How Institutions Change*, edited by Walter W. Powell and Dan L. Jones. Chicago: University of Chicago Press.

Schön, Donald A., and Martin Rein. 1994. *Frame Reflection: Toward the Resolution of Intractable Policy Controversies*. New York: Basic.

Schulze, Gunther G., and Heinrich W. Ursprung. 1999. "Globalization of the Economy and the Nation State." *World Economy* 22(3): 295–352.

Schumpeter, Joseph A. [1934] 1983. *The Theory of Economic Development*. New Brunswick, N.J.: Transaction.

Scott, James. 1990. *Domination and the Arts of Resistance: Hidden Transcripts*. New Haven: Yale University Press.

Scott, W. Richard. 2001. *Institutions and Organizations*, 2nd ed. Thousand Oaks, Calif.: Sage.

———. 1992. *Organizations: Rational, Natural, and Open Systems*. New York: Prentice Hall.

———. 1966. "Professionals in Bureaucracies: Areas of Conflict." In *Professionalization*, edited by H. M. Vollmer and D. L. Mills. Englewood Cliffs, N.J.: Prentice-Hall.

Scott, W. Richard, and John W. Meyer, editors. 1994. *Institutional Environments and Organizations: Structural Complexity and Individualism*. Thousand Oaks, Calif.: Sage.

Scott, W. Richard, Martin Ruef, Peter J. Mendel, and Carol A. Caronna. 2000. *Institutional Change and Healthcare Organizations: From Professional Dominance to Managed Care.* Chicago: University of Chicago Press.

Selznick, Philip. 1949. *TVA and the Grass Roots.* Berkeley: University of California Press.

Sheingate, Adam. Forthcoming. "Political Entrepreneurship, Institutional Change, and American Political Development." *American Studies in Political Development.*

Shepsle, Kenneth A. 1986. "Institutional Equilibrium and Equilibrium Institutions." Pp. 51–81 in *Political Science: The Science of Politics*, edited by Herbert Weisberg. New York: Agathon.

Shonfield, Andrew. 1965. *Modern Capitalism.* New York: Oxford University Press.

Shore, Bradd, 2001. "Making Sense of Change." Unpublished manuscript, Department of Anthropology, Emory University, Atlanta, Georgia.

Sik, Andre. 1992. "From the Second to the Informal Economy." *Journal of Public Policy* 12(2): 153–75.

Simmons, Beth. 1999. "The Internationalization of Capital." Pp. 36–69 in *Continuity and Change in Contemporary Capitalism*, edited by Herbert P. Kitschelt, Peter Lange, Gary Marks, and John D. Stephens. New York: Cambridge University Press.

Skocpol, Theda. 2000. *The Missing Middle: Working Families and the Future of American Social Policy.* New York: Norton.

———. 1992. *Protecting Soldiers and Mothers.* Cambridge: Belknap / Harvard University Press.

———. 1985. "Bringing the State Back In: Strategies of Analysis in Current Research." Pp. 3–44 in *Bringing the State Back In*, edited by Peter Evans, Dietrich Rueschemeyer, and Theda Skocpol. New York: Cambridge University Press.

———. 1984. "Sociology's Historical Imagination." Pp. 1–21 in *Vision and Method in Historical Sociology*, edited by Theda Skocpol. New York: Cambridge University Press.

———. 1979. *States and Social Revolutions: A Comparative Analysis of France, Russia, and China.* New York: Cambridge University Press.

Skocpol, Theda, and Edwin Amenta. 1995. "Redefining the New Deal: World War II and the Development of Social Provision in the United States." Pp. 167–208 in *Social Policy in the United States*, edited by Theda Skocpol. Princeton: Princeton University Press.

Skocpol, Theda, and G. John Ikenberry. 1995. "The Road to Social Security." Pp. 136–66 in *Social Policy in the United States*, edited by Theda Skocpol. Princeton: Princeton University Press.

Skowronek, Stephen. 1995. "Order and Change." *Polity* 28(1): 91–96.

———. 1982. *Building a New American State: The Expansion of National Administrative Capacities, 1870–1920.* New York: Cambridge University Press.

Skrentny, John David. 1998. "The Effect of the Cold War on African-American Civil Rights: America and the World Audience, 1945–1968." *Theory and Society* 27:237–85.

————. 1996. *The Ironies of Affirmative Action: Politics, Culture, and Justice in America*. Chicago: University of Chicago Press.

Smith, Michael R. 1992. *Power, Norms, and Inflation: A Skeptical Treatment*. New York: Aldine de Gruyter.

Smith, Rogers M. 1995. "Ideas, Institutions, and Strategic Choice." *Polity* 28(1): 135–40.

Snow, David, and Robert D. Benford. 1992. "Master Frames and Cycles of Protest." Pp. 133–55 in *Frontiers in Social Movement Theory*, edited by Aldon Morris and Carol McClurg Mueller. New Haven: Yale University Press.

Snow, David, Burke Rochford, Steven Worden, and Robert Benford. 1986. "Frame Alignment Processes, Micromobilization, and Movement Participation." *American Sociological Review* 51:464–81.

Sørensen, Aage. 1998. "Theoretical Mechanisms and the Empirical Study of Social Processes." Pp. 238–66 in *Social Mechanisms: An Analytical Approach to Social Theory*, edited by Peter Hedström and Richard Swedberg. New York: Cambridge University Press.

Soskice, David. 1999. "Divergent Production Regimes: Coordinated and Uncoordinated Market Economies in the 1980s and 1990s." Pp. 101–34 in *Continuity and Change in Contemporary Capitalism*, edited by Herbert P. Kitschelt, Peter Lange, Gary Marks, and John D. Stephens. New York: Cambridge University Press.

Soysal, Yasemin. 1994. *Limits of Citizenship*. Chicago: University of Chicago Press.

Stark, David. 1996. "Recombinant Property in East European Capitalism." *American Journal of Sociology* 101:993–1027.

————. 1986. "Rethinking Internal Labor Markets: New Insights from a Comparative Perspective." *American Sociological Review* 51:492–504.

Stark, David, and Laszlo Bruszt. 1998. *Postsocialist Pathways: Transforming Politics and Property in East Central Europe*. New York: Cambridge University Press.

Stein, Herbert. 1996. "The Fiscal Revolution in America, Part II: 1964–1994." Pp. 194–286 in *Funding the Modern American State, 1941–1995*, edited by W. Elliot Brownlee. New York: Cambridge University Press.

————. 1990. *The Fiscal Revolution in America*. Washington, D.C.: American Enterprise Institute Press.

Steinmo, Sven. 2002. "Globalization and Taxation: Challenges to the Swedish Welfare State." *Comparative Political Studies* 35(7): 839–62.

————. 1993. *Taxation and Democracy*. New Haven: Yale University Press.

Steinmo, Sven, Kathleen Thelen, and Frank Longstreth, eds. 1992. *Structuring Politics: Historical Institutionalism in Comparative Perspective*. New York: Cambridge University Press.

Steinmo, Sven, and Caroline J. Tolbert. 1998. "Do Institutions Really Matter? Taxation in Industrialized Democracies." *Comparative Political Studies* 31(2): 165–87.

Stephens, John D., Evelyne Huber, and Leonard Ray. 1999. "The Welfare State in Hard Times." Pp. 164–93 in *Continuity and Change in Contemporary Capi-*

talism, edited by Herbert P. Kitschelt, Peter Lange, Gary Marks, and John D. Stephens. New York: Cambridge University Press.

Stinchcombe, Arthur L. 1998. "Monopolistic Competition as a Mechanism: Corporations, Universities, and Nation-States in Competitive Fields." Pp. 267–305 in *Social Mechanisms: An Analytical Approach to Social Theory*, edited by Peter Hedström and Richard Swedberg. New York: Cambridge University Press.

———. 1997. "On the Virtues of the Old Institutionalism." *Annual Review of Sociology* 23:1–18.

———. 1968. *Constructing Social Theories*. Chicago: University of Chicago Press.

Stone, Diane. 1999. "Learning Lessons and Transferring Policy Across Time, Space and Disciplines." *Politics* 19(1): 51–59.

———. 1996. *Capturing the Political Imagination: Think Tanks and the Policy Process*. London: Frank Cass.

Strang, David. 1990. "From Dependency to Sovereignty: An Event History Analysis of Decolonization." *American Sociological Review* 55:846–70.

Strang, David, and Ellen M. Bradburn. 2001. "Theorizing Legitimacy or Legitimating Theory? Neoliberal Discourse and HMO Policy, 1970–1989." Pp. 129–58 in *The Rise of Neoliberalism and Institutional Analysis*, edited by John L. Campbell and Ove K. Pedersen. Princeton: Princeton University Press.

Strang, David, and Michael W. Macy. 2001. "In Search of Excellence: Fads, Success Stories, and Adaptive Emulation." *American Journal of Sociology* 107:147–82.

Strang, David, and John W. Meyer. 1993. "Institutional Conditions for Diffusion." *Theory and Society* 22:487–511.

Strang, David, and Sarah A. Soule. 1998. "Diffusion in Organizations and Social Movements: From Hybrid Corn to Poison Pills." *Annual Review of Sociology* 24:265–90.

Strange, Susan. 1997. "The Future of Global Capitalism: Or, Will Divergence Persist Forever?" Pp. 182–91 in *Political Economy of Modern Capitalism: Mapping Convergence and Diversity*, edited by Colin Crouch and Wolfgang Streeck. Thousand Oaks, Calif.: Sage.

Stråth, Bo. 1990. "Introduction: Production of Meaning, Construction of Class Identities, and Social Change." Pp. 1–23 in *Language and the Construction of Class Identities*, report no. 3, edited by Bo Stråth. Project on Continuity and Discontinuity in the Democratization Process, Gothenburg University.

Streeck, Wolfgang. 1997. "Beneficial Constraints: On the Economic Limits of Rational Voluntarism." Pp. 197–219 in *Contemporary Capitalism: The Embeddedness of Institutions*, edited by J. Rogers Hollingsworth and Robert Boyer. New York: Cambridge University Press.

———. 1991. "On the Institutional Conditions of Diversified Quality Production." Pp. 21–61 in *Beyond Keynesianism: The Socio-Economics of Production and Full Employment*, edited by Egon Matzner and Wolfgang Streeck. Aldershot, U.K.: Edward Elgar.

Streeck, Wolfgang, and Philippe C. Schmitter. 1985. "Community, Market, State—and Associations? The Prospective Contribution of Interest Governance to Social Order." Pp. 1–29 in *Private Interest Government: Beyond Market and*

State, edited by Wolfgang Streeck and Philippe C. Schmitter. Beverly Hills, Calif.: Sage.

Suchman, Mark C. 1997. "On Beyond Interest: Rational, Normative, and Cognitive Perspectives in the Social Scientific Study of Law." *Wisconsin Law Review* 1997(3): 475–501.

Swank, Duane. 2002. *Global Capital, Political Institutions and Policy Change in Developed Welfare States*. New York: Cambridge University Press.

————. 1998. "Funding the Welfare State: Globalization and the Taxation of Business in Advanced Market Economies." *Political Studies* 46:671–92.

Swank, Duane, and Cathie Jo Martin. 2001. "Employers and the Welfare State: The Political Economic Organization of Firms and Social Policy in Contemporary Capitalist Democracies." *Comparative Political Studies* 34(8): 889–923.

Swank, Duane, and Sven Steinmo. 2002. "The New Political Economy of Taxation in Advanced Capitalist Democracies." *American Journal of Political Science* 46(3): 642–55.

Swedberg, Richard. 2000. *Entrepreneurship: The Social Science View*. New York: Oxford University Press.

Swidler, Ann. 1986. "Culture in Action: Symbols and Strategies." *American Sociological Review* 51:273–86.

Sztompka, Piotr. 1993. *The Sociology of Change*. Cambridge: Blackwell.

Tanzi, Vito. 1995. *Taxation in an Integrating World*. Washington, D.C.: Brookings Institution.

Tarrow, Sidney. 1996. "States and Opportunities: The Political Structuring of Social Movements." Pp. 41–61 in *Comparative Perspectives on Social Movements*, edited by Doug McAdam, John D. McCarthy, and Mayer N. Zald. New York: Cambridge University Press.

————. 1994. *Power in Movement: Social Movements, Collective Action and Politics*. New York: Cambridge University Press.

Temin, Peter. 1999. "Globalization." *Oxford Economic Review* 15(4): 76–83.

Thelen, Kathleen. 2000a. "Timing and Temporality in the Analysis of Institutional Evolution and Change." *Studies in American Political Development* 14(Spring): 101–8.

————. 2000b. "How Institutions Evolve: Insights from Comparative-Historical Analysis." Unpublished manuscript, Department of Political Science, Northwestern University.

————. 2000c. "Why German Employers Cannot Bring Themselves to Dismantle the German Model." Pp. 138–69 in *Unions, Employers and Central Banks*, edited by Torben Iversen, Jonas Pontusson, and David Soskice. New York: Cambridge University Press.

————. 1999. "Historical Institutionalism in Comparative Politics." *Annual Review of Political Science* 2:369–404.

Thelen, Kathleen, and Ikuo Kume. 1999. "The Effects of 'Globalization' on Labor Revisited: Lessons from Germany and Japan." *Politics and Society* 27(4): 476–504.

Thelen, Kathleen, and Sven Steinmo. 1992. "Historical Institutionalism in Comparative Politics." Pp. 1–32 in *Structuring Politics: Historical Institutionalism in Comparative Analysis*. New York: Cambridge University Press.

Thomas, George M., John W. Meyer, Francisco O. Ramirez, and John Boli, eds. 1987. *Institutional Structure: Constituting State, Society, and the Individual.* Newbury Park, Calif.: Sage.

Thornton, Patricia H. 1999. "The Sociology of Entrepreneurship." *Annual Review of Sociology* 25:19–46.

Thornton, Patricia H., and Katherine H. Flynn. Forthcoming. "Entrepreneurship, Networks, and Geographies." In *The International Handbook of Entrepreneurship,* edited by Zoltan J. Acs and David B. Audretsch. Amsterdam: Kluwer.

Thornton, Patricia H., and William Ocasio. 1999. "Institutional Logics and the Historical Contingency of Power in Organizations: Executive Succession in the Higher Education Publishing Industry, 1958–1990." *American Journal of Sociology* 105:801–43.

Tilly, Charles. 1994. "The Time of States." *Social Research* 61(2): 267–95.

———. 1984. *Big Structures, Large Processes, Huge Comparisons.* New York: Russell Sage.

Tolbert, Pamela S., and Lyne G. Zucker. 1983. "Institutional Sources of Change in the Formal Structure of Organizations: The Diffusion of Civil Service Reform, 1880–1935." *Administrative Science Quarterly* 28:22–39.

Tushman, Michael L., and Philip Anderson. 1986. "Technological Discontinuities and Organizational Environments." *Administrative Science Quarterly* 31: 439–65.

Useem, Michael. 1996. *Investor Capitalism: How Money Managers Are Changing the Face of Corporate America.* New York: Basic.

Uzzi, Brian. 1996. "The Sources and Consequences of Embeddedness for the Economic Performance of Organizations: The Network Effect." *American Sociological Review* 61:674–98.

Vanberg, V., and James Buchanan. 1989. "Interests and Theories in Constitutional Choice." *Journal of Theoretical Politics* 1:49–62.

Van de Ven, Andrew H., and Raghu Garud. 1993. "Innovation and Industry Development: The Case of Cochlear Implants." *Research on Technological Innovation, Management and Policy* 5:1–46.

Van de Ven, Andrew H., and D. N. Grazman. 1999. "Evolution in a Nested Hierarchy: A Genealogy of Twin Cities Health Care Organizations, 1853–1995." Pp. 185–212 in *Variations in Organization Science: In Honor of Donald T. Campbell,* edited by J. A. C. Baum and B. McKelvey. Thousand Oaks, Calif.: Sage.

Van de Ven, Andrew H., and Tim Hargrave. Forthcoming. "Social, Technical, and Institutional Change: A Literature Review and Synthesis." In *Handbook of Organizational Change and Innovation,* edited by Marshall Scott Poole and Andrew Van de Ven. New York: Oxford University Press.

Van de Ven, Andrew H., and Marshall Scott Poole. 1995. "Explaining Development and Change in Organizations." *Academy of Management Review* 20(3): 510–40.

Veblen, Thorstein. [1914] 1964. *The Instinct of Workmanship and the State of the Industrial Arts.* New York: Augustus M. Kelley.

Vogel, Steven K. 1996. *Freer Markets, More Rules: Regulatory Reform in Advanced Countries.* Ithaca: Cornell University Press.

Wade, Robert. 1996. "Globalization and Its Limits: Reports of the Death of the National Economy Are Greatly Exaggerated." Pp. 60–88 in *National Diversity and Global Capitalism*, edited by Suzanne Berger and Ronald Dore. Ithaca: Cornell University Press.

Wade, Robert, and Frank Veneroso. 1998a. "The Asian Crisis: The High Debt Model Versus the Wall Street-Treasury-IMF Complex." *New Left Review* 228:3–24.

———. 1998b. "The Gathering World Slump and the Battle over Capital Controls." *New Left Review* 231:13–42.

Waters, Malcolm. 1995. *Globalization*. London: Routledge.

———. 1989. "Collegiality, Bureaucratization, and Professionalization: A Weberian Analysis." *American Journal of Sociology* 94:945–72.

Weber, Max. 1978. *Economy and Society*, vol. 1. Translated by Gunther Roth and Claus Wittich. Berkeley: University of California Press.

———. [1927] 1995. *General Economic History*. New Brunswick, N.J.: Transaction.

———. [1915] 1958. "The Social Psychology of the World Religions." Pp. 267–301 in *From Max Weber: Essays in Sociology*, edited by Hans Gerth and C. Wright Mills. New York: Oxford University Press.

Weir, Margaret. 1992. *Politics and Jobs: The Boundaries of Employment Policy in the United States*. Princeton: Princeton University Press.

Weir, Margaret, Ann Shola Orloff, and Theda Skocpol. 1988. *The Politics of Social Policy in the United States*. Princeton: Princeton University Press.

Weir, Margaret, and Theda Skocpol. 1985. "State Structures and the Possibilities for 'Keynesian' Responses to the Great Depression in Sweden, Britain and the United States." Pp. 107–67 in *Bringing the State Back In*, edited by Peter Evans, Dietrich Rueschemeyer, and Theda Skocpol. New York: Cambridge University Press.

Weiss, Linda. 1998. *The Myth of the Powerless State*. Ithaca: Cornell University Press.

———. 1988. *Creating Capitalism: The State and Small Business Since 1945*. New York: Basil Blackwell.

Wejnert, Barbara. 2002. "Integrating Models of Diffusion of Innovations: A Conceptual Framework." *Annual Review of Sociology* 28:297–326.

Wendt, Alexander. 1992. "Anarchy Is What States Make of It: The Social Construction of Power Politics." *International Organization* 46(2): 391–425.

Western, Bruce. 2001. "Institutions, Investment and the Rise in Unemployment." Pp. 71–93 in *The Rise of Neoliberalism and Institutional Analysis*, edited by John L. Campbell and Ove K. Pedersen. Princeton: Princeton University Press.

———. 1997. *Between Class and Market: Postwar Unionization in the Capitalist Democracies*. Princeton: Princeton University Press.

Western, Bruce, and Katherine Beckett. 1999. "How Unregulated is the U.S. Labor Market? The Penal System as a Labor Market Institution." *American Journal of Sociology* 104:1030–60.

Westney, Eleanor D. 1987. *Imitation and Innovation: The Transfer of Western Organization Patterns to Meiji Japan*. Cambridge: Harvard University Press.

Whitley, Richard. 1997. "The Social Regulation of Work Systems: Institutions, Interest Groups, and Varieties of Work Organization in Capitalist Societies." Pp. 227–60 in *Governance at Work: The Social Regulation of Economic Relations*, edited by Richard Whitley and Peer Hull Kristensen. New York: Oxford University Press.

Whitley, Richard, and Peer Hull Kristensen, eds. 1997. *Governance at Work: The Social Regulation of Economic Relations*. New York: Oxford University Press.

Wilensky, Harold L. 1964. "The Professionalization of Everyone?" *American Journal of Sociology* 70:137–58.

Williamson, Oliver E. 1985. *The Economic Institutions of Capitalism*. New York: Free Press.

———. 1975. *Markets and Hierarchies: Analysis and Antitrust Implications*. New York: Free Press.

Witte, John F. 1985. *The Politics and Development of the Federal Income Tax*. Madison: University of Wisconsin Press.

Woods, Ngaire. 1995. "Economic Ideas and International Relations: Beyond Rational Neglect." *International Studies Quarterly* 39:161–80.

World Bank. 2001. *World Development Indicators*. Washington, D.C.: World Bank.

Yee, Albert S. 1996. "The Causal Effects of Ideas on Policies." *International Organization* 50(1): 69–108.

Yonay, Yuval P. 1998. *The Struggle Over the Soul of Economics: Institutionalist and Neoclassical Economists in America Between the Wars*. Princeton: Princeton University Press.

Zald, Mayer N., and Patricia Denton. 1963. "From Evangelism to General Service: The Transformation of the YMCA." *Administrative Science Quarterly* 8(2): 214–34.

Zald, Mayer N., Calvin Morrill, and Hayagreeva Rao. 2002. "How Do Social Movements Penetrate Organizations? Environmental Impact and Organizational Response." Paper presented at the conference on Organization and Social Movement Theory, University of Michigan.

Zeitlin, Jonathan. 2003. "Introduction." Pp. 1–30 in *Governing Work and Welfare in a New Economy: European and American Experiments*, edited by Jonathan Zeitlin and David Trubek. New York: Oxford University Press.

Zerubavel, Eviatar. 1997. *Social Mindscapes: An Invitation to Cognitive Sociology*. Cambridge: Harvard University Press.

Ziegler, J. Nicholas. 1997. *Governing Ideas: Strategies for Innovation in France and Germany*. Ithaca: Cornell University Press.

INDEX

Page numbers in italics refer to figures
or tables.

Abbott, Andrew, 45
Abrahamson, Eric, 122n
academicians. *See* theorists, as actors
accelerating change patterns, 32
action: choice-within-constraints theory
  of, 15–16, 24; constraints on, 6, 14, 19,
  26, 62, 72, 77, 100, 109–10, 149, 151,
  173–74; embeddedness and, 62; en-
  abling/empowering of, 6, 62; logics of,
  14, 18, 27, 57, 69–70, 73n.12, 84, 88–
  89, 113, 174, 186
actors, 12, 28; brokers as, defined, 104–7;
  carriers/gatekeepers as, 103, 110; constituents as, defined, 104, 107–8; decision-
  makers as, defined, 101–2; endogenous/
  exogenous problems and, 57, 174–75,
  185–86; entrepreneurs as, 65, 74–77,
  80, 101, 103, 177–80, 182, 184, 186–
  89; framers as, defined, 102–5, 110; historical institutionalism and, 27, 100n,
  182, 184; ideational roles of, 91–92,
  100–107, 121; locations of, in institu-
  tional/social networks, 65, 74–77, 80,
  86, 107, 178–79, 182, 184, 186–88; organizational institutionalism and, 18,
  22–23, 70, 101, 182, 184; power distribution concerns of, 12, 83, 175–77; rational choice institutionalism and, 14,
  16, 18n, 29–30, 33, 100–101, 182–83;
  regulative institutions and, 146; theo-
  rists/academicians as, 102, 105, 153–54,
  157, 159, 163; trust generation and,
  76n, 116
advertising firms, 103
affirmative action, 3, 43
AFL-CIO, 75
agency theory(ists), 45
airline industry, 102
Aldrich, Howard, 75, 186–87
Allen, Michael, 50n
American Economic Review, 157
American Enterprise Institute, 153

American Farm Bureau Federation (AFBF),
  106
analysis: case study, 55–56, 79, 149;
  cluster, 52–53; counterfactual, 119–21,
  149; data sources and, 46–47, 51, 58;
  interrupted time-series, 53; levels of,
  14, 19, 23, 38–40, 45–47, 58, 87–89;
  process tracing, 119, 121; qualitative,
  33, 48–50, 55–57, 119n; quantitative,
  33, 50–57, 119n; scale of, 44n; textual,
  121n; time-varying parameters regression, 53
anti-terrorist programs, 109
appropriateness, logic of, 18, 27, 70,
  73n.12
Arthur, Brian, 13
art museums, 3, 19
associations, trade/business, 12, 106,
  146–47, 149
Atomic Energy Commission, U. S.,
  113–14, 176
Australia, *140, 142, 144*
Austria, *140, 142, 144*
automobile industry, 166

Babb, Sarah, 118n
background assumptions, 93–95, 156, 159
Bartley, Tim, 81, 85
behavioralism, 24
Belgium, *140, 142, 144,* 164
Berman, Sheri, 121–22
Blair, Tony, 110
Block, Fred, 108–9
Blyth, Mark, 27, *94,* 98, 122, 159
bonds markets. *See* portfolio investment
Boston, Mass., 111
bounded rationality, 16, 30, 33
Bradburn, Ellen, 84–85
Bretton Woods agreement, 25, 125, 134
bricolage, 28, 30, 69–74, 80, 172; in evolu-
  tionary/revolutionary change, 65, 70–75,
  77, 86, 178; framers and, 103, 110; globalization and, 29; institutional/social locations and, 65, 178, 187–88; organizational institutionalism and, 184; path